Roller Derby: The Sensation That Caused a Book

Confessions of a Roller Derby Mascot

As experienced by Bane-ana

Copyright © 2012 Bane-ana

ISBN-13: 978-0615692456
ISBN-10: 0615692451

All rights reserved. No part of this publication may be reproduced, stored in a retrieval system, or transmitted in any form or by any means, electronic, mechanical, recording or otherwise, without the prior written permission of the author.

DEDICATION

Per il mio Capitana, grazie per tutte le avventure.
E per Butterscotch Cripple, per la convinzione che mi hai dato.

> *He is totally annoying.*
> MINNIE MAYHEM

I'm going to punch that banana in the snout!
RANDOM LONG ISLAND TOUGH-GUY

> *You need to stop with this roller derby nonsense and start thinking about a real future.*
> RELATIVE

That's it! I'm calling the cops! Let's see how you like sitting in jail in that banana costume, asshole!
ROLLER DERBY FAN THAT I "ASSAULTED" WITH A DEADLY POMPOM

> *So what are you, some kind of gay super-hero?*
> CLOSET CASE

Contents

	Ad Lectorem	ix
I	The Other Side of the Purple	1
II	Rabble in Skates	24
III	Women who Skate with the Wolves	45
IV	Yellow Bellied	62
V	There and Back Again: A Mascot's Tale	89
VI	Mods and Dolls! Just a Buncha Crazy Mods and Dolls!	95
VII	Vague As	106
VIII	Lone Star Skate	141
IX	How the West was Fun	161
X	Pissing Excellence	187
XI	Lit Up, Knocked Down	205
XII	Althea on the Dark Side of the Moon	231
XIII	Coalition of the Rolling	250
XIV	The Banana Monologues	264
XV	On the Cusp of Revolution	269
	Appendices	275
	Selected Bibliography	302
	Acknowledgements	307

AD LECTOREM

Before moving forward, I must tell you that this book is not about roller derby as a sport. It is a book about the experiences, people, and the experiences of the people that I have had the good fortune of encountering during the short years I have donned a banana costume as a roller derby mascot. It is about how I learned that there is a difference between how an audience member sees the sport and how those who are involved see it; how I used to think that there was a common thread sewn through the life of every derbyist whether she or he skated, refed, EMT'd, mascoted, or volunteered in one form or another. And how I was wrong about that.

Several writers have described roller derby as a sport[1]—from the groundbreaking ideas originating in Texas strewn through the pages of Melissa "Melicious" Joulwan's *Rollergirl: Totally True Tales from the Track* to the growth of the sport post *Rollergirl* found in Catherine Mabe's *Roller Derby: The History and All-Girl Revival of the Greatest Sport on Wheels*, and most recently, the definitive *Down and Derby: The Insider's Guide to Roller Derby* by Jennifer "Casey Bomber" Barbee and Alex "Axles of Evil" Cohen. These books include excellent chapters that discuss roller derby history, from its Great Depression origins to the present day. If after reading these above mentioned works you still want to read more about roller derby, I offer the following.

---

[1] See Appendix 1: Useful Terminology for a basic introduction to how the sport is played.

A Tale of Two Derbys

Although several writers have used the word "revival" to describe the 21st century roller derby launch, I feel it is a misnomer.[2] Revival implies that the same thing sprung up a second time. In my opinion, the sport, completely revamped by the Texas Roller Girls, more closely resembles not an athletic "revival" but an athletic "revolution." To be certain, roller derby has roots extending back to the 1930s, but then, so do radios; are iPods the same thing? When America seceded from England in 1776, no one in Parliament said, "There is a *revival* happening across the Atlantic." If anything, the sport jumped ahead in its evolution because of "an awfully good idea" born in Texas this past century's turn.[3] Revival. Evolution. *Revolution.* And nowhere in roller derby is the athletic revolution more prominent than in the subculture that has sprung up alongside the sport.

Such is the subject of this book. The subculture that grew alongside 21st century derby is inextricably woven into the sport itself and differentiates it from previous versions. My position is that the Texas Rollergirls' Great Idea set a precedent that roller derby had never enjoyed (i.e., "the skaters ... manage the league") and revolutionized the sport not as a cultural-athletic *phenomenon* (as in the past) but rather as a cultural-athletic

---

[2] For example see Catherine Mabe, "Roller Derby: The History and All-Girl Revival of the Greatest Sport on Eight Wheels," Denver: Speck Press (2007) – although Mabe does also refer to it as a "revolution," too (p. 17), La'Vicious (2008) in *Five on Five: The Official Magazine of the Women's Flat Track Derby Association (WFTDA)*, Volume 1, Issue 2, p. 38, Lemon Drop (2008) in *Blood and Thunder Magazine: Women's Roller Derby Magazine*, Issue 9, p. 31.

[3] Melissa "Melicious" Joulwan, "Rollergirl: Totally true Tales from the Track," New York: Simon and Schuster, (2007) p. 52.

movement.⁴ Therefore, I leave to posterity this first-hand account of the greatest sport on eight wheels, as experienced by me, a person of no real significance in it.

I am a mascot. That's all I am. Every year, hundreds of roller derby bouts commence without me (or any other mascots) and will continue to do so for many years to come. Bouts require several things: rollergirls and referees. Oh! And score keepers, statisticians, bands, D.J.s, bench coaches, assistant coaches, penalty box timers and other NSOs (Non-Skating Officials), beer, fans, technicians, EMTs, free labor volunteers, and announcers. Bouts, I admit, do not need mascots. The sport is changing for the better by attracting more fans, sponsors, and dynamic personalities. The circus-like roots of the 21st century revolution are being pulled, allowing more room for the sport itself to blossom. The so-called "bawdy hijinks" of roller derby might be what first caught the interest of many skaters and fans.⁵ However, as the sport has grown, a lot of that has been discarded. As Rat City Rollergirls' mascot Dirty "Rat Man" Houllahan has observed, "As Rollerderby has become less of a theatrical event and more of a sport, a greater burden has fallen on the support cast to provide the theatrics while the women concentrate on playing."⁶ This "burden ... to provide the theatrics" is a small part of the roller derby revolution that has allowed me (and countless other mascots) to evolve our bits and acts in a supportive environment—so long as we <u>never</u> interfere with the bout itself.

This book attempts to deal with roller derby in both objective and subjective ways. It is objective because I tried my

---

⁴ Ibid., p. 80.
⁵ Quoted in Paul Wachter, "You Just Can't Keep The Girls From Jamming," *The New York Times Magazine*, (Feb. 1, 2009), p. 21.
⁶ "Meet the Girls (and Boys) of Rat City Rollerderby," Accessed via: www.prostamerika.com/Rollerderby.html

best to view the culture from every way I could and at times, was forced to abandon several misconceptions I had about it; and subjective because I couldn't possibly be everywhere at once and couldn't interview every derbyist out there. As such, I do not want anyone who reads this book to define every derbyist's experience by the next few hundred pages. The following exploits are mine and mine alone. Although it is possible that some themes may strike familiar with some skaters, refs, etc., I do not speak for all derbyists. Those who make up the sport are as diverse as delegates debating at a United Nations meeting.

The phrase I have used to describe my approach is "analysis through anecdote." I wrote some of the following in "real time," i.e. as it historically unfolded before my bewildered eyes—me, feverishly looking for a pen and a piece of paper, bar napkin, or if these weren't available, my forearm to record the scene. Some of it was written just post "real time," i.e. when I finally made it home to my notebook stinking of sweat, cigarettes, beer, and a host of other odors that signify a pleasant evening. Still, other parts were written post "post real time"–I had sobered up, purged my hang over, finally ate something that my stomach wouldn't reject, and recorded the shenanigans of yesterday.

What makes this sport so special to me? To all involved? Why do we put ourselves through such outlandish ordeals without hope of pay, prospect, or salvation? Why do I, with full knowledge of how easy a target I am for drunken assholes to pick apart bit by bit, continue to put on a banana suit and cheer for roller derby? Who is attracted to this sport and why? The answers surprised me, assuming that I even discovered them at all.

After all my travels, I learned that the sport, despite the endless list of motives by those who play it, is meant to be enjoyed. Years from now, people may speak of an "in between" time, when the roller derby revolution wobbled in its 'tween phase. I am all too aware that when and if this work ever sees the light of publication, much of what is described might have already come to pass. In Malcolm Galdwell's *The Tipping Point*, he speaks of a specific time in any new ideas' life when it goes from underground to mainstream.[7] I do not know what the sport will look like in the future but simply wish to leave a record of the days before it "tipped" through my experiences as a roller derby mascot.

Every derbyist does her or his part to bring roller derby into public consciousness. As such, every derbyist has a story to tell of what they did to bring the sport from a few people sitting around a living room dreaming of derby to the national phenomenon it is becoming. The following is the small part that I played within our "culture unto itself."[8]

Many names have been changed to protect the guilty. The veeeerrrry very guilty ...

---

[7] Malcolm Gladwell, *The Tipping Point: How Little Things Can Make a Big Difference*, (NY: Little, Brown and Company, 2002), p. 12.
[8] Mabe (2007), p. 97.

I

THE OTHER SIDE OF THE PURPLE

*What I want to be most when
I grow up is a kid again.*
ME

"Should … uh … we be doing this right now?"

Half ignoring my question, Jenna Fiesta measured a shot of Southern Comfort into an empty beer bottle. I knew the answer but vainly hoped my question would cause her to rethink our actions, maybe even prevent the next few minutes from unfolding.

"Of course not," Fiesta answered, still calculating the shot with the precision of an alchemist. She gave me the answer I desired; only, I had asked the wrong question. Or rather, I asked the right question to the wrong person.

Jenna "Fiesta" wasn't just her derbyname—it was her way of life. That, coupled with a matter-of-fact simplicity to everything she said, left me defenseless. Apparently, I couldn't foresee how un-psychic I was. I searched my mind for an arbitrary point of commonality—music, movies, books—anything to build a bridge. Nothing came to mind. And we already had one thing *not* in common—I can't stand Southern Comfort, Fiesta's tonic of choice.

Bane-ana

I looked over my body, which was covered by a moldy, integrity-snuffing, yellow—save a few stains—banana costume. My hands caught my attention. They simultaneously shook and profusely sweat, making it impossible to wipe the perspiration from my brow without reinforcing it. It sure was hot in that car despite February's cold window patter. At 5 o'clock in the evening, the sun had already retreated from the cold; its fading residue of light met the natural blue of the sky, dyeing it a purple so opaque that even the stars disappeared behind its veil. I wished to join them. I sat motionless (my nerves notwithstanding) in Fiesta's car behind Skate Safe, a large hockey rink out in Bethpage, Long Island. It was the 18th of that month—my burfday. I had forgotten all about it and started to feel nauseous—the first phase of my defense mechanisms. That night, I was to mascot for one of the newly formed Long Island Roller Rebels' home teams, The Wicked Wheelers of the West. Our rivals that night, The East End Ladies of Laceration, held no vendetta against us; there simply weren't any other teams to play yet. Eventually, our league would have enough girls for three teams: The Wicked Wheelers of the West, The East End Ladies of Laceration, and The Mid Island Rolling Thundercats.

When Fiesta had first conscripted me to her car, the parking lot had been near empty. Now, little by little, spectators infiltrated our refuge. I could hear the still few disparate voices talking in the parking lot; every comment from the authoritatively nostalgic: "I remember roller derby from the 70s..." to the chauvinistically stupid: "Man, am I gonna fuck me some pretty little lass on wheels tonight..."

... or kick a banana's ass, I thought.

Despite my silent hopes that a small audience might amount to more of a dress rehearsal setting than a full-on roller derby production, the parking lot steadily filled with ravenous fans, family members, and those who were simply curious about roller derby. I too was curious about roller derby. After the Texas-bred roller derby revolution had finally moseyed up to New York, I never imagined that one day I would participate in a bout. Hell, I'd just found out that the sport existed. Yet there I sat, suited up in a banana costume, fretfully waiting. My edginess had an easily identifiable origin: I didn't fully understand my job that day—*roller derby mascot? What the fuck is that?* A minor position, for sure, yet I still would have appreciated a roller derby-mascot instruction manual. None existed. There was no script. My romantic thoughts over the past three months of what I would do as a mascot all seemed like bad ideas now. I had some jokes prepared to tell audience members in case of a lull in the bout; but why would anyone want to hear jokes? They came for roller derby, not comedy. I wanted out. I wanted to join those outlying stars, floating safely on the other side of that deeply purpled sky.

As I opened my mouth to explain my concerns to Fiesta (and state my intended parting from the whole affair), she broke her fixation with the bottle and turned to face me. Her glasses slid down towards the tip of her nose. Peering above the rims, she bore her eyes into my insecurities and quipped, "Look, shit is gonna go down whether you're *here*"—referring to my lucidity and tapping my head for effectiveness—"or not."

She was right. I realize now she said that to relax me, but at the time, I couldn't help but feel unnecessary. What business did I really have at Skate Safe? It had all seemed like a fun idea at first: dress up like a banana, mascot for a cool new sport, and maybe take a few pictures with roller derby fans. *February will never come.* But it came quicker than I thought it would. Three-month's time was not nearly long enough to have made the transition yet from "acquaintance" to "friend" with the league. Several of the girls and refs had given me a warm welcome, but there remained others who viewed me with suspicion, or at least cordial caution.

I had no idea where Fiesta fit into all this. Friend? Foe? Was she trying to get me in trouble? I quickly scanned her for clues. She was calm. Stoned? *Not yet.* Stoic? *Perhaps.* Why let a simple thing like my continued sanity ruin a good time? She put the two SoCo shots on the dashboard and packed her bowl with sticky green herbs. Bejeweled throughout were small THC crystals whose sparkles rivaled those of the frosted windows. On an ordinary day, my lips watered for such a delicacy; but that day, at the Long Island Roller Rebels first bout, getting drunk and high beforehand seemed like a terrible idea. For reasons that escape me, marijuana doesn't make me so much lazy and dim as hyper-motivated, productive, silly, and outrageous. It releases the American worker in me. In one personally legendary night, while dealing with my bizarre reaction to this supposed "depressant," I wrote a song, a poem, and edited my Master's thesis. I alphabetized my books (several hundred) for no real reason, cleaned *behind* furniture, and as a grand finale, shoveled the walks of my entire block in the middle of the night, much to the surprise of my neighbors when they woke the next morning. I've heard that this response to THC—although not commonplace—does happen to some people; less enjoyable is it's negative counterpart—a hellish, introspective (but far from illuminating) panic attack.

"Grab a beer," ordered Fiesta.

I apprehensively reached to the floor, grabbed one from the box between my feet, and popped it open.

"We call this a 'strikeout.'[1] Ever done one?"

---

[1] A "Strike Out" consists of taking a sip off of a bowl or joint, taking a shot of hard liquor, drinking a full beer, exhaling the smoke, and embracing the delirium.

"Yes, but we didn't call it that back in high school."
"What did you call it?"
"Chicago."
"Chicago? That doesn't make any sense. It's called a 'strikeout,' which if you think about it, is logical."
I thought about it. "Why is it logical?"
"It's because ..." Fiesta stopped. "It just is. Now stop being such a pussy! Got the lighter?"
I glanced at the lighter sitting in the center cup holder.
"No."
I was stalling, waiting for some miracle to intervene and deliver me from the scene. A fire, a car crash, a lost and wandering child—any last minute crisis would do splendidly. I glanced out the iced windows in desperation. *C'mon! C'mon! Something's gotta go wrong to make this all right!* More and more people showed up. I remembered that I was supposed to be out by the front door, freezing my nuts off, pumping up fans as they waited on line to enter Skate Safe. Instead, I was holed up in Fiesta's car, ignoring the fans, about to imbibe my regret, and freezing my nuts off. What would happen if someone noticed I wasn't by the door? This thought was fleeting as I was saved by the calming, yet equally disappointing, fact that I wasn't important enough for anyone to notice my absence. Still, I hoped that at any second, a Roller Rebel was going to run out of Skate Safe, catch Fiesta and me before the act, and reprimand us—maybe even tell me to go home! Seemed preferable, and I eagerly awaited the dressing-down. *Any second now. Any second ...*

Fiesta reached into the cup holder, grabbed the lighter, and handed it to me. "Got the lighter?" she asked rhetorically.
"Yes." *Fuck.* I put the bowl up to my mouth and inhaled; as the smoke swirled around and polluted my lungs, I took my shot and pounded a beer. Exhale.

Bad idea. Chronic, Corona, and 'Co—three hits and I was out. Fiesta was right; "strikeout" was totally logical.

I opened the door and fell out of the car in a stupor. Fiesta stayed to polish off another beer. Stumbling back to Skate Safe, I mumbled to myself that walking shouldn't give me this much trouble. I'd done it thousands of times before after all. But walking is relative, and despite a few staggers, I was amazed at how well I was doing. *One foot at a time.* The considerable attention I paid to each step was interrupted just outside the front entrance by a young girl I pegged at around seventeenish.

"Hey Mr. Banana!" she yelled.

Human contact felt alien. I had to proceed with caution. I couldn't pretend not to hear her, but I hoped she was referring to some other banana mascot. She wasn't. She grabbed my elbow, "Lemme get a picture with you." Trapped. I stood beside her and faked a smile. Then another kid came up to me.

"Can I get a picture with you?"

"Sure," I said reluctantly.

Riddled with guilt, I felt like a poster board for a D.A.R.E campaign: "Drugs Make You Bananas." Welcome the second phase of my defense mechanisms: self-deprecation. I pretended not to notice another kid—a camera dangling from his wrist—approaching me with his friends. I quickly ran inside.

Skate Safe had filled up in the meanwhile. The large metal bleachers were reaching their maximum seating capacity as some spectators willingly headed trackside. Were they looking to have a rollergirl land on their laps? Probably. Everywhere I looked, girls on skates either tried to keep themselves upright or skated confidently around the spectators. Some Ladies of Laceration skated towards me, flailing their arms like they were going to crash into me. Only, they gained control and dodged me at the last moment, chuckling while I cowered.

The click was tocking—*clock was ticking* damn you, SoCo!—and the Ladies of Laceration had temporarily suspended all allegiances. Yet before the bout, there existed a cohesive unit of preparation. Like soldiers tilling their own battlefield, both Wheelers and Ladies set up the track. We created a skeleton for the skate path out of long ropes and then covered them with hockey tape. We also collectively set up the DJ booth, iced the kegs, and helped unload the band gear. It was shortly after sound check when Fiesta decided how she was going to spend my post set-up time. But the marijuana had released my inner Protestant; I now frantically wanted a job to do. Something private, preferably. But everything was just about ready. I couldn't take it. I needed something to take my mind off the fact that it was eating itself; a distraction to ameliorate my marijuana-induced productive urges. The one thing I was *supposed* to do—meet and greet fans at the door—seemed too harrowing an affair. I saw some cuts in the track tape that the coarse, underlying rope had rubbed against and broken through. *Salvation*! I grabbed a roll of tape from a milk crate and started to reinforce the track outline, hoping no one would question what I was doing.

"What are you doing?" asked a voice from behind me. Padded up and ready to skate, Killer Tofu towered over me.

"The ... uh ... structural integrity of the tape ... is ...uh—needs fixing," I babbled.

She glanced over the track. "Looks good," she smiled and skated away.

Wait? What? What looks good? The track as it is or my fixing of it? Should I keep doing this?

"Bane!" Another voice yelled from behind me. I turned just as Butterscotch Cripple, pivot for the Wicked Wheelers, skated up to me. She pushed the tips of her skates down to stop and grabbed my arm to keep balance. "We need the monkey suit! Cappa's looking for you!"

Shit! *The monkey suit.* In addition to my banana debut, the girls asked Frank Cappa to take on the role of "Furious George," the Wicked Wheelers' flying monkey mascot. The costume included wings and a beanie a la the flying monkeys in *The Wizard of Oz.* I ran out to my car to get it. I had died a little that day sitting in hours of Van Wyck gridlock to get that fucking outfit from Rubie's Costume. Now I thought about just staying in my car, pushing the driver's seat back, and laying low. But the task had calmed me down a bit. It gave me a reason to go back into Skate Safe: *Cappa needs the suit.* I had a job—no, a mission!—to deliver the monkey costume to the rightful wearer—that strikeout would not be in vain! I found Cappa in the changing area, which was really just a back room for hockey equipment storage and kid's birthday parties. Small orange cones and goalie gear littered the floor alongside makeup kits and shards of torn fishnet stockings. As Cappa pulled the costume out of the bag, I stood there waiting for him to tell me what we were supposed to do. He had already been friends with Captain Morgan (Captain of the Wicked Wheelers), Butterscotch Cripple (Co-Captain), and several others from the Roller Rebels before the league even existed. I assumed someone had given him some advice for us, told us what to do. And decidedly more important, what we *cannot* do. As I opened my mouth to finally broach the subject, he looked up at me.

"So, do you know what we're supposed to do out there?" he asked, pushing his right foot through the foot hole of the costume.

Good question. I froze. I wanted to answer him but I didn't know what to say. *You* were supposed to tell *me* that.

"I believe we're supposed to rev the crowd up," I finally muttered. I hoped that he wouldn't press the issue; that "rev the crowd up" would suffice as an answer in and of itself.

"How?" he asked.

Shit. "I hadn't really thought about it. I guess we're supposed to cheer when our girls do something good and boo when they do something bad."

Cappa pushed his left foot through the bottom of the suit. "Oh ... okay."

I didn't know the rules yet; from the wobble in Cappa's voice, I gathered he didn't know them either.

Suddenly, the door swung open and a young man dressed in a blood-drenched white butcher's smock—the Ladies of Laceration "boutfit"—skated into the room.

"How's it going?" he said amicably. He was Pee Wee Hurt 'em, the Ladies of Laceration mascot, and damn did he seem confident in his position, what with the roller skates and all. At the time, he had been dating Ladies of Laceration blocker Holly Cide. Their blood-smock uniforms harmonized, a match made in hell. *Surely, he would know the rules.*

"Do you know what we're supposed to do out there?" I asked Hurt 'em. Cappa, too, awaited his response.

"I dunno." He shrugged. "I guess just have fun."

Perfect. Nice and vague ...

The door swung open again. Mary Jane Rottencrotch stuck her head inside the room. "We're starting," she yelled, "get out there!"

Hurt 'em turned to the door and skated out, leaving behind a perplexed monkey and banana. Cappa pulled the costume over his shoulders, creating a fur-lined "V" down his back that looked like a vagina turned inside out. We looked over at each other, waiting for the other to interpret whatever "just have fun" meant. He struggled with the back zipper for a few seconds before I took over. My hands shook as I fastened flesh under fur. Adrenaline flooded sensibility, capsizing reason in its sweet natural bourbon. Bout time was here, and we were lost. Nervousness gave way to an acute—almost primitive—awareness of my surroundings. Despite the screaming fans and the music, I could hear every metallic tooth of the zipper clink shut, swallowing Cappa into Furious George.

"What do we do?" asked Cappa. He pulled his flying-monkey wings out of the Rubie's bag and handed them to me.

"I don't know," I said fixing them on his back. "Just *wing* it, I guess." Cappa slipped an edgy chuckle, put his huge papier-mâché monkey head on, and together we walked out to the track. We tried to find a position on the Wheelers' side, where we wouldn't be in anyone's way. A futile attempt as some of the girls didn't exactly know where to situate themselves either. In retrospect, Cappa and I weren't the only ones unsure of what to do that night—this whole business of roller derby was new to all of us.

What I remember from that first period comes in small bits and pieces usually triggered—like most pleasant and forgotten memories—with random, seemingly unrelated stimuli. I mostly recall everyone yelling at me: rollergirls, refs, fans, and especially photographers. But interspersed throughout the screaming and confusion bubbled up an underlying serenity—the final phase of my defense mechanisms. Such blissful moments were tentative, cut short by sizeable bitchslaps from reality. I remember my first one well. The Wicked Wheelers called a timeout. I focused my attention on the middle of the track where Captain Morgan, several other Wheelers, Ladies, refs, and officials scratched their heads over the rules. Leaning in closer to hear them, I didn't notice Felon of Troy (a Lady of Laceration whose face, it has been said, once launched a thousand fists) slowly rolling up from behind me. Like a falcon over a mouse, she pounced, talons out, tackling me to the ground, drowning out the shouts of the crowd ... oww. I assumed this was part of my initiation into the league, as no ref came to my aid. The EMTs pointed and laughed. The audience, so easily amused by cartoonish pain, gaffed childlike taunts as Felon hazed me. Apparently, roller derby has no rules against pureeing bananas. Then again, what could I expect from roller derbyfans? Ancient Romans had nothing on them. This crowd had assembled into our modest coliseum for one sight: *blood*. Mine would do. I couldn't imagine what further pledges I would have to endure. For now, Felon had just given me my first lesson in roller derby ... mascoting is full contact.

At halftime, The Wicked Wheelers stole away into the kid's party room. I sat steaming in that suit and looked over at Cappa; he must have been in hell. And that smell! An odorous sweat emitted from the girls' knee and elbow pads, caking onto the air like a fire in Heaven, polluting our pores, and suffocating our nostrils. Our cilia didn't stand a chance; noses have long ago evolved away from their defensive capabilities in favor of a more domesticated approach to smell: locating apple pies and enjoying flowers. Half gagging, I looked around the room. Where fifteen anticipating girls once eagerly strapped their gear on only an hour earlier, a new legion of roller warriors now sat before me.

I needed air. I walked out the back door into the cold night. The parking lot overflowed with fans smoking cigarettes and other things, drinking beers, and yelling about the bout. I was elated; they actually care enough about the game to bark over it.

"Hey, Banana Man! You look like a douche!" yelled some drunk guy. He lifted his beer to toast the genius of his comment. The girl he had his arm around laughed with her friends. Another girl from the group ran over and asked me for a picture.

I obliged and smiled. She handed the camera to her friend and put her arm around my shoulder.
Maybe this isn't so bad.
"Thank you," she said. As the camera flash went off, she lipped under her breath, "My friends think you're stupid."
"Thanks," I muttered. Second lesson of roller derby: banana costumes come equipped with a built in target sign on the back. *Perfect.*

I didn't know where to go; the temperature outside was colder than the company but going back into Skate Safe proved just as distressing a trial. Once inside, fans yelled and cheered all around me. More people cornered me for a photo or an autograph, or to tell me they were happy when Felon kicked my ass, or that they wanted to do the same. I felt trapped—crooked. I couldn't find a point of level floor to stand on. I looked up at the electronic billboard. Twelve minutes left to pull myself together for the second half. I saw an area that was roped off to the public and dipped into one of the smaller changing rooms. I slid down the wall and crumbled on the floor in a perfect mess.

I started panting loudly. I was immersed in my own private little hell of strikeouts, meatheads, and an inescapable winter. Every cell on my flesh ached. I was hungry but had no appetite. This was no moment of Zen; this was a panic attack. We're old friends, these spells and I. They don't last long; they just *feel* like forever. Water helps, as does slowing down the breath and focusing on the interrelationships between inhale and exhale. Soon I was able to stand again; hunched over, I paced around the room. Inhale; exhale ... slowly. The now very maddening buzzer rang, signifying the start of the second period. I composed myself enough to emerge from isolation and elbowed my way back to The Wheelers, keeping a watchful eye out for Felon of Troy.

Furious George was already standing beside The Wheelers' bench. Saying nothing, I took my position beside him. He asked me a question, but I couldn't hear him through the large monkey head. Furious, George pulled his monkey head off and suggested we run around the outer part of the track. With the start of the next jam, we raced around the buffer zone between the skaters and the spectators, cheering with anyone holding Wheelers placards. The idea was half-planned, as The Ladies scored several points during that jam. We didn't want people thinking we were cheering for The Ladies. That, after all, would be treasonous. We were still learning and quickly decided that first a Wheeler would have to take lead jammer before we got excited; or, a Wheeler would have to annihilate a Ladies jammer.

Furious and I patiently waited. And lo! Aunty Christ took lead and scored several points. We roared off around the track screaming, "Aun-ty Christ! Aun-ty Christ!" Getting in on the bit, Pee Wee Hurt' em chased after us. He caught up to Furious, pushed him into me, and skated away. I fell on my side and rolled over, landing like a splatter of yellow paint on the floor. My cape flipped over my shoulders, covering my head. The crowd responded. They seemed to enjoy it. Furious jumped on me and we began to scuffle on the floor near the track. I managed to get up, stand with my foot on his chest for all but a second, and then ran around the track goading him. He wouldn't have it. He caught up to me and tackled me to the floor. I started to laugh profusely. I couldn't help myself. It was like the gods were tickling my soul; only, it was really a flying monkey knocking me in the head. My endorphins couldn't tell the difference. I can't fight when I'm laughing and so, surrendered. Now it was his turn; he stood with his foot on my chest in triumphant victory and waved to the crowd. They continued to roar for our little display. We finally understood our position. It was all so simple. *Just have fun ...*

For the rest of the bout, every time a Wheeler took lead jammer or knocked the shit out of a Lady, Furious and I ran around the track and gloated like *we* were the players. I blew Miss America kisses to the fans as I rode atop my imaginary parade float. It was all tongue-in-cheek, of course, but perhaps that's what made it so amusing. We had a silly confidence, like two cocky magicians who don't realize the supposedly "vanished" bunny is nipping at their feet. The crowd ate it up, and I joined my star brothers and sisters on the other side of the purple.

Like our skating counterparts, we were on a roll now.[2] We hadn't discussed anything at all. No routine, no script; yet it all started to fall into place. When a Lady took lead jammer, I shook my ass at the crowd or let Furious George spank me. A monkey spanking a banana! I rubbed my eyes in a crying motion when one of our girls received a penalty—and there were plenty of penalties! Of the four fights that erupted between The Wheelers and The Ladies that night, I vividly remember one that happened right at my feet.

Miss Murder Heart (a Lady) took down Allison Chains (a Wheeler), fanning the flames of a growing personal rivalry. Still new to the league, I was not yet aware of any contention between the skaters. It had all just been derby parties and fundraisers up until this point—preparation for this day. I thought all of these girls were friends outside of derby and only took their aggressions out on the track. Like so many other assumptions I had about roller derby, this one was quickly discarded. Allison Chains rolled on top of Miss Murder Heart and used her knees to pin her to the floor. Chains started to

---

[2] I know, I know. Bad pun.

punch her in the face right in front of me. Murder Heart returned the blows in kind.

"Wow!" I screamed. I laughed and hopped up and down in an effort to draw the crowd's attention to the catfight.

"Whee-lers! Whee-lers! Whee-lers!" I shouted. I heard that sometimes girls would fake fight to entertain the crowd. I figured that Allison Chains and Murder Heart were playing up the whole "brawling derbygirl" stereotype for the fans, so it was only natural that I cheer Allison Chains, my teammate, on. Only, they weren't playing anything up for anybody. They were really beating the shit out of each other.

"Stop laughing you idiot and help me break them up!" yelled a girl beside me. This we did. After a few more intense jams, The Wicked Wheelers emerged victoriously.

After the bout, we cleaned the track thoroughly. We pulled up all the track tape, wound the underlying track rope, and threw out every last bit of garbage. Furious and I returned to the hockey equipment room to change out of our costumes. We quickly ducked back out of the door when we saw the girls still changing out of their boutfits.

"Hey guys! Get back in here!" someone yelled from inside.

We walked back in to loud cheers. Butterscotch went back and forth giving Cappa and me hugs and kisses. "Good job," said Fiesta as she handed us shot glasses overflowing with Southern Comfort. We all got into a huddle. Captain Morgan counted to three, and we all screamed a resounding "WEST SIDE!" That became our team's mantra.

Good 'ole Wicked Wheelers.

The Munchaba Lounge, a sizeable live music club not far from Skate Safe, hosted the after-party. Loud music, post-bout shit talk, dark ales, and good times rang through the clinking of beer glasses. Black Eye Barbie, one of our fresh bloods,[3] told me that the banana costume was both stupid and cute. The band was rocking out until Sissy Facekick (a Lady of Laceration) jumped on stage and helped herself to the microphone. The singer's girlfriend didn't much care for her show-womanship and pushed Ms. Facekick off the stage, causing one final scuffle that was quickly broken up.

At about 3:00 am, with the party winding down, Captain Morgan, Jefferee, Allison Chains, Ruby Redrum, and Cherry Deville piled into my car to leave.[4] Captain lost a long-held

---

[3] Though this is not a universal term. Other teams, like NYC's Gotham Girls, call new girls "fresh *meats*."

[4] Jefferee is Captain's brother and one of our refs. Ruby Redrum skated for the Wicked Wheelers that night, but became a Mid Island Rolling Thundercat once the team formed. Cherry Deville was a blocker for the Ladies of Laceration.

record. She had boasted a flawless drinking career, having never puked in a car in her life. Until *that* night. On *my* car. She felt a little woozy and sat up front. Unable to find the window in time, she leaned over and heaved. No actual vomit yet. But her spittle buckshot blasted the side of my neck—a feeling akin to roughly one hundred tiny bee stings. My nerves receded from the inner walls of my skin and desperately sought refuge in the middle of my neck. I scrambled to open her window from a switch on my door. Captain quickly leaned over to the window and spewed her whiskey-wreaked projectile onto the outside of the passenger door. A puke-lear missile! Cherry Deville had had enough. She jumped out of the car and opened the passenger door. Captain spun out and continued to expunge half-digested alcohol onto the street. I heard Captain's glasses hit the pavement. I grabbed the tissues and napkins that I kept in the glove box and frantically wiped the spit off the side of my neck. I then jumped out of the car, picked the glasses off the ground, and snapped a picture to commemorate the occasion. When she felt better, we climbed back in the car and took off.

As I drove everyone home, I tallied the night I had in my head: a strikeout, the leagues debut, flying monkeys, human butchers, a beat down by a girl on roller skates, four fights at the bout, a barroom scuffle, and a vomit-smelling car—I was a Long Island Roller Rebel.

I returned home, showered, and slipped into bed just as the sun peered above the curvature of the earth to faithfully relight the world again. As exhausted as I was, I knew my night wouldn't end there. Over the past several years, I had developed fickle sleep patterns that could be couched in either of two words: worry or excitement. After my first bout experience, the latter happily overwhelmed me. Restlessness never felt so good. Dreams were unnecessary, as the longest line cast into the deepest abysses of sleep could never trawl such thrills. I had roller derby on my mind.

I lay awake in bed savoring both the most pleasant moments of the bout and the most reveling expectations of bouts to come. *Were there more adventures on the other side of the purple?* I placed my hand over my heart, surprised to feel it still beat sweet summer breezes. A revived corpse, I danced with a spring-risen Persephone. The air in my room sang a long forgotten reprise; I hummed along.

Outside, winter's chill desperately tried to dissolve my elation as easily as her rains had worn the gray snow. Try as she did, she couldn't drag me from the serenity of the sun-kissed meadow in my mind. We've all felt "under the weather" at times. But I'd like to introduce a new term: "over the weather." Butterscotch had warned me that this would happen.

I Fall Amongst Pirates ... Sort of.

"So, like, what's a banana have to do with roller derby?" is the question I get asked more than any other. At every bout I've ever mascoted, I've answered it at least ten times for ten different people, who always preface the question with the disclaimer, "I'm sure you get asked this all the time, but ... ." The best answer I have ever heard came from Manhattan Gotham Girl, Ginger Snap. When a fan asked her that question about me, she replied, "Well, other than 'duh,' we need a lot of potassium." I think what she meant by that was, "Because it's roller derby ... 'nuff said."

Good 'ole Ginger Snap.

However, there is a deeper reason I got involved with the Roller Rebels, and a little background is in order at this juncture. You see, I come from a cesspool called Nassau County, Long Island. The taxes are too high, while the IQs drag way too low. There's everything to do, and no one does a thing. Everyone goes to church, but no one loves thy neighbor. Smiles are frowned upon and so perceptibly phony, it's as if the smiler were deciphering a foreign language called "sincerity." No one is happy or sad. Picture a bunch of self-centered halfwits who live in vaunted sardine tins and act with zero consideration for the rest of humanity. Extrapolate such a moral and intellectual disappointment onto an entire county and call it Nassau; sell the T-shirts, pay the taxes.

Of course, not everyone fits this description. There are some beacons of light, many of whom I have had the pleasure of basking in; but we are hopelessly outnumbered. A place like this forces a lot of alone time amongst the sane as we grasp to understand the insipidness around us; if one is so inclined, one can foster a fertile imagination. Some kids join gangs or commit suicide. Enticing as these things sound, they simply aren't for me. I found my serenity in performance art. I dabbled in writing and reciting poetry, playing in every genre of band, and performing standup comedy and music at local open mics; I now added mascoting as my newest form of expression in the otherwise aesthetically barren slice of hell known as Nassau County, Long Island.

So here's how it all happened: A month or two before our first bout, I had attended a party at Captain's house. I'd heard of roller derby, but the extent of my familiarity ended with knowing that the game involved roller skates. An old friend of mine, now renowned roller derby ref Mr. Rawk, invited some buddies and me along. He had had a long friendship with Captain Morgan and became one of the league's first refs.

I showed up at Captain's house with some friends of mine around ten o'clock on a Friday night. As we walked up to the house, we could hear the party from inside the walls. One of the few things Long Island does well is throw house parties. The set up of this particular house begged for celebration. Doors didn't separate the rooms downstairs—save the bathroom—so that left a lot of open space. The house was breathable, comfortable. I hoped that the people were as open as the residence. The dining room was converted into a gambling den. Out back, the yard panned a considerable size and came complete with a deck, pool, and that night, a king's bounty in alcohol; a perfectly middle-class abode. Beer pong ruled the back patio. I walked into the maelstrom and merriment of a good ole' fashioned kegger. Folks put hands upon hips and when one dipped, the other dipped. And then they dipped, and dipped, and dipped. As is my way whenever I arrive at a house party socially naked, I wanted to meet the host. I quickly sought out Mr. Rawk to introduce us.

"I think Jeff is upstairs," he shouted above the music. He pointed his thumb upwardly as if hitchhiking. Jeff is Captain Morgan's brother and derby ref, known amongst rollerfolk as Jefferee; though, the name is used here anachronistically. In those days Jefferee's ref name was "Zerba," a humorous hold over from a misspelling of the word "zebra" during his childhood. But someone else caught my attention; meeting Jefferee would have to wait. A girl with a shaved head, artsy nerd-hot librarian glasses, and an inquisitive look—Butterscotch Cripple—appeared just as misplaced as I was. We were both lost in a crowd we knew nothing about, silently saying, "Yes, I'm available for conversation! Plus, I'm non-threatening, hard-working, and will be a real asset to this organization." People brushed by her and I saw a look of small-talk excitement on her face that turned just as quickly to a sigh when the passersby just passed on by. She couldn't have missed the same expression in my face. Eventually (or naturally), our oddities caught eyes and the two people beyond the awkward began to talk-ward. We got along swimmingly and thus began a friendly relationship.

The party was coming to an end; after-hours bong rips and whiskey shots loomed twenty minutes or so over the horizon. As I sat on the living room couch talking to Butterscotch, a punk rock girl spun around and around on a computer chair. She yelled loudly and totted her beer high in the air like an outlaw waving a six-shooter in old western flicks. Wholly inebriated, and susceptible to high-speed swivel chair motions, she succumbed to gravity and the laws of motion. She flew off the chair and crash-landed into an old, wooden coffee table. The impact smashed it to pieces.

Worried, I dropped the conversation and picked her up.

"Are you alright?" I asked, concerned. Butterscotch grabbed her other arm to help lift her up.

She looked up at us with the largest smile I had ever seen. "Party foul!!" she yelled at me.

"We've got to find the owner of the house," I said. "I think he might still be upstairs."

"*He*?" she asked. "This is *my* house! Woo Hoo!!!!"

'Twas Captain Morgan.

I could tell already that I liked her. She had a punk flair that seemed genuine and old-school. After most had moved on, Captain retained her "don't forget your roots" credentials—an irresistible trait.[5]

Appeal of a Peel

By and by, I solidified a relationship with the league, not as a mascot or ref or anything, but as someone who was there. I was fascinated not only by the sport itself but also by the dedication of the members. Twice a week the girls assembled at a skate rink, beat the crap out of themselves and each other, and

---

[5] H2O, "Family Tree," *H2O* (1996).

showed up again the following week for more. The Long Island Roller Rebels league consisted of three teams: The East End Ladies of Laceration, The Mid-Island Rolling Thundercats, and The Wicked Wheelers of the West.[6] This last team concerns my personal roller derby story. Playing off the name, The Wicked Wheelers decided to incorporate a flying monkey mascot to stir up not only trouble but also the crowd. At some point unknown to me, someone posited the question, "Well, what goes with a monkey?" Only to be returned with: "A banana!"

One of the Roller Rebels, Percy Cute, had an old dirty banana costume decaying in the trunk of her car. The league set about finding someone to be the Wicked Wheelers' banana. The first person that they approached agreed to do it, albeit reluctantly. When I caught wind that a banana would be added to the bunch, I jumped on the opportunity. I love performing and proudly count myself a veteran of the class-clown army. I pleaded with them to let me try out, but it was for naught. It simply wouldn't be fair to the first guy they commissioned. In order to get the job, the original banana-hopeful would have to bow out.

"I can't believe you needed a banana and didn't ask me first," I complained to Butterscotch.

"I know, I'm sorry, but he's Captain's friend and he said he'd do it."

"Yeah, but he's not sure about it and here I am jumping up and down excitedly telling you I'll do it!" I jumped up and down excitedly to prove my point. "The job should go to the person more anxious because, by default, that person'll bring more to it!" *Flawless logic.* Still jumping up and down, I

---

[6] Known informally by our foes as the "Wasted Wheelers," due in no small part to our after-party bravado.

flapped my arms wildly to further confirm my sincerity. "I'll do it! I'll do it! I'll do it!"

Much to my fortune, the first banana's initial "yes" had been made in haste; it seemed he was rather happy to escape the gig. He gladly turned the job down, and when it came time to choose a new banana, Butterscotch Cripple pressed the team to give me a chance.

Good 'ole Butterscotch Cripple.

I had the job and figured instructions would surely follow. They never did. So, in answer to the question asked of me more times than my limited math skills can calculate, that's what a banana has to do with roller derby: nothing, really.

II

RABBLE IN SKATES

> *Can you imagine that call to the police? 'Um, yes, I'd like to report about a dozen girls in short skirts and knee socks skating around—they must be stopped!'*[1]
> BUTTER SCOTCH CRIPPLE

We didn't always call ourselves The Long Island Roller Rebels. The first name of the league was The Rockabetty Bruisers. When founding member Dirty Gertie quit The Bruisers, she took the name (it was her brainchild after all). While still The Rockabetty Bruisers, the team—no more than a dozen girls—skated on tennis courts, as no skate rink owners wanted to take a risk on roller derby. Other practices took place outside on public skating rinks after the public had retired for the evening. Sometimes neighbors called the cops (those damn Long Island soccer moms!) to come deal with that rabble in skates that made too much noise. The profanity that resulted from rink rash and fish net burn did nothing to strengthen the girls' discretion, and only further roasted the soccer moms' hotline to the fuzz.

---

[1] Quoted in Taylor Long, "Roller Derby League Blows Off Steam," *The Chronicle* (Dec. 15, 2005), B4.

And then there were the injuries. No one knew if insurance companies would cover roller derby related expenses.[2] When our girls sustained ER-worthy injuries they had to ... uh, get creative with the doctors about how they broke this or that bone. Sometimes all the creative language led to more serious charges. For example, Lady of Laceration Holly Cide's doctor thought she was in an abusive relationship. I remember laughing at that: *Imagine someone hitting Holly Cide and she not breaking his face.* Even after the team established itself as a serious organization and started to skate at Skate Safe, the owner at the time remarked that his "core business [was] hockey, not roller derby" and moved the Bruisers' practices to 11 p.m. on weekdays.[3] Captain Morgan adapted; she stopped soliciting rinks for "roller derby practice" and chopped her request down to the more generic "practice space." This created confusion and an uncertain future, causing a revolving door of skaters, refs, and officials. I'm sure most leagues go through this: a new member joins, swears s/he is down for the long haul, and disappears within a few weeks, unable to handle the frustrations of skating for a fledgling enterprise and unwilling to be part of a solution. The Long Island Roller Rebels dealt with this monthly, but nonetheless, we were determined to make our league work. As girls dropped out due to one reason or another, new girls stepped up to the skate.

Amid our ranks, several skaters stood out from the rest. One of our most notorious was Anna Tramp—our Roller Rebels ruffian. Her thigh bears a tattoo of one rollergirl pounding on another. "That's me, the one on top," she told me as she pointed to her tattoo. Her inked-likeness had the girl on the bottom in a

---

[2] See Appendix 2: Don't Show Me The Money.
[3] Quoted in Katie Thomas, "A Bruising Beginning," *Newsday* (Jan. 2, 2006), G7.

headlock; I was sure I'd seen the image before, but not in a magazine, a comic book, or on TV—no. This was a scene straight out of *The Life and Times of Anna Tramp*! Tramp was our eviction queen. I don't recall many a' bout that she wasn't ejected from for unnecessary roughness.

She didn't play nice off the track either. I remember one New Year's Eve party when Tramp, Fiesta, and Captain shared a house.[4] Tramp, drunk off her ass, decided to ring in the New Year with boxing gloves and a bathrobe. She pounded her gloves together and went to find Captain, who busily prepared shots in the kitchen. Tramp yelled absolute gibberish and swung drunkenly as if trying to kick the shit out of the air. By accident or luck, she landed several good punches on Captain and then fell into the open refrigerator door. Beers spilt on the tile floor, and someone shouted the obligatory "party foul!" The brawl then spilled into the hallway. Tramp took another series of swings and then, in a state of victorious bliss occasioned by alcohol, fell flat on her rump. To this day, I still remember her garbled "I won, right's?" as we lifted her up and placed her on her bed; on quiet nights, I can almost hear them.

Captain Morgan was no pushover. A powerhouse skater, she sailed as the flagship of our fleet, albeit one that had left her anchor back at port. After meeting her, I finally understood why the finest vessels have historically been referred to in the feminine. Captain Morgan carried the torch for those such as La Marquise de Frèsne and Lady Killigrew—women who have ruled the waves throughout the ages. The scourge of the seven

---

[4] Sometimes called "derbyhouses." Essentially, this is a house or apartment rented by two or more derbyists. Usually these are the places that are the first to open their doors to you when on the road. The Long Island Roller Rebels had two derbyhouses: Captain, Tramp, and Fiesta's pad; and the "Dark Side" where Roxie Heartless, Ruby Redrum, and Carnage Electra lived.

speeds, Captain, unlike her predecessors, has no taste for treasures. She thirsts only for the blood of other rollergirls—a terribly insatiable craving. I am not one to believe the often exaggerated "rollergirl bios" but Captain's always seemed plausible to me.

On the track, Captain skated with the power of a cast-iron cannon ball, ripping holes into hauls. Just as the opposing jammer thought she'd made it through the pack, Captain would zero-in on her. I would gasp, cover my ears, close my eyes, duck, and say a novena for the poor jammer. Within seconds, the premature celebration of the jammer would be cut short—Captain having smashed her into the next bout. The poor jammer never saw her coming and soon spiraled down into the dark depths of Davy Jones' locker. I'd smile. That's my Captain Morgan; the *Jolly Roger* on wheels.

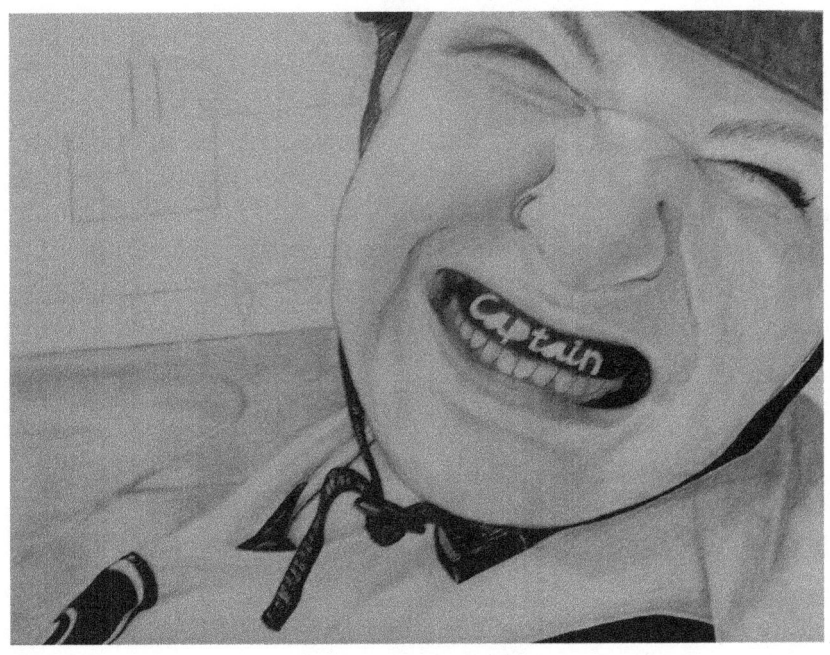

Any good Captain needs a crew. Always eager for the next adventure in life, Butterscotch Cripple signed on as first mate. She had just returned from Israel that 2005 feeling that she was missing something in her life. She needed that next voyage. Although she lived in New Jersey, she wouldn't let distance and geography stop her. She drove at least 400 miles every week (100 or so three to four times a week back and forth from practice on Long Island to New Jersey) and rarely showed any sign of fatigue. Butterscotch and I had an odd relationship. She was my best friend in the league, yet I didn't even know her real name. It sort of became a running ... rolling joke. When I would speak of her to my friends, they would instinctually ask me her real name. "I have no idea," I'd respond. Eventually (I think maybe two years after our first encounter), one of our girls slipped and called her by her real name. I fell to my knees and screamed an embellished "Noooooooo!"

During an interview with her university's newspaper *The Chronicle*, Butterscotch remarked, "You don't understand how differently you walk, how differently you view yourself after you get into derby ... you know you can take a hit. ... That's really important. I think a lot of women who have been through hell and back, they need that confidence."[5]

One of our Wicked Wheelers learned this lesson all too well. Carnage Electra had left her boyfriend's house after a heated argument back on Halloween night 2005. Sitting on a bench in a baseball field, she was attacked by a stranger. Thankfully, several people playing baseball saw the assault and chased the asshole away. "I felt completely disempowered," Carnage told me. "So, to try to gain back some sense of respect for myself, I needed to take back this confidence ... I needed to rebuild me. I didn't really know what could possibly happen ...

---

[5] Long, B4.

with what goes with trying to get to that place."[6] Not long after the encounter, a flier caught Carnage's attention: New York City's Gotham Girls Roller Derby league sought new recruits. Carnage prepared herself to try out for Gotham, but with the start of the Rockabetty Bruisers, felt that a league closer to home better suited her. This worked out well for the newly rechristened Long Island Roller Rebels—Carnage has been a dedicated skater, and since her ball field incident, become a force to be reckoned with.

We also had Chairman Meow who helped us out on our administrative end—he handled much of "our promotion, sponsorship, made a lot of phone calls, talked to screaming girls and venue owners, and did basically the derby office work." At first Mr. Chairman (as I called him) didn't have a derbyname because, "I wasn't one of the girls, and I didn't think I needed one." However, after one of the girls started to call him "Kung Fu Kitty" because of his martial arts background and love of cats, he rethought the name idea, settling on Chairman Meow because, as he says, "I sit in a chair and do paperwork." Butterscotch's trips to and from Jersey to practice and back again impressed us, as did Chairman's travels; a Chicago native, Chairman flew to New York whenever we needed him there. "The distance didn't matter," he told me, "I loved my league."[7]

When Chairman was absent, which given the distance between Long Island and Chicago was actually less often than one might expect, we had Heidi Ho-bag to make up the difference. I suppose that most leagues have one or two saviors who can be counted on, whether rain or shine, to make all the ins and outs of derby run more smoothly; Heidi Ho-bag was our messiah as evidenced by her numerous "Unsung Hero" awards

---

[6] Bane-ana, *Interview with Carnage Electra*, 29, March, 2000Great.
[7] Bane-ana, *Interview with Chairman Meow*, 14, August, 2000Great.

that she collected at our Roller Rebel Holiday Party every year. Although I always felt that there was a certain incongruence to presenting an "Unsung Hero" award (after all, one cannot receive an award and be "unsung" at the same time), I will make an exception for Heidi. Her addition to the league was also great for me. She could take a joke and—holy shit!—actually understood my sense of humor. She gave delicious and filling hugs and had some kind of intuition of bestowing them just when my tired soul needed them most.

And then there was Killer Tofu with that deceptive smile. Sporting a disarming look, I knew her to actually be a ruthless calculator and executor of strategies. This dichotomy was evidenced in her name. A vegetarian by trade, she broke her own veggie rules dishing up rollergirl flesh for breakfast, truly earning her moniker, "The Vegetarian Barbarian." I would often joke about her cannibalistic ways on the track. "Well, they get in my way,"[8] she told me. Meat isn't murder; Killer Tofu is. Like most other girls in the league, she also had a wonderfully sweet side. When Carnage Electra first joined the league, Tofu held her hand to help ease her nerves at the first bout. Her boyfriend (now husband) Thor became our head ref, though he was more like a god. As Captain remembers Thor: "We basically tried to copy Gotham's rules and did whatever the fuck Thor told us to do. We asked him everything."[9]

We also had announcers unlike any I'd ever heard. Matthew Scott La Rock and Jake Steele made a fantastic duo, fusing sports casting and comedy. They both possessed an iron wit; during some timeouts I couldn't even do a track run because their remarks had me in hysterics. I wasn't alone; others have felt the announcer's wrath as well. For example,

---

[8] Bane-ana, *Interview with Killer Tofu*, 29, March, 2000Great.
[9] Bane-ana, *Interview with Captain Morgan*, 29, March, 2000Great.

Steele would go on to have a bout-stopping moment later in his career. During one bout, the refs had to put the game on hiatus because they couldn't stop laughing.

The Long Island Roller Rebels looked anywhere for outlets to promote our league, in one such instance even appearing in that Bible of drug magazines *High Times* (Chairman Meow henceforth called us the "Bong Island Stoner Rebels"). Most of the girls had no palate for the paradisiacal plant but understood the necessity of getting the word of the Roller Rebels into a mainstream "news" outlet. Even the ruff and tumble Anna Tramp, who enjoyed an occasional smoke, didn't puff before bouts. As she put it, "I like being on edge, even angry, so I play more aggressively." Jefferee offered a slightly more liberal approach: "I smoke before, during, and after the bout."[10]

Earning WFTDA status changed all that.[11] The Women's Flat Track Derby Association (or "WFTDA" for short) is the governing body of the modern roller derby revolution, amending the rules as the growth of the sport necessitates. As the Roller Rebels matured as a league, we developed some of our own rules regarding pre-bout conduct. The Wicked Wheelers used to ceremoniously take a team shot of whiskey before every bout; the practice stopped once we sought WFTDA status. We developed a rule that barred anyone from drinking the night before a bout. There would certainly be no more smoking "before and during" bouts. As for the "after," well, the Roller Rebels became after-party queens, taking on (and down) any and all challenges to our title.[12]

---

[10] Bobby Black, *High Rollers*, High Times Magazine (Oct, 2006) p 60.

[11] We owed a big thank you to Gotham Girls Roller Derby for supporting our WFTDA initiative. That a bigger league helped a smaller one always stuck with me as an essential component of the "grass roots" revolution roller derby is supposed to be.

[12] See Appendix 3: After-Parties.

The more we practiced, played, and talked, the more the league became a unit. We would gather at Captain's house and watch bout footage from a league we were scheduled to play. As the girls studied their opponents' moves, I asked questions about the rules. Several Roller Rebels told me that I need only concern myself with the basics. But the truth was I wanted to know the rules. I liked ... *loved* the sport and wanted to know the ins and outs of how it worked. Moreover, if I didn't know the rules, how would I be able to work with them during game time? For example, the girls have only thirty seconds to line up on the track in between jams. If I thought that there was a full minute in between jams, one of my bits might have overlapped into the jam. Mascots, I have always maintained, are not supposed to interfere with the bout itself.

Briefly, I considered reffing. They got to whistle while they worked, and rules regarding ref conduct were already laid out—simply follow them. And it is a more respectable position than a mascot. No one fucked with the "zebras"; bananas were fair game. I even marshaled possible ref names for my transition: Home Reffer, Nick Name, A.C. Skater, Frank Lee Scarlet (the ref who just don't "give a damn"), Mark Mywords, Carmichael Weapon, Full Metal Jack, and probably scores of others long since forgotten. Captain's response to my reffing possibilities was simple: "No! You're our banana!" No one argues with Captain.

Before the Roller Rebels' first bout, the practices I attended had piqued my interest in roller derby; after the first bout, I was enthralled. I decided to pay league dues. Captain told me that, as a non-skater, I didn't have to shell out anything. I wanted to pay them though. The Roller Rebels was my league, and I wanted to support it any way I could. Killer Tofu, an inspiration to us all, could "barley" afford her own seeds, roots, tree bark, and whatever the hell else vegetarians ate, yet she too faithfully paid her monthly dues. When money was plentiful (the exception), we donated to various human interest groups[13]; when money was tight (the rule), we held fundraisers.

One such fundraiser took place at McCoys, a bar far out east in the abyss of Suffolk County. I usually wouldn't trek that far out east for anything—too confusing. It's as if the people who live in Suffolk want rustic, but can't (or won't) fully commit. Growing up in Nassau at least afforded me a twenty minute drive on the parkway into the greatest city on the planet. Going the other direction seemed ... I dunno. Suffolk just always seemed so far away—both geographically and aesthetically.

But in those nascent days of Roller Rebeldom, everyone had to contribute to survive. I walked into McCoys to find what can only be called an outpost for the fleeting Long Island heavy metal scene. The weighty, bearded dude in the Slayer shirt and his local-band shirt-sporting skinnier counterpart sat at the bar—the last vestiges of a dying culture. How sad. I used to love going to metal shows, but the whole thing had sort of dried up. Everyone needs something beautiful in life, and these fellows were hanging onto their skulls and mutilations the way post-70s hippies hang onto being full of shit. Not that I equate the two—I refer here only to *the struggle*.

On the stage to the back of the bar, Killer Tofu danced in her skates while an unruly crowd cheered on her performance. Behind them, other people danced to the music that was louder than the speakers could audibly amplify. Amongst them, I saw some guy who had his collar curved in such a way that it waved over the back of his neck like a fin. I ordered a drink and said hello to Captain, Tofu, and others. I made my rounds, but kept going back to that dude with the flipped collar. *Why would*

---

[13] See Appendix 4: Community Based, Community Baste.

someone purposefully set out to look like an asshole? Then it hit me; *Oh ... right. Long Island ...*

In the corner opposite the stage, the girls set up an "arm wrestle a rollergirl" table to make some extra cash for the fundraiser. I decided that if we were truly serious about arm wrestling strangers, we should take off our clothes. "We should get naked," I yelled.

I took all my clothes off, parked my ass behind the table, and offered to arm-wrestle any takers. The guys declined, but shit did the girls love it. One-by-one, they stepped up to the plate to arm-wrestle the unpeeled banana. It was a lot fun until Anna Tramp almost broke my wrist.

"Uncle!" I screamed in pain, half bent over the table.

"You mean *Aunt!*" she yelled as she squished my hand.

Dedly Weaponz, a Thundercat, grabbed a thick black marker and wrote "Property of Dedly Weaponz" on my chest. When I protested, she raised her hand like she was going to slap me. I shut up. It took me two days to scrub her territorial scribbles off my chest completely.

These fundraisers weren't solely about raising funds. They are essential to league building. Working together on the track was one thing; working off the track was something else entirely. Fundraisers, I always felt, served a surrogate role between bouts and the off-season. We all wanted the league to work. We had to—no one else gave a shit yet.

Derbyfolk know that skating is only half the job at a bout. There are also specialized committees such as coaching, promotion, fundraiser organizing, bout production (and many more). I signed up for the bout production committee. I worked closely with Holly Cide, and together, we ensured that our bouts went off as close to "without a hitch" as possible. We solicited bands to play the bouts, set up the track, brought enough water for everyone, set up chairs and merch tables, spoke with special

Roller Derby: The Sensation That Caused A Book!

interest groups to donate proceeds to, and did a zillion smaller jobs like simply bringing girls a last minute safety pin or hairspray. I offered my P.A. system for free to save the league the rental fee. Twice, I had my P.A. destroyed by a band we hired to play the bout.

Feelings of exhaustion came in waves. I found that the more I involved myself in roller derby, the more complicated my life became. This seems to be the one "universal" of all derbyists, and nearly all will freely tell you about the hell that derby has made of her or his life (just keep the shots coming). Boyfriends, girlfriends, jobs, careers, families, friends all will eventually get in the way and you will constantly have to make choices between the enumerated and roller derby. It is a truism that most derbyfolk are forced to live two lives: professional by day, derbyist by night. Derby awarded me the opportunity to juggle four lives: derbyist, (not-so) gainfully employed American, graduate student, and bandleader. Eventually all four of these roles collided. I remember one particularly disastrous weekend well: After a night of cramming for a midterm, I took said midterm, went home, packed up my guitar and amp gear, and played a gig at The Bitter End in Manhattan. From there, I went home, took a shower, lay awake in bed for all of three hours, got up, and went to work. After work, I reloaded the band equipment into my car, drove out to a Roller Rebels' fundraiser, played an awful set, and after two hours of sleep, woke up Sunday morning hung over and went back to work. This hectic routine, more or less, was my life until I graduated.

Pun Crock: Fun Intended!

Some of the girls (and guys) in roller derby have certain songs that they listen to ritualistically before a bout. The songs are usually (but not always) fast, aggressive, and—like the girls who listen to them—hard-hitting. Adrenaline-spiked punk rock, warrior-esque Goth-Viking black metal, or bone-crushing hardcore could be heard bursting out of car windows as girls arrived to the venue. I don't have any such play lists. When I arrive at the venue, I'm usually so nervous that I say as little as possible (which is good because I talk too much anyway). After set up, I patiently wait for the back "locker" room to empty before I slip into my peel. When the cacophonous mix of girls and heavy metal has vanished, I turn out the lights and sit there. I don't meditate or anything like that; I don't pray or contemplate; I don't do anything at all; I disappear. It can be a scary thing—to not exist, to be just awareness—but a piece of me embraces such feelings as part of the natural order. Any music or sound would ruin these fleeting moments before a bout; tapping into the certainty of mortality demands complete attention. Retrospectively, I cannot think of a single reason I did that other than needing those moments of silence to appreciate the gifts of all that was about to commence. I tried to remain there for as long as I could. No grind of a song could ever pump me up more than the silent recognition that I will be dead one day. It forced me to be wholly alive while I was there.

Outside my little world, Furious George and I decided that our job was not only to amp up the crowd but also to act as a bridge between the audience members and the skaters. Bring them as close to the action as possible without, say, one of the girls swan diving into a trackside onlooker.[14] I don't know what possessed us to think we were even allowed to do this. Upon reflection, it seems kind of like a dick move—were we overstepping our boundaries? I could just hear the heads of WFTDA scrambling in a meeting shouting, "Who authorized

---

[14] Though, no one ever complained when that happened.

these idiots?!" Happily, we weren't that important or known to the larger derby world to be on anyone's radar.

Or maybe the answer to why no one cared lies in the difference between old roller derby and the roller derby of today? Before WFTDA, the hits in derby were theatrical; the outcomes, predetermined. We figured that since the girls were all business on the track (and not fake at all), we mascots should keep the old theatrics alive. Nostalgia never goes out of style. Following the model of the Texas Rollergirls, we kept the theatrics off the track and relegated it to the sidelines—a sideshow. That way fans could separate the sport of roller derby from the aesthetic of it.

Besides the fact that "every cliché has a morsel of truth" is itself cliché, its cousin, the courageous, all-American "practice makes perfect!" also discredits it; for the latter is without truth—at least for Furious and me. The more bouts we attended, the more we started to wonder how soon the crowd would grow weary of our antics. Furious would chase me around the track or jump on my back and together we would run around the sidelines for fans, ending with a wrestle. Other than waving pompoms and screaming, we didn't have much else to go on. But the crowd never seemed to bore with it, so long as we timed our antics properly. Any comedian will tell you that delivery is key; same rule holds true for mascoting. You need to know how much space to give the girls, the refs, the fans. You need to know when to scream and when to shut the fuck up. Before every bout, I would find the head refs and let them know that Furious and I would always be aware of them and they needn't worry about us. If we ever seemed like we weren't paying attention, we were—it was all part of the act. Sometimes, the whistle would blow after a timeout before Furious and I made it back to the Wheelers' bench. At that point, we would jump into the crowd and cheer from behind it. We never had to be told not to run around the track while a jam was in session; we simply figured as much. Sometimes rollergirls would chase us down and give us a good walloping; I started to look forward to them because the crowd always responded so loudly. I never cared about getting hurt, only about applause.

On some particularly scary occasions, Furious wouldn't be able to make a bout, and I would have to go alone. Since no one gave me any ideas or advice (the girls, after all, had their own bout necessities to worry over), I decided that the roller derby mascot's job was open to interpretation. Girls often told Furious and me to just "get out there and do your thing." Only I didn't have a "thing" without my mascot counterpart.

But there was hope. Other than getting picked on in high school, fifteen years of writing will also accustom someone with the fine skill of wordplay; thus, I gave small comedic bits a try. I made up goofy sentences that revolved around a single word and recited them to audience members: "Joan of Arc cross dressed so she could cross swords all for the glory of the Cross, then she was burned by men of the Cross who were cross with her because she crossed them," and "We're aware of where the werewolf's wares wear and tear"; others that revolved around a single idea: "Did the stool pigeon rat on the loan shark to the big dog for playing a deadly game of cat and mouse with the pigs? Or was the little weasel so chicken he cowed and felt sheepish?" and "I make pillow talk about putting blanket statements concerning cover bands that use sheet music to bed"; and puns too: "I quit deli meats … cold turkey"; "I have a scab … I made it from scratch!"; "to stop Queens from going to shit, keep Flushing!"

I would directly interact with audience members, a tactic that an internet search of "mascot etiquette" deemed against policy (if an audience member asks you a question, you are supposed to just stay silent and shrug your shoulders like an asshole). I never was good with convention—mascot or otherwise—and whenever I saw someone at a bout wearing a yellow shirt, I couldn't help but approach them, in full banana garb, and say something smugly to the tune of, "Pfft! What kind of an idiot wears yellow?" When someone would ask why I dressed like a banana, I'd reply, "Well, it has 'a peel.'" Later, I added, "Although it has 'a peel,' sometimes I feel like a fruit." One of my favorite things to do was spell my name out for derbyfans the way a receptionist spells a name (let's say, Adam) over the phone: "'A' as in 'apple';'D' as in 'dog' ...." I'd say: "Bane-ana. That's 'B' as in 'Botulism in Belfast; 'A' as in 'Ane-bana'; 'N' as in 'Nigerian freedom fighters'...." Taking a bathroom break became "draining potassium." Autographs became "slaughter-graphs." Every slaughter-graph that I signed came with some kind of positive message for balance: "*Stay in school, Bane-ana*"; "*Live life to its fullest, Bane-ana*"; "*Keep an open heart and mind, Bane-ana.*"

On the more risqué side of things, if my banana hood limped over my head and someone commented about it, I would say, "I know, I know, I ran out of Viagra this morning." This joke helped me out a great deal, as wear on the outfit made keeping the hood upright almost impossible. Likewise, on the odd chance that the hood behaved itself by staying vertical, questions like, "How does that thing stay up?" were met with, "I remembered to take my Viagra this morning." Kids got the G-rated answer: "Cause I'm full of hot air."

The problem with the jokes was that they only worked before and after the bouts and during halftime. I needed something physical to do during the thirty-second jam hiatus if Furious couldn't make a bout. With the following spring came not an answer, but a start towards one. Spring 2006 saw another season of kickball. My friends and I had played kickball for years and eventually joined Brooklyn Kickball July of that year.

I had emerged from winter a fully rested beast, woken from my decades-long slumber via roller derby. At McCarren Park, where we played kickball, I happened upon a youngling—about 13 or 14 years old—doing front handsprings, backwards somersaults, cartwheels, and other amateur circus tricks.

As a kid, I too had dabbled in minor acrobatics. Not because I aspired a future in gymnastics, but because I wanted to duplicate the nimble moves of Jackie Chan and the elegant ass kicking of Bruce Lee. My brother Frank and I used to rent their movies and slow-mo the fight scenes in order to learn exactly what they were doing. We didn't play video games and opted to make our own kung-fu movies with our friends instead, "borrowing" our dad's video camera while he was at work. We were young and made of rubber. Back then, learning a front handspring didn't take long at all; I simply convinced myself that I could do one and did it. *Ahhhh ... youth.*

Moving forward to summer 2000 aught 6, I strutted into my backyard on a particularly sunny day, convinced that I could still execute a front handspring. But my 26-year-old body was not the same as my prior 13-year-old one, and on my first attempt, I promptly broke my ass. *Okay. What about a cartwheel?* These I could still do, albeit sloppily; a problem that a little practice would straighten right out. I sighed with relief and stubbornly refused to accept that I couldn't execute a front handspring anymore. After my muscle memory sobered up and a few days of tenderizing my derriere, I was able to perform a front handspring again. I practiced over and over so as not to lose it and even pulled off a one-handed handspring as well.

Although handsprings and cartwheels wouldn't be enough, sadly, that was all I could do. To make up for this, I added pompoms, and Jenna Fiesta also gave me little black and green Wicked Wheeler flags, one of which I whitened-out with whiteout. If The Wheelers' had a substantial lead in the game, I would hand the flag to a member of the opposing team so that she could "wave the white flag." At one of our later bouts, one of the skaters from the Thunder Cats snatched the flag from my hand, snapped it in two, and threw it at me.

The Roller Rebels, eager to play other teams outside of New York, arranged our first interleague bout against Boston Massacre that summer. I was anxious to try out my modest acrobatics. As I ran around the track, I broke the predictable routine that running around the track had become. Instead of just plopping myself back on the Roller Rebels' side, I decided to end my short journey with a handspring. I was sure I could do it! Just when I got around the third turn of the track, without slowing down even a tad, I tried the handspring and fell flat on my rump. I felt embarrassed, but the audience cheered. I guess they thought I had meant to fall. I hadn't. Or maybe they preferred that my move didn't work? Seemed more likely. Whatever the reason, I got a reaction and made my way back to The Wheelers bench and waited for a good run. I didn't have to wait long. Allison Chains took lead and had a spectacular jam. Going on my new insight into roller derby fan psychology, I did a cartwheel—something I could certainly land—and "unintentionally" fell into some audience members. Did they get mad? No, they cheered! I looked into the eyes of the girl I fell into and asked, "Am I a banana in your lap or are you just happy to see me?" She resonated with the most heartwarmingly intoxicating sound that the gods had ever concocted—the female giggle.

As time went on, more and more girls would attack me and give me a walloping. One time it was Toxic Shock, the next time it was Sissy Facekick; another time it was both. Then, one night, a young girl—a relative of our best jammer C-Roll—started punching me in the leg. I went with it. Her friends ran over and they started beating me up too. I fell to the floor clutching my knee tightly and screaming in exaggerated pain. Later, at the after-party, The Rebels informed me that the kids enjoyed beating me up and convinced me (i.e. poured shots down my throat) to go along with it. Thus began a staple prepubescent flogging at every bout.

Sometimes Furious and I simply improvised. During halftime at the 2006 season opener (Thunder Cats vs. Wicked Wheelers), Furious, Chairman Meow, and I swept up the track as the Wheelers talked strategy in the backroom. Sensing an improv-ortunity, we didn't just brush track rubbish into the dustpan, but instead kneeled on the floor, turned the brooms around, and like pool-sharks, shot the empty bottles and loose papers into the pan. At first, no one noticed. Then a few disparate chuckles could be heard from a few audience members. After several good shots, we managed to get applause out of the crowd every time we sunk a piece of trash. I turned the broom back around, bristle-side down, and now had my very own putter. I continued to knock more pieces of trash into the bin.

"Nice shot, Tiger," yelled a fan, making a loose reference to the golfer.

"Your compliment is too late!" I said in an imposing voice. "It's not a golf club, it's a croquet mallet." I placed my foot on an empty water bottle, arched back, and wound up to hit it. I swung the broom passed the bottle, 360 degrees, clunked myself in the noggin with it, and fell down on my bottom. The crowd still cheered as Furious, Meow, and I walked into the back meeting room.

"Is the track ready?" asked Butterscotch.

" 'Twas a sweeping success," I beamed.

But it was at this bout that I also made my first big mistake. Upping the ante for The Roller Rebels' season opener, I bought two bags of confetti and threw handfuls of it at the crowd. Not everyone, of course: derby-crazed applause was spared; those sitting quietly received the full onslaught of my confetti wrath! I would keep dowsing them with my pixie dust until they cheered; then I would move on.

While The Thunder Cats held the lead, my confetti nonsense didn't seem to bother anyone, save a few shy folks who didn't like being egged on to cheer (one girl rather angrily told me to "fuck off already"). Once The Thunder Cats started to trail behind The Wheelers' by a little, Thunder Cat captain Raven Madd flipped on me.

"My skaters can't skate with you acting like an idiot all the time! They're gonna break their necks on your stupid confetti!" she blasted at me.

She was right, and I knew it. I hadn't thought about that. A girl could easily slip on the confetti and hurt herself, so I discarded the bags until after the bout. It was important for me to consider the skaters' safety when contemplating new gags. Raven sort of did me a favor there; she stopped me from causing an injury.

Also at this bout, the drinking had started to spiral into problems. No, not my drinking—the audience's. Usually, drunks in the crowd were merry and often conveniently blinded by their beer goggles to the un-necessity of mascots. Other times, I'm less enthusiastic to report, a sauced spoilsport would shout a loud "these guys suck!" at us. I'm fully aware that my attire makes for an easy target. To combat this, I would usually hang around the parking lot before the bout killing any would-be heckler with kindness. I hate to admit it, but a little bit of profiling did go into play. If fans were already drunk and loud in the parking lot, chances were good they would be even drunker and louder inside where the action was. *Get them while they tailgate*—everyone was happy then; their team hadn't lost yet. During ½ time, I might even buy ½ wits a beer at ½ price in a ½–hearted attempt to cut their ill-will towards me in ½. I also started carrying around a lighter. If I saw someone pulling a cigarette out, I'd run over and unexpectedly light it. This would not only assure heckling-silence but also would get her or his friends—whose cigarettes I often lit as well—on my side. Then we would take a picture, I'd sign a flyer or a program and badda boom badda bing, I could rest easy. Buy 'em a beer, smoke 'em out, do whatever it takes.

Our audience turnouts grew with each bout and we needed a bigger after-party bar to house all the fans. Resting conveniently down the road from Skate Safe, El Loco Donkey was a spacious bar that could easily fit all the skaters, refs, support staff, and all their friends, family members, and fans. Only problem was that the owners didn't bother to tell the league that there was a dress code for the guys (not the girls, mind you) and some of us were denied entrance into the bar. Furious and I stood outside in the rain frantically calling Butterscotch, who enjoyed herself inside, unable to hear the ring of her phone over the music. We watched dudes with hedgehog haircuts (lame), pre-ripped store-bought jeans (lamer), and popped-collared shirts (the absolute lamest) douchebagingly stroll into the bar. Apparently, Furious and I didn't look enough like jackasses to get into El Loco Donkey. When Butterscotch finally received our frantic call, she rounded up what girls she could find, gave a "thanks but no thanks" fuck you to the managers of El Loco Donkey, and we all sped off to Mr. Beery's, a bar more suited to our tastes.

III

WOMEN WHO SKATE WITH THE WOLVES

Roller derby: same shit, different state.
CYANIDE KISSES

*You know roller derby—
this week's bullshit is next week's joke.*
LAYLA SMACKDOWN

Undoubtedly, my favorite aspect of roller derby is the travel bouts, a euphemism for "derby weekend." For me, the travel bout begins the Thursday night before the weekend with some kind of nightmare. I dream that I forgot something, or no fans show up at the bout, or The Roller Rebels get booed, or the most nefarious of all: mascoting naked. After a brief 5 am wake up to check if, at the very least, I have all of my costume and won't mascot nude, I fall back to sleep for a few more hours. On Friday afternoons, I'd join the rest of the entourage that would assemble at Captain's house and hyperventilate until the last Roller Rebel arrived. Then off we went.

Usually The Roller Rebels would show up in some city the night before the bout and spend the evening in our m/hotel rooms polishing, coloring, stickering, fine tuning, adjusting, *everythinging* the girls' equipment. The next day, we would arrive at the rink early to help with the set up. Then bout time, clean up, after-party, after-after-party at the hotel, wake up, nurse hangover, throw up, and drive home. Stored in the recesses of my memory are random snippets and pieces of The Roller Rebels' first two seasons.

Night of the Rolling Dead

> *This is not Vietnam, there are rules.*[1]
> *Walter Sobchak*

Sometimes it seemed like roller derby didn't have any rules at all. It did, of course, but the many adjustments to the rules caused numerous mishaps along the way of the sport's evolution. Sometimes different leagues had different rules, which also led to problems. Such was the case with The Roller Rebels' first travel bout. Three days before Halloween in 2006, we chartered a bus to southern New Jersey to play The Penn-Jersey She Devils. We adopted a pirate theme, "The Scally-hags," and played The Penn-Jersey She Devils, cast as the "Zombetties." Some Roller Rebels even changed their derbynames for the bout: Aunty Christ became "Jack's Spare Hoe," Iris Carbomb became "One-Eyed Willa," and Allison Chains became "Treasure Chest."

Butterscotch had been a friend of some of the She Devils and acted as liaison between our two leagues. She met them at an earlier bout between The She Devils and Virginia's Dominion Derby Girls. It was Dominion's first interleague bout, and they played by WFTDA rules; The She Devils did not. As the game progressed, Butterscotch noticed that a lot of

---

[1] *The Big Lebowski.* Dir. Joel and Ethan Cohen. Polygram Filmed Entertainment, 1998.

fouls—at least fouls by way of standard WFTDA rules—went uncalled by the Penn-Jersey refs. Since Dominion hadn't yet played outside their own intra-league bouts, they didn't contest any of the Penn-Jersey refs' calls. At the after-party, Butterscotch asked The She Devils if they planned on playing by WFTDA rules when the Roller Rebels came down to bout them. She was met with blank faces. "From then on, I knew it was going to be a disaster," she told me. At our next practice, Butter explained to us, "They aren't going to know the rules ... but it's okay because they're going to get called on them and spend the whole time in the box, so it's all good. Let them hit you—just let them foul out. 'Cause when half the team is gone they are going to have to forfeit."

Several of us couldn't make the bus departure time. So Mr. Rawk, Furious George, Sissy Facekick, and I drove my car to the bout. This worked in our favor as reports of plentiful vomit on the bus ride later leaked out. At some point on the way, we got lost, and when we finally arrived, the bout was one jam in. Skaters from both teams had situated themselves in the center of the track. Up until then, I had only seen referees patrol that area—not skaters. Furious George and I had grown comfortable in our fur and peel by this time and took our position with The Scally-hags in the middle of the track. "Get the fuck out of here!" yelled one of the Penn-Jersey refs. There was a foul air looming. Furious and I ran across the track to the far side of the rink.

'Twould be unfair to demonize the whole of The She Devils due to the transgressions of only one or two skaters, so I won't. The Zombetties (for the most part) didn't play dirty or anything like that, and their refs weren't assholes to our girls (just to Furious and me). They simply didn't know and/or play by WFTDA rules.

For the first time in our short careers, Furious and I didn't run around the track to charge up the crowd. Dogs can sense thunderstorms, cats can detect rain, and mascots can feel crowd disapproval. The place was rife with it! Many timeouts, bitching, and a lot of yelling from the middle of the track had the audience pissed. The distending tension between the two teams had heated up to the point of combustion. The bout took a cruel turn. I fell back into my defenses and started to feel uneasy, vulnerable.

Over in the middle of the track where the girls, coaches, and refs readied themselves for the next bit of nonsense, a commotion stirred. Suddenly, the rink filled with loud "boos." Jefferee was battling the whole of Penn-Jersey! Refs, coaches, girls, fans, everyone! Fists cut the air, skates kicked violently, and I shit myself. Jefferee was thrown out of the rink and several She Devils fans followed close behind him. No fight erupted in the parking lot. Jefferee got onto the bus, pounded a few beers, and cooled down.

Back inside, the Roller Rebels talked of forfeiting the bout. I thought it a bad idea because we were trailing in points. I suggested we make up the point differential first and then bail. Not so that we could leave as winners, but rather, so that we wouldn't look like sore losers. Raven Madd got raving mad with me because, clearly, the whole debacle had been *my* fault. I don't know whether Raven got ejected or quit, but at some point she took her skates off and stormed out of the rink. As for what happened next, I have two conflicting accounts: According to one version, with two minutes left in the game, Madd pulled out The Roller Rebels, which is why she stormed out. In another version, we finished out the bout and quickly left. I remember the former unfolding. Either way there was no grand finale, no after-party. The girls joined Jefferee on the bus; Rawk,

Facekick, Furious George, and I got into my car. The drive home was silent.

Mob Town

Later that season, The Long Island Roller Rebels lost a lot of key members. Some girls transferred to Manhattan's Gotham Girls (or others leagues) or quit roller derby altogether. The timing couldn't have been worse; we had a bout scheduled against the Baltimore League, The Mobtown Maulers. To make matters more of a pain in the ass, some of our most seasoned players couldn't make the bout for reasons ranging from family obligations to possible jail terms, as crossing state lines violated Anna Tramp's parole agreements. Our team consisted mostly of fresh bloods, girls who had made it into the league but were still in training. We decided to play anyway and took a road trip to Baltimore.

At the time, The Mobtown Maulers could only bout on Sundays due to the arrangements made with the rink, Puttyhill Skateland. A flier on the door of the entrance promised fans a "heated head to head-banging battle"[2] between The Maulers and us. The Mobtown Maulers was a team of exceptional skaters, most demonstrated in the performance of star jammer, Joy Collision. The few bouts I'd attended hadn't prepared me for her moves. She fluttered around The Rebels, displaying what I am convinced was, and still is, the most highly evolved sense of echolocation a human being can obtain. Aware of every inch of her body, she contorted her remarkably malleable extremities carefully around our blockers, finding the short synapses in our defense and swamping them with her adrenaline. Readjusting

---

[2] Promotional Flier, *Taped on the Front Door of Puttyhill Skateland*, 14, March, 2007.

her position within seconds if she felt even the slightest breath of a Roller Rebel crawling down her neck, Joy Collision danced through the pack like a ricocheting rubber bullet. It was as if the entire bout had already been scripted beforehand and only Joy had shown up for dress rehearsal. She need only remember her lines and let the show play out. Never ad-libbing, never delaying or forgetting a response, she smeared Shakespeare over the track and rolled over the poetry of her own movements.

The Rebels were having a rough time out there. I looked over at Captain. Hands on her hips, she surveyed the track with the cold skepticism of a general. Her eyes carefully combed the pack looking for any sign of a possible tactic to be deployed in a desperate situation. Suspended in a hopeless struggle, she hung over the edge of two irreconcilable possibilities: doubt and hope. Winning, you see, was as unthinkable to her as giving up.

Good 'ole Captain Morgan.

Amaretto Sourpuss, one of our more promising fresh bloods, skated over to the jammer line. She had put up a hell of a fight but looked tired, distraught. Yet she stood proudly on the jammer line awaiting the executioner's whistle. The sweat dripping down from beneath her helmet polished her face to a shiny glow; the worried look in her eyes spoke of a mind that juggled between the task at hand and her three-ring circus of nerves. The Mauler jammer beside her, Lady Quebeaum, stood differently than Sourpuss—and with good reason: she knew what she was doing. I looked at Sourpuss with anxiety and hope. She had taken a lioness' share of licks during the bout and never complained once, never refused to take the line, never once didn't give everything she had. I thought to myself—even as she was pummeled from all sides—*there is a future queen of the track.*

The pack lined up ten feet in front of the two jammers. The Roller Rebels, however, needed a fourth blocker. With the jam about to start, Fiesta yelled, "Holly Cide! Get out there!" We all turned to an empty bench. Wait a minute ... *where is Holly Cide?* She had left. An old injury, courtesy of Anna Tramp, had unstitched itself from deep within her belly. She left the bout and bought a plane ticket back to New York, thus ending her roller derby career.

Amaretto Sourpuss

Back on the track, the whistle blew, and Lady Quebeaum exploded through the pack, leaving Sourpuss to deal with Charm City's seemingly impenetrable blocking force. Suddenly, a whiff of refined horseshit pummeled my nostrils. I looked behind me as Raven Madd puked into a small garbage can behind the bench, the stink of her breath rivaling that of her kneepads. I gagged, not noticing that Lady Quebeaum was on a collision course with me. She flapped her arms around violently and tried to catch herself. I tried to move, but there was no place to go. I braced myself as Quebeaum crashed into me, taking us both to the floor. I thought she was going to kill me for getting in her way. She didn't. She dove back into the pack, never missing a beat. She had bigger fish to fry: our skaters.

I got up and continued to cheer, trying not to become disheartened by the unfolding slaughter. Furious and I ran around the track. Acting oblivious to the scoreboard, I approached Maulers' fans and yelled such absur–dittys like, "You guys are going down! ... to the morgue to drop off our carcasses." Another person got: "I knew this would happen! I knew our amazingness would rub off on your team ... can we have it back now, please?" Some people laughed; others thought I was stupid. I did a cartwheel. A kid yelled at me, "Why are you cheering? You guys are losing! You suck!" Furious jumped on me. I ran with him around the track. When the whistle blew we quickly jumped into the crowd to avoid possibly obstructing the players—my brush with Lady Quebeaum still fresh in my mind. But this led to another problem: possibly obstructing a fan's view. In a matter of moments, a derby photographer flipped on us.

"Get the fuck out of the way!" he put his camera up to his face and then pulled it back down. "Fuck! Did you see that block! I missed it! Stay the fuck clear of this area!"

Furious and I hurried back to The Roller Rebels' side. I felt something solid and sticky on my left knee. I looked down; I was bleeding. The blood acted like a natural adhesive, gluing my knee to the yellow leggings, adding a spot of orange. *Fuck, Butter gave me these. She's gonna be pissed.* I assumed I got cut when Lady Quebeaum fell into me; I must have opened the wound up further as I ran around cheering.

Aside from our slaughter on the track, I didn't feel intimidated off the track. The fans were, for the most part, cool, and Maulers' refs Johnny Zebra and Justice Feelgood Marshall had a calm but assertive handle on things. I would even go as far as to call them sticklers for the rules. Mobtown Maulers jammer Betty Beatdown told me that she was my "biggest fan." The air of this bout, even with our humbling performance, was pure and inviting.

The Mobtown Maulers' announcers had me rolling on the floor hysterically. Dirty Marty and Jimmy Valentine made quite the witty pair, with an announcing style more like that of comedians than that of sports anchors. Such lines like, "And the crowd goes … mild," if the audience wasn't cheering loud enough, and "Joy Collision, the jammer without a pause!" had me laughing to the point that I couldn't stand up straight.

In the third period, The Maulers' decided to add one final insult to a bout's worth of injury, jamming blockers Rosie the Rioter, Cindy Lop-her, and Australian native Berzerker to score a cumulative seventeen points. We brought the largest point spread in derby history (289-16) back as a souvenir.

After our upset, I helped clean up the track. I pulled the track tape and rope off the floor, and collapsed all the folding chairs, setting them neatly against the wall. As I cleaned, a little girl asked me for my autograph. "You're silly!" she laughed. I signed her program and reminded her to always follow her dreams. Her father shook my hand. With a big smile, he swapped a "thanks" for a, "Boy, you guys really suck!"

"Nah, that's just our odor. We don't suck"—I sniffed under my armpit—"we stink!"

"Well better luck next time."

I had almost finished stacking all the chairs when two kids ran up to me and started kicking me in the ass. I fell over and pretended that I was dying. Apparently, word had spread that pounding on the banana was a fun way to end the night for kids. Forgetting the chairs next to me, I rolled over and knocked into one. The first one slid down off of the others, ending abruptly when the two crunched right legs punched me in the side of the head. Then, like tree branches in a hurricane, they all started to come down on me with a loud "clang!" The kids laughed and ran away. Some maintenance people heard the crashing chairs and ran towards me to help ... by laughing their asses off. I picked up all the chairs and restacked them against the wall. By this time, I figured everyone was wondering where the hell I was and what I was still doing inside. I grabbed my sports bag and ran outside still dressed like a banana.

Captain and the others had been waiting patiently for me in Captain's car.

"You still haven't changed?" asked Killer Tofu.

"I didn't have time. I started messing around with some kids and ended up knocking all the chairs over," I said anxiously.

"Well, knock this over," said Captain handing me a flask.

When we arrived at the after-party, I stayed behind in the car to change my clothes while everyone else went inside. I started to unpeel when I remembered the maintenance men's reactions. I pulled my banana cover back down over my body. An idea dawned on me: *why not mascot the after-party too?* I waltzed into the bar still in costume and received a warm welcome from the patrons.

I spent the first part of the after-party telling jokes to people, performing barroom magic tricks, and trying to juggle saltshakers. I spent the second half of the after-party justifying the point spread; I ran from table to bar stool explaining that a lot of our veterans weren't there for whatever reason. I don't think anyone really cared though. The bout was over; it was time to party. That night, I started a tradition with Essie Ecks, one of The Maulers' fresh bloods. My banana suit was color-coordinated with their yellow and black boutfits, so Essie and I traded clothes. I walked around the bar self-aggrandizing about how wonderfully I had played in the bout.

East Coast Derby Extravaganza '07

My phone rang. The caller I.D. read "Cap Tin Morgue." I anxiously answered. As was always the case when she called, some adventure laid waiting for me on the other side of the ring. It wasn't Captain though; it was Butterscotch Cripple calling from Captain's phone.

She wasted no time. "You coming to E.C.E?"[3]

"What's E.C.E.?"

I could hear Butterscotch talking to other people in the room. A faint, "Banana's coming?" came through the phone to my end. "Yeah, he's in." After some garbled noise, Captain got back on the phone.

"Hello?"

"Easy E ... like the rapper?" I asked. "Isn't he dead?"

---

[3] The true abbreviation for the East Coast Derby Extravaganza is "ECDX." Apparently, that tremendous shortening of the name is still too long for our zippy new millennium, and the event is universally referred to as "E.C.E" by rollerfolk the world over.

"No, it's the East Coast Derby Extravaganza!"

The first ECDX was in 2007. Hosted by the Philly Roller Girls, it provided a meeting ground for over thirty different leagues across America to convene for an onslaught of roller derby action throughout St. Patrick's Day weekend. Fun as the event would prove, it also promoted serious derby objectives. As more and more cities and towns discovered roller derby, it became paramount "to foster interaction between established leagues and newer leagues in a fun, yet competitive, environment,"[4] which included sanctioned bouts, challenge bouts, and scrimmages.[5] Events like this also helped introduce roller derby to wider audiences.

C-Roll, Roxie Heartless, and Ruby Redrum piled into my car, and we battled both snow and shitty drivers down to Pennsylvania. When we finally arrived in Feasterville, we checked into the hotel and made our way to the ECDX host Sportsplex, a three-track jumbo skating rink, complete with a huge swimming pool and barbeque area. I looked around, dumbfounded by the size and scope of the event. Girls and guys from more than thirty leagues had shown up to represent. I was excited to mascot. No bouts would commence yet, as everyone still needed to register, but I could at least change into my costume, tell some jokes, and just cheer for the affair as a whole. I walked to the bathroom to change. Moments after I stepped on line—a good mile away from the nearest bathroom stall—I saw a bunch of refs and other officials walk into a back room behind one of the tracks. *Fuck this.* I walked over to the entranceway. A large Sampsonite in a black and white lined shirt (who was, phrenologically speaking, not too far removed

---

[4] Philly Roller Girls, "Welcome to the East Coast Derby Extravaganza," *East Coast Derby Extravaganza* (Program), March 17-18, 2007, p. 5.
[5] See Appendix 5: Challenge Bouts.

from our australopithecine progenitors) guarded the door. I walked past him, hoping my trepidation would somehow come off as authoritative.

"Whoa there, fella. You a ref? Where's your pass?" he asked.

"No. I'm a mascot. I don't have one."

"Refs only," he said, crossing his finely sculpted arms.

"But I have no place to change except the bathroom ... and it's really crowded in there ... I thought that it might be different this time," I pleaded.

"Well, it isn't ... Carry on."

Fourth lesson of mascoting: Rollergirls, refs, and officials get dressing rooms; mascots get bathroom stalls. I slugged back to the bathroom line, which, in the short time I was gone, had doubled in size. After about ten minutes or so, I entered a stall. I had changed in one dozens of times and learned how to switch clothes in tight quarters while balancing myself on top of my sneakers to avoid stepping on urine-covered floors. This stall, unlike many others, didn't have a coat hanger. There were, however, two rusty holes in the back of the door where a coat hanger used to be. I made due and changed my clothes while simultaneously juggling my sports bag, making sure that nothing—*nothing!*—I owned touched the floor.

A person came to the stall door, pulled on it, and after seeing that it was locked, proceeded to bang on it like he wanted to break the door down and pee on whatever's (or whomever's) inside. I've never understood this, especially how often it happens. Stall doors can't lock themselves; wouldn't he assume that a person was inside? This phenomenon is only as baffling as its frequency, and when it does happen, only merits an "occupied" squeaked by me, half-naked in the stall.

I walked out of the now line-less bathroom to rejoin my league and saw a girl carrying two twelve-packs of water, one stacked on top of the other. I asked her if she needed a hand with the load.

"Whatdayathink?!" she snapped. "That a girl can't lift some water bottles? ... Typical man."

We both continued walking at the same pace in the same direction back towards the track. *Well, this isn't awkward.* We passed by another girl walking the opposite way. She rolled her eyes at the sight. "Typical man," she hissed. "Make the lady do all the work. You need a hand, girl?"

"Oh, yes, thank you," said the first girl. She slid the top bottle pack off the bottom pack into the other girl's hands. She then turned back towards me and metaphorically kicked me in the nuts with a devilish smirk. The two walked away rather quickly. I felt like shit. *Was it the phallic nature of my costume? Was I in the movie PCU? Was she fighting the "phallacracy?" Was a candlelit chant of "Hey hey, ho ho, this penis party's got to go!" about to break out?*[6] *Were guys not allowed to participate in an all-female sport?*[7] My mood changed, though, when the Mobtown Maulers showed up. Lady Quebeaum had her leg in a cast. She told me she got the injury when she crashed into me at the Maulers/Roller Rebel bout. Tongue-tied, I started to apologize with incoherent babbles.

"Relax. I'm fucking with you," she laughed.

We exchanged hellos and hugs, but then I left to find my team. After registering, watching some bouts, and drinking some beers, we retired to the hotel. We had a bout the next day.

We woke up Saturday morning and after breakfast (and a desperate, futile attempt to find me a decent cup of coffee) drove back to the Sportsplex. We were supposed to play the Dominion Derby girls, but for reasons unknown to me (I heard

---

[6] Hart Bochner, "PCU," *Twentieth Century Fox Film Corporation*, (1994).
[7] See Appendix 6: On the Notion of Guys In Derby.

both that Dominion had too many injuries and that many girls couldn't show up for myriad reasons), we ended up playing Steele City in a grueling balls-to-the-wall bout.

As the Roller Rebels warmed up, I bought two beers from the vendor inside and retreated to Fiesta's car with her. After downing one of the brews, I tipsily went to place the other in the cup holder but accidentally spilled it on the edge of the passenger seat. The beer quickly found my butt and the back of my costume and soaked itself into me. I ran inside to the bathroom and found a hand dryer to put my ass up to while frantically shoving paper towels down my boxer shorts. The bout was beginning; I had to go! I ran to the track and situated myself beside Furious George and Chairman Meow. I mascoted that Roller Rebel/Steele City bout with the worst case of swamp-ass imaginable. Even the subtlest gyrations felt like I was sitting in jelly.

Furious called my ear close to his monkey mask. "Mrrhff muwah suwan," he said in a voice that reminded me of Charlie Brown's teacher.

"What?" I asked. The whistle blew, and I started my cheering. Furious pulled on my arm.

"What?!" I asked again.

"Murff muwah suwan!" he repeated, pointing behind me.

I turned around. Nothing. *Maybe he wants to do a track run?* I took off around the track to loud laughter from the crowd. Halfway across, I turned around. Furious was still next to the Roller Rebels bench, head in his hands. I ran back to the bench area. Furious ripped his mask off.

"Dude!" he shouted, pointing behind me again.

Then it caught my eye—a long strip of toilet paper was hanging out the back of my ass. *So that's what the crowd found so funny during my run.* Much to my embarrassment, I quickly pulled the TP out and discarded it in the trashcan behind the bench.

Now toilet paper free, I jumped up and down with Furious George screaming for the Roller Rebels. A man taped Furious on the shoulder. "You and the banana are in my shot. Move!" He quickly shooed us and aimed his camera at the skating girls. "Shit!" he yelled. "I missed them! Try to stay the hell out of the way!" We moved ten or so feet down the track, closer to the first turn. "Get the fuck out of the way!" yelled another photographer.

At one point during the second half, Furious jumped on my back and started stabbing my head with a banana. We ran around the track, leaving both laughs and jeers in our wake. Fired up from the girl's grand performance, I did a series of cartwheels. My last one was poorly executed and I fell into a fan. He got pissed. I put up my dukes in a Popeye fashion, wound up, swung, and "accidentally" knocked myself in the back of the head. I fell over and waved my prop white flag, saying, "You win …." Dude bought me a beer!

The Roller Rebels emerged victoriously. We happily celebrated the win, taking the party from the Sportsplex back to the hotel.

The good times were not to last. After ECDX, our league changed again. More and more girls left for one reason or another. Eventually, even Butterscotch sought greener pastures with The Philly Roller Girls. New girls came in to fill the void but they were hardly as enthusiastic as those of us who remained. Roller derby simply didn't matter that much to them. Though we certainly had picked up girls along the way who were hardcore for the sport, the majority of the newer girls only feigned interest at best. As time went by, I noticed that our league resembled more of a recycling plant than a tightly-knit confederacy. One of our fresh bloods' boyfriends started a fight with one of Captain's friends and me at one of her parties. He thought he was funny but he really just sucked. His girlfriend quit the Roller Rebels shortly thereafter.

    I stayed on. Fiesta still coached and was always willing to stay up with me until the wee hours of the morning when we were on the road. Butterscotch helped coach the new girls at our practices from time to time and still hanged with us whenever she could. I was happy about that; I thought her departure from the league would mean an end to our friendship. It didn't.

    But none of this could prepare me for the biggest blow to come. When I heard that Furious George had decided to move to California, I didn't know what to do. My heart broke. We had finally grown passably comfortable with our positions, calculating the short moments between jams to rile the crowd up and executing our bits near-flawlessly. We fought each other while skaters contested ref calls, and took pictures and signed slaughter-graphs with roller derbyfans at halftime. I tried to work out a routine with another Furious George, but to no avail. He was a good guy, who did a good job, but chemistry is chemistry; I decided that without Cappa as Furious George, I had nothing to go on. I contemplated hanging up the ensemble for good. Butterscotch caught wind of this and threatened my life; I reconsidered. She can be quite persuasive, but now I was all alone out there.

IV

YELLOW BELLIED

> *This is a different breed of girls. They're not your run of the mill, everyday females. Who you are and what you are ... whatever, derby still loves you.*
> MOKO LOKO

I didn't know RollerCon existed until just a few days before I left for it. Birthed in 2004, RollerCon unapologetically engenders the defining soirée of the new derby milieu—another ingredient that, to me, separates today's roller derby from every version that came before Texas' Great Idea. Although RollerCon is the brainchild of several girls from several leagues, a Texas Rollergirl gave it its name. Derbyfolk from all over the world convened in Vegas at the lips of August for the event. As grand as RollerCon is, the values from which it grew were fairly straightforward: "have some fun, some drinks, some skating."[1] But there is more to it than that. There are also the scrimmages at Flamingo Banks, skating and gear workshops, punk shows at the Double Down Saloon, a scavenger hunt, and the crème de la crème of derby dances, the Black and Blue Ball. A splendid assembly hosted by Sin City Roller Derby and a

---

[1] Ivanna S. Pankin, "History of RollerCon," *RollerCon: Official Information Packet and Desert Survival Guide*, (August 8-12, 2007), p. 3.

spectacular attraction to derbyists the world over, RollerCon was first dreamt up as an affair for only a handful of leagues that existed in the US. A mere three summers later, we counted over forty domestic leagues and several others from countries like Canada, England, and Australia. Details of RollerCon madness will always suffer, smothered by the sheer oddness of trying to describe what is happening all around you. According to B.ay A.rea D.erby (B.A.D) blocker Mötley Crüz, sometimes all the skating, booze, and merry Hell of RollerCon can make "the events clump together in [one's] mind like cat shit in a litter box."[2]

I had never been to Las Vegas, and truth be told, had avoided going my whole life. I simply didn't think I'd find anything of interest there. I don't gamble and strippers aren't my thing. But my experiences at E.C.E. had me addicted to roller derby gatherings. I threw two league mates (who asked to remain anonymous) some last minute loot to haul up in their room. We only had two room keys, and as the latecomer, I had to make do without one over the five-day roller stretch.

Sometime after checking into our room, my phone rang. I excused myself while my roommates relaxed after the long flight. Although I recognized the number and hesitated answering the call, I flipped my phone open nonetheless and said hello. The details of the conversation would impede on another person's private matters, so they will not be addressed here. I will only say this: Someone close to me was in serious condition at the hospital. I hung up and leaned against the wall. A strip of memories unraveled in my mind like a broken movie projector spitting out film. I cursed the gods. They cared not.

---

[2] Mötley Crüz, "RollerCon 2006: Kind Of Not That Awesome," in *Hellarad: Cali's Most Ignaceous Skate 'Zine*, V.1.1, 2008, p. 21.

Bane-ana

By the time Fiesta, Captain, Rawk, Jefferee, Masta Kate (one of the Roller Rebels' new skaters) showed up, I was a wreck internally but managed to pull myself together externally. Masta Kate, however, could sense something was wrong with me. Later that night, while at the Double Down Saloon, she asked what troubled me. I told her I had had a rough few days and just wanted to go back to the room and sleep. She managed to keep me at the Double Down and bought me a beer. Then another. I started to drink. Heavily. I bought beers for rollerfolk, the bartender, and strangers, trying vainly to enjoy myself during a time of uncertainty. My throbbing would be quelled by excess, I foolishly thought. A girl took me outside and smoked a bowl with me. I made for terrible company.

After I went back inside Double Down, another girl and I caught eyes. We had met before at this bout and that event, and I found her both smart and oh, so beautiful. On the other end, there was me—a stupid male. After playing catch-up, we started to kiss right there in the bar. I couldn't resist.

"I feel like a teenager kissing you in a bar," she said.

"Well, with all due respect," I said slurrier than an Irish poet, "teenagers aren't allowed in bars."

"Shut up, you know what I mean."

"So what do you want to do?"

"We can't go back to my room. My people are already there ... long flight and all. What about your room?"

"Well, I guess we have no choice then, do we?" I said using the most stained of logic.

One of my roommates was involved in a conversation and I hated to bother her for the key card, but what was one to do? The lady and I boarded the shuttle back to the hotel and were back in my room in twenty minutes.

Was I disrespecting the integrity of the sport? My internal witness waved a protest poster that read: "Remember Your Derby Ethics!!"

Still, I surrendered to a biological impulse that ran deeper than my notions of derby etiquette, fell to my knees, and looked at the playground between her legs. My core trembled, tickled by the tempting tongue of an Eden serpent. Too nervous to say "yes," too curious to say "no," I whet both our appetites and feasted on her forbidden fruit. After several convulsive twitches, she lifted herself over me, and then, this Rosie riveted herself down onto me. I moved closer to kiss her, and as our foreheads touched, her eyes cyclopsed into one giant iris; her eyebrows *uni-ed* into one strip of brown. A billion years moved between us—the original split from the first single-celled organism demanded the return of its estranged counterpart. Dowsed in Precambrian gunk, we rolled in celestial chemistry until the molecules became whole again; now we are grasses and wheat fields; now insects; now fearful mammals; now Cro-Magnons, hunting the plains of Africa; now humans, and now, at long last, representatives of The Great Conjunction between the Skeksis and the Mystics.[3]

Yet, my confliction continued. Our bodies had twined into perfect unison; all the while my mind was split in half, distancing itself from my body's actions. A stoic I am not. At one moment, I could have sworn Zeno was looking crossly at me from some ancient stone steps in Athens. I guiltily glanced up. He failed me—or rather, I him. My defenses refortified, and I ached for liberation; but I was unable to shake from my thoughts how wonderful it all felt ...

---

[3] See Jim Henson and Frank Oz, "The Dark Crystal," *Universal Studios ITC Entertainment*, (1982).

I lay awake flagellating my conscience after she left. The next day, I called her and desperately tried to find her to apologize. She didn't answer her phone and no one seemed to know where she was. The message was clear: I had fucked up; disrespected the sport. I wanted to tell her that I still valued the sport but sulked to the buffet to grab breakfast instead. I sat there alone, feeling undeserving of any company.

After eating, I went back to Fiesta and Masta Kate's room where a joint passed from person to person. Fiesta's sips of the Lord's plant were strictly medicinal. She woke up complaining that she hurt her back in the same spot she hurt it a year ago. One of the problems with roller derby (as many ladies know) is that old injuries recycle themselves and can spring up like the weeds you thought you pulled last summer. Our party was too collectively hung over to even say the word "hospital," let alone accompany Fiesta there, so I volunteered. Masta Kate accompanied us as well. We called a cab; it picked us up in the area behind the hotel where the buses loaded up with rollergirls. They were on their way to Fremont Street for the challenge bouts. I looked on jealously as I climbed into the cab.

We turned off a mile or so down the road onto the misnomered Rainbow Blvd (not a cloud in sight). The Spring Valley Hospital, about a hundred paces down the road, looked like a yoga studio on the outskirts of the Age of Aquarius—post-apocalyptic. Humans had triumphed over cyborgs, and this place stood as ruins of a great spiritual war. The red rock bricks of the building matched the land all around it, as if some previously imprisoned wizard had waved a magic wand over the ground causing it to materialize up from the dirt—ensuring victory and a bright future for humans. It was the sort of place that I imagined had a little old man with a long beard tucked away in a janitor's closet somewhere that only the worthy were allowed to approach to contemplate the secret of life. I expected the nurse that greeted us to be a serene, angelic being who would lead us through Grecian columned corridors with busts of great leaders lining the walls. "There is no pain here; there is no death anymore," she would peacefully explain.

"Sigh-un-in" said the receptionist, looking displeased that an injured person would have the audacity to go to a hospital and ruin her easygoing day. Fiesta asked the nurse if either Kate or I could join her in the O.R. for moral support. Kate, as the girl, was invited.

I sat in the waiting room. I sat and waited, and I waited and sat. I twiddled my thumbs; I tried to justify what I'd done the night prior and attempted to think of other reasons why the enchantress was avoiding me other than because I fucked up. None came to mind. I also tried not to think about my friend back in New York, but she kept bombarding my present mind with pleasant and perturbed memories. Was she alright? Just as quickly, my head zoomed back to the night before. *Had I really dishonored the sport*? I knew not the answers to either question, and juggling them became too much to handle; I eventually ran to the bathroom and lost it. Regaining composure, I sat back down in the waiting room again.

I wanted to get away for a while. Far. I remembered that a friend of mine was moving to Italy that autumn. He invited me along. I decided in that waiting room that I would go. The move would mean no Regionals or Nationals; but after my actions, I thought my mascoting future was uncertain. Finally, after a mere six hours sitting in a chair that grew less comfortable with each minute, Fiesta and Kate emerged from the O.R. Fiesta would be all right. A few beers, some painkillers, and a fat joint would alleviate any residual pain. We called a cab and went back to the hotel. After arriving, we went up to Fiesta's room where she literally took a page out of the Bible that was conveniently placed in the hotel nightstand. She did unto others by rolling page 666 into a joint and passing it along.

I can't tell if Vegas nights come quickly or just play on a continuous loop. With our bellies craving munchies, we decided to eat a good dinner at one of Las Vegas' fabulous restaurants. Even though I hadn't even mascoted a single bout or scrimmage, I was beat. I didn't even want to. I didn't know what to do with myself. My friend's imminent departure from this world and a strenuous six-hour wait in a deceptive paradise had left me emotionally drained only a day and a half into RollerCon. After our meal, I opted to go back to the room and pass out.

"What?!" exclaimed Jefferee. "But it's Friday night at RollerCon! C'mon, wake up! I'll buy you a coffee."

"I think it'll take a little more than that," I mumbled.

"Okay!" Jefferee called the waiter over. "Three cups of coffee!"

By the time we left the restaurant, I was wide-awake. We split ways after dinner—Mr. Rawk and Captain went straight to the Flamingo Banks, which had a skating rink that Sin City arranged for use in night scrimmages; Fiesta, Jefferee, Kate, my roommates, and I went back to the hotel for gambling and drinks. I put my costume on and then caught a shuttle to the Flamingo Banks. I sat quietly in the back as the shuttle filled with rollergirls and took off into the warm Vegas night. Beers popped open, cigarettes lit up. I didn't know what I was doing there. I hadn't arranged anything with anyone from Sin City about mascoting at the Flamingo Banks scrimmages and didn't know if I was even invited to the Banks as a non-skater. Furthermore, what if the girl from the night prior—that enchantress—was there? After a day of ignoring me it would have been awkward to see her. I ruminated on this, and by the time the shuttle arrived at the scrimmages, I wasn't really in the mood to mascot. Three cups of coffee, and still no life; there is no such thing as emotional caffeine. The shuttle emptied, and the riders eagerly ran trackside for the best seating. I stayed behind until the bus driver asked me if I was planning on riding around with him all night. "I'd happily trade places with you," he joked as he studied the tuckus of a girl in purple booty shorts and glittering blue tights who was bent over lacing up her skates. "Go have fun before I quit my job and take yours."

I exited the bus but stayed in the parking lot. *Why did I come here*? I sighed and sat on a concrete parking divider. Mr. Rawk must have spied me because he skated over to my outpost. "Hey buddy, we were going to end the scrimmages but one of the girls said, 'We can't stop, the banana just got here.'" I mean, I *wanted* to enjoy myself, and with no clear sign of Enchantress anywhere, I traded sulk for perk.

Good 'ole Mr. Rawk.

The scrimmages were shortly extended (only a handful of jams), but I gave 'em mascot-hell! I enjoyed the scrimmages because the only people attending were rollergirls, refs, and the like. So everyone was cheering for everyone—all I had to do was merely fill in the gaps. This made my job easy—almost too easy—as the fans were only too willing to scream louder at my urges.

I excitedly thought about impressing a team present at the Flamingo Banks. Maybe someone would ask me to mascot for them at Fremont Street—the RollerCon equivalent of primetime. No one came. I decided it was up to me to offer my services and looked around at the hundreds of skaters, wondering who looked approachable enough to query. But the lack of rollergirls' interest in my Fremont possibilities suddenly had me too scared to ask any of the teams. I was on a mascot-high (a delicate place to be, indeed!) and didn't want to end the remarkable night turnaround by getting laughed at by my inquest. I was too satisfied to expose myself to anyone. Maybe it was for the best; I wasn't ready for primetime. By the time we all boarded the shuttle to head back to the hotel, my soggy costume was stuck to me, and I smelled like a helmet after a bout. Still no invites to mascot at Fremont Street, but it mattered not. For the first time since my arrival in Vegas, I was smiling.

I found one of my roommates in the casino, grabbed the room key, showered, and changed back into regular clothes. When I got back downstairs to the casino, everyone—as I found was becoming customary—had assembled around the Maui Bar. I sort of hid out there, sitting in a large reddish armchair behind the bar that allowed me to see anyone coming before they saw me. I had a drink. Then another. As my inhibitions broke down with each drink, I started to feel exposed. *What if Enchantress showed up at the Maui Bar?* I was invited back to a ▮▮▮ Roller Girls' room for a puff, which I accepted; the chances of channeling Enchantress would be even slimmer if I were quarantined somewhere, I hoped. A few elevator flights later, we arrived at the smoky room filled with girls and guys wearing an array of roller derby team shirts. I found myself involved in a dozen or so conversations; no one recognized me without the banana costume on. A relief, until one of the girls mentioned how she couldn't stand "that loser wearing a banana costume" back at the Flamingo Banks. Some guy chimed in, "Yeah, that guy's a douche ... probably needs a good asskicking." He passed me the bowl.

I didn't say anything. The girl who invited me to the room didn't say anything either. She just glanced an "I'm sorry" look in her eyes, which did nothing to palliate the stabbing sensation I felt in my chest. *Am I really just a loser wearing a banana costume?* Suddenly not feeling very welcome, I said my goodbyes, returned to the Maui Bar, and sunk back into that large armchair in the dark corner.

Now that I wasn't mascoting (and several intoxicants had stirred my deeper poetic sensibilities), I started to think about my friend in New York, and how it all didn't jive with the vibe around me. I turned desperate. One can only hold on for so long before realizing, *Shit, everyone is else is having fun, and here you are a sucker—a prisoner—to your own ideologies; a loser wearing a banana costume. How was wasting your money on a flight and hotel going to make things alright? Stop banging on the bars and realize that you have the key to your cell in your pocket. No one knows who you are. No one cares.* I chased my thoughts with shots of whiskey and stopped caring if I saw Enchantress. Better to get the whole thing over with.

I moved out of the corner and sat at the bar completely exposed. A girl with rainbow colored hair and a mischievous smile sat down next to me. "Hey," she said.

"Hey ..." I repeated.

She ordered a martini, the color of which matched her head. She turned to me and let her knee ever-so-slightly touch mine. A gentle brush, mind you, but enough to rouse waves in a pheromone surf. With each sentence of small talk, she drew herself closer and closer, until she had crossed the safe distance I had tried to keep between us. I kept looking at her martini glass, which dangled haphazardly over my legs. She leaned in; some of her drink breached the rim of the glass, splattering on my thigh. I pulled back. "Sorry," she said seductively, "... for getting you wet." She grabbed a small black straw off the bar and sipped up the spill from my shorts. Another girl sat next to her, and after a hello (and some suspicious whispering), bought a martini as well. Rainbow Hair kissed me and then turned to her friend and kissed her. Then we three exchanged lips and fingertips. They were an aggressive pair. We were falling over on our bar stools. Rainbow Hair laid down on the bar itself, knocking over other patrons' drinks, violating the Maui Bar.

Bane-ana

I didn't even know who I was anymore. I just knew who I didn't want to be: some loser in a banana costume; some loser that Enchantress had gotten the best of. I wanted to be someone that was somewhat desirable—like a ref or a coach or something. My heart raced as lust erased heart. *Fuck chivalry.* I hit bottom, pulled out my shovel, and kept digging. What did I care anymore? I was moving to Italy anyway. My mascot days were over. Nothing mattered, only Freudian lust. If these two lovelies wanted my company, who was I to judge? I was sick of being played with; I forgot myself and left my cowing ways out to pasture. A man came over and tapped my shoulder.

"I just want to say, man, that you are the luckiest guy in the world right now."

I couldn't have agreed less.

"He knows!" shouted Rainbow Hair. "Go away!"

If only you both knew ...

We continued our display. A small crowd gathered. Camera flashes went off. *What happens in Vegas, stays on Facebook.* This was not good, but it all happened too fast for me to stop it ... part of me, admittedly, didn't want to. Another man approached us. *Just another guy here to tell me how lucky I am.*

He didn't say anything for a moment but just stood there watching.

"Can I help you, perv?" asked Rainbow Hair's friend. The man pulled his shield out from under his shirt. Flashing it in our faces, he said, "Look, you have three options: stop what you are doing, get a room, or we all go down town." I told him that I admired his nostalgic cop "down town" colloquialism. He didn't care; he certainly wasn't in the mood for me.

We stopped. Rainbow Hair's friend gave us exaggerated good-bye kisses that were clearly aimed at pissing off the cop. *Ahhh ... derbygirls.* She ordered another drink and left. Rainbow Hair smiled at me. "So ... what's good?"

"I was supposed to wait here for my friends," I said, hoping that someone from the Roller Rebels would magically materialize at the Maui Bar for confirmation. Sometimes the gods throw a little luck your way. Jenna Fiesta emerged from the elevators with a group of others. *Yes*! Piña colada in hand, bedecked with colorful red, green, silver, and gold bead necklaces, and a plastic crown on her head, Fiesta was ready to, well, fiesta—the queen of the after-party had returned to regain her throne! We all ran off and got lost in RollerCon lunacy. But under all the bacchanalian behavior, a foreboding feeling began to bubble up from deep inside me.

When I finally woke up later that Saturday afternoon, Hell came calling to collect. I couldn't get over what I had done. I felt like a cad. A largely unknown fact about the word "hypocrite" is that one can unravel each syllable, re-knot the letters into a noose, and hang oneself with it. I had gone from zero to Caligula in a matter of days. *Three girls in two nights? And rollergirls?!? What the fuck was I thinking*? My stomach twisted as guts found new territory in my throat. In fact, I'm sure I had other body parts up in there too, not least of which was my foot. After a dip in the pool to relax, I sat in a hallway alone writing my thoughts of the incidents. I was trying to get things out on paper in an effort to, if only symbolically, get them the hell out of me. I was running short of paper because, needless to say, I had much to atone for. I couldn't speak and I didn't want to see anyone. But you can't stay at RollerCon for too long without someone finding you.

Dame Nation, a Carolina Rollergirl whom I had met at the after-party when the Mobtown Maulers slaughtered us Roller Rebels back in Baltimore, walked over to say hello.

"What are you writing?" she asked.

"My transgressions," I replied. Then an explosion of babbling: "I can't get over what I have done here! I always wanted to believe that I could control myself! Not get involved ... but I ...," I paused, "... and rollergirls too! I've violated the integrity of WFTDA! The integrity of the sport itself! I'm just another douche! No character! Why do rollergirls have to be so alluring? So beautiful? So strong? So amazing? I broke, Dame, I broke! And I just never ... I guess I never felt so ... so"

"Human?" asked Dame.

Epiphany. I clammed up. Man, did I need to hear that. Dame was right. I *was* human. A stupid human that, like all stupid humans, fucked up! *Everyone fucks up.* Why did I think that the world would end? As we can all surely attest to, the world hasn't ended; and when it eventually does end, it won't be because of what happened at RollerCon. *How solipsistic*! With one word, Dame definitely dammed the ditch in my damn mouth. *Dang.*

Good 'ole Dame Nation.

I had just felt badly for those who were involved. But after Dame Nation and I rejoined the relentless party at the Maui Bar, I saw Rainbow Hair and her friend carrying on and enjoying themselves like nothing happened at all. I felt a lot better. I asked Rainbow Hair if everything was alright. She looked at me confusedly. "Why wouldn't everything be alright?"

"Well, you know, last night ... the integrity of the sport ..."

"What? Do you think you were the only one to hook up with someone this weekend?"

Point taken.

But I still wanted to make things right. I approached Rainbow Hair's friend. "So are we derbywives now?"[4]

"Should we not consummate it with a wedding? At the Double Down. Tonight. Midnight."

---

[4] See Appendix 7: With This Ring I Bled Thee.

I ordered a beer, and was about to call Fiesta, or Kate, or Jeff, or whomever, when I got a text from Captain: "Fremont Street bouts. One Hour. We're here."

Not wanting to waste a moment, I downed my beer as I walked to the shuttle pickup area. There was already a handful of people waiting; a bus would probably come by shortly.

"When's it expected?" I asked.

A girl with pink hair covered in tattoos looked up. "Schedule said it should have been here twenty minutes ago."

"Which means it should be here any minute," another girl assured the group.

A half-hour later we were on our way to Fremont Street—my first visit to that legendary alcove. But like everything else in Vegas, Fremont Street looked like our hotel lobby—even the sidewalks did. Con artists set up ad hoc booths to relieve naïve tourists of whatever money they hadn't lost yet. I only had twelve dollars and wasn't about to stupidly sacrifice my slim savings to some shady sidewalk shark. I met up with Fiesta and Captain in a small casino, the kind of which was conveniently placed *everywhere*—the General Store had a slot machine for fuck's sake!—on Fremont Street. I don't gamble, but sat beside Fiesta at one of the automated games she had parked herself behind. She refused to move until she either earned her fortune or the bouts started. A waitress, who could have easily doubled as a porn star, took a beer off her tray, placed it before me, and walked away.

"Uh, I didn't order this," I said.

"Ssh!" whispered Fiesta. "She thinks you're gambling."

"So?"

"So? Gambler's drink for free. Don't you know anything?"

A light turned on; over my head a maintenance man fastened a florescent tube in the ceiling. "You mean I only have to pretend I'm gambling and I'll get to drink?" I asked.

"No," said Fiesta, diverting her eyes to the security cameras. "They are watching us."

I did a little math in my head: *If I can recycle these twelve dollars for as long as it takes the porn-waitress to feed me drinks, I can get drunk for a fraction of the cost*!

I put a dollar in the slot machine and with a glacial pace, started to play. I wasn't gambling, I was channeling—*Pavlov*: A loss, a win, porn-waitress brought me beer; a loss, a win, porn-waitress brought me beer. After drinking four free beers (estimated worth: twenty-some odd dollars, tips included) and watching my cash dive and rise like a seagull fishing in the bay, I stopped when I accumulated fourteen dollars. Drunk for free and two more dollars than I began my day with. Bane-ana: five points; Casino: zero. *House always wins, indeed ...*

Captain, Fiesta, and I left the casino to meet up with others who had already situated themselves around the Fremont Street track. Fiesta bought me a large piña colada and we found our seats right up on the outside ref line—where the action is! I wanted to mascot so badly now but wouldn't dare ask anyone in my inebriated state.

After the challenge bouts ended, we went back to the hotel for a nap. I wanted to get a good rest for my fast encroaching wedding in a few hours. I had finally passed out, but by the time I woke up, I was an hour late for my wedding. I quickly ran to the shuttle pickup and caught a bus to the Double Down. I arrived, and the Elvis im-priest-onator said he would "shot gun" it for us. Rainbow Hair grabbed me. "Marry her in this dress," she said, referring to the dress she was wearing. We ran into the filthiest women's bathroom I have ever seen and swapped clothes. Then, back outside in the parking lot, Elvis quickly read over the vows like an auctioneer.

Our matrimony was short lived. Rainbow Hair's Friend's other derbywife threatened me with bodily harm when I got back to the East Coast.[5]

That night, I ran into Enchantress at the Double Down. We walked across the street and spoke about what had happened. As it turned out, she hadn't been avoiding me; she had just been busy with her RollerCon weekend. She assured me that I hadn't dishonored roller derby and that if hooking up with rollergirls really killed the sport, it never would have made it this far. "We would have died off a long time ago," she gaffed. We hugged, went back to the bar, ordered some drinks, and rejoined the reception. I can be a real idiot sometimes.

I woke up the next morning, packed my shit, and flew back to New York a blissfully bemused, but bewildered, banana. With perhaps less thought than someone should put into such a drastic move, I worked several odd jobs that summer to make extra money, packed my things, and left for Italy, unsure if I was ever coming back. And I wouldn't have to miss derby; while at RollerCon, I met London Roller Girl (LRG) blocker Slice Andice and her husband, LRG ref Ballistic Whistle. I told them of my move to Italy that autumn, and they invited me to mascot an LRG bout. Plane tickets, they told me, were cheap within and throughout Europe.

And of what I can remember from ECDX 2000Great

Italy doesn't work like America. Since I was not an Italian citizen, I couldn't find a job anywhere. Euroless, I played my guitar on the Milanese streets for spare change daily. With no

---

[5] But that wasn't the shortest derbymarraige, or the shittiest. I'd heard that the year before, Daddy's Girl (Sacred City Derby Girls) tattooed her first derbywife's name on her foot to commemorate the occasion. The girl quit derby the very next week.

roller derby community in Italy and no way to get to England to mascot, I came back to America that January 2008. I wanted to restart my roller derby mascoting off the right way in the new year and referred to it as "2000Great."

I spent the next few months picking up where I left off, looking for work, practicing acrobatics, writing mascot material, and attending Roller Rebel practices. Soon, spring sprang sweet summer skies. This time it was I who frantically called Captain.

"When's E.C.E? Are you going?! We're going, right?! Split a room?"

The answer to all these questions was "yes"; we were going, of course, but this year the Roller Rebels hadn't signed up in time to play. However, several Roller Rebels like Captain, Régine Bull, and Amaretto Sourpuss made it onto different challenge teams and would get to skate that weekend. But that still left me without a team to root for, and I wanted to mascot for somebody. Since leagues often borrow skaters from other leagues when they are short players, I figured mascots could be borrowed too. The league that I wanted to cheer for was the MobTown Maulers, newly rechristened as the Charm City All-Stars. I gave myself two missions: First, convince the Charm City girls to let me mascot for them. Second, find different leagues from all over the US to query about a mascot tour that summer. ECDX would be the perfect place to work out such a venture, as I would be able to speak directly to league representatives for schedules, bouts I would be welcome to, and the like. I wanted to find that ambiguous element within roller derby culture that truly revolutionized not only the sport itself but also our understanding of what makes someone an athlete. A tour of the top leagues in the nation would surely end with an answer to these questions. I needed only to seek it out. My hunt began at ECDX that year.

I also volunteered for two jobs: penalty tracking and guarding Philly Roller Girls statistician Statisfire's burritos. I didn't know anything about penalty tracking so Number 2, a Roller Rebels' statistician, taught me as we sat in traffic on our way to Pennsylvania. It wasn't too difficult; infinitely easier than my second job, as guarding the burritos didn't include eating them.

We arrived in Feasterville; our itinerary included the usual: check into the hotel, start the party, and pass out. The following morning Captain, Jefferee, Sourpuss, Number 2, and I drove to the Sportsplex early. The chaotic parking situation at the venue served as testimony to ECDX's success the previous year. Last year, we had parked down a little dirt path adjacent to the pool; this year, we must have parked about a mile or so away from the farthest edge of the parking lot, which was a mile or so away from the front doors of the Sportsplex. We trudged along in the blistering heat, and by the time the entrance (and air conditioning!) was in reach, we looked more like a troupe of damp dishrags than a roller derby team. I met Statisfire, who told me to meet him by Rink 3 at 2 o' clock for burrito duty. After registration, we split up; the girls found their respective rinks, and I reported to Rink 2 for penalty tracking, the ease of which was only exceeded by its boringness. With penalty tracking, one has to pay close attention to the bout without committing oneself to enjoying it, like going to a baseball game on a hot summer day and filling out insurance forms (although I'm sure some asshole would enjoy that). I wanted to cheer, not take notes. Brandish pompoms, not a pen. I felt trapped behind that officials' foldout table while my tracking partner couldn't have been more enthusiastic about it. "We're so official!" she beamed. "Officially bored," I mumbled.

When the bout ended, I quickly signed my name to my penalty tracking sheet and ran away—fast! I had a few hours to kill before my next job so I couldn't buy a beer. I made my way to the pool and temporarily passed out on a sizzling poolside recliner. When I woke up, all the people who had initially surrounded me had been replaced by a fresh crop. How long had I been out for? What time was it? *Shit! 1:58*?! I had two minutes to find Statisfire and command my burrito post. I frantically ran around the huge complex asking if anyone had seen him. *1:59. Fuck*! Desperate, I screamed "Statisfire!" in the crowded theatre. I found him waiting at Rink 3 for me, 2 o' clock on the dot. Precisely where he said he'd be. *Right* ...

Statsi had stashed the burritos in a loft between Rinks 2 and 3—clearly this was a sensitive mission.

"Everyone," he said, "Ev-ery-one you know here is going to ask you for a burrito. Your answer will be ...?"

"¿No hablo Ingles?"

He smiled and left me to my station.

There was one person I had counted on definitely wanting a burrito—me. I hadn't eaten yet that day and found myself simultaneously reaching into the large brown burrito box with my right hand while slapping it with my left. I suddenly wished I were back on the rink penalty-tracking—no internal conflicts (just internal dullness). But I couldn't let Statisfire (and the whole of Philly Roller Girls) down. They worked hard to ensure that ECDX was a splendid affair. I chastised my tongue by thinking about eating mud. When that didn't work, I mentally undressed one of the old nuns from elementary school. Sister Angelina, that craggy old crone, finally served a useful purpose. Appetite? Suppressed. Burritos? Safe!

After my burrito guarding job ended, I ran into a girl who told me that her league also featured a banana mascot. I had just read Steve Martin's *Born Standing Up* and found one of his bits—the "mock self importance" bit—hilarious and wanted to try it out.[6] I figured that if I put on my own "mock self-importance" act while dressed like a banana, I would get a chuckle out of her. Doctrinaire and self-righteous, I began to pontificate about how I—and only *I*—was worthy of donning a banana costume. "There can be only one banana, and it's me!" I finished my tirade, trying not to crack up. The girl didn't get the joke; I had forgotten that (Heidi Ho-Bag notwithstanding) most people don't really get me; this girl was no exception. She got peeved and stormed off before I could explain that it was just a goof; that I love the idea of other mascots in derby—banana or otherwise. It might even be funny to set up a bout between her league and the Roller Rebels. We could call it "Battle of the Bananas." I couldn't find her anywhere, lost in an ocean of roller girls. *Oh well. Maybe after she skates around a little she'll lighten up.* After all, some girls—even the sweetest—can be a little high-strung before a bout; hell, I usually was too before mascoting. I am one of the few who does not believe that a person only has one chance to make a first impression. We are all entitled to a bad day; perhaps I caught her on one. I shrugged off the encounter thinking she must have as well and walked back out towards the pool area where Fiesta and several others were just about to take a walk an' shots an' smoke.

    We left the Sportsplex property limits and gathered by an old railway track, maybe half a mile away from the venue. The smoke didn't help. I still had no mascot gigs lined up, and as the smoke consumed me, the thought of mascoting for Charm City descended into a debilitating fear—the kind of which quickly turns into a panic attack. I grew alarmed. I didn't know if my stomach was collapsing on itself or if I was just experiencing a fit of the "munchies" worthy of a digestive apocalypse. After

---

[6] Steve Martin, *Born Standing Up: A Comic's Life*, (New York: Scribner, 2007) p. 167.

we walked back to the parking lot, we assembled for a few moments around Fiesta's car. Suddenly the fear of asking Charm City to mascot for them overwhelmed me. Before I knew it, I had sunk deep into that familiar oubliette of my subconscious designs. I asked Fiesta for her keys and retreated alone into her car, closed the door, laid my head back on the seat, and braced myself for the mania. I had fallen too far. Wholly besieged by the idea of mascoting for Charm City, I couldn't even salivate; forget cottonmouth, this was drought mouth. I needed water. By the time I opened my eyes to ask someone for a drag of water, everyone had gone. I left Fiesta's car, locked it up, went inside the Sportsplex, found my bag among Captain and Fiesta's stuff, and pulled out a large bottle of water. I ran to Rink 1 where the bathroom was empty. I refilled my bottle from a water fountain by the front door—the first water load had not even remotely cured my parched throat. This second one did little more than make me have to pee my brains out. I entered an empty stall to unload, and hide out until the trepidation subsided.

Twenty minutes (and about a hundred knocks on the stall door) later, I exited the bathroom and headed back outside. Just passed the door, I ran into Leggs Benedict, a Philly Roller Girl. Butterscotch Cripple had introduced us at a Philly bout I attended earlier that year. I had made a running joke about never calling her "Leggs" Benedict: "Arms" Benedict, "Ben Leggs-a-stick," and so on. She was always cool about it, so I kept it up. *Alright now, stay together old man. Everything is fine.* "What's up, Arms Benedict?" I said to test if I could still communicate with humans. She stopped me—*fuck!*—and asked me why I never referred to her as "Leggs" Benedict. My panic resurfaced and I forgot how to speak properly. I could still form words in my mind just not sentences in my throat. I felt the pull of my descent, my regression into naught but a vapid animal.

What was I supposed to say to her? I had joked in such a way for a while now with 88 Fingers Benedict and now she stood before me, leggs and all, wanting an answer.

Terrified, I replied rather Faulkner-esquely: "I don't know, I don't know why I do anything at all. I just think that you're a good person, and I constantly need to joke, and I thought that a joke wouldn't bother you because you don't seem threatening, and I don't mean to sound like some New-Agey person, but you really do emit a comforting vibe, and I really don't mean to be babbling on like this, but you asked and ti' tis my duty to let you know, so I call you all that stuff just because no one gets my humor except Heidi, and some girl with a banana mascot hates me, and I thought you might get my humor and not hate me, and I'm sorry if you do, and I don't mean to offend you and please don't hate me, and I really like other banana mascots."

Benedict looked at me unsure of what to say. "Oh. ... okay," she replied in such a way as to make me unable to understand if it was a good "okay" or a bad "okay." I could feel my skin melting off my body. I must have sounded like an idiot. I was about to pass out. I bolted out the door and ran across the parking lot to the pool area.

The sun, beating upon my apropos yellow belly, scorched my outfit, and I now further descended into a mushy pile of platanos. I couldn't focus on anything. I needed water. Cool, quenching, refreshing water. As I entered the pool area, Texas Rollergirl Muffin Tumble and a bunch of others tried to grab me and throw me into the pool.

"Get the banana!" Tumble yelled.

"Please, nnnnn ...ot now!" I cried. Stuck in a fearful state with people actually trying to tackle and throw you into a pool is absolutely petrifying! *Ahem*: *"Just because you're paranoid, don't mean they're not after you."*[7]

"Whatever man! Get 'em!" Muffin Tumble yelled back. One girl grabbed my cape; another, my arm. I felt like a fly struggling through a viscous black widow's web of derbygirls. I don't know how (survival instincts maybe?), but I managed to evade them and run into the men's bathroom. Knowing that rollergirls would be inclined to ignore the "Men's" room sign, I took additional precautions and locked myself in a stall to hide; I swore I was never going to leave my encampment. Images of derbyfolk pulling my dead body out of that stall flashed across my psyche. I couldn't breathe or swallow. *Was this the end*?

Then, as if in answer to my pleadings, the gods machined a deus ex machina: Chairman Meow took position up at the urinal beside the stall. Perhaps he noticed my dangling cape or shivering yellow legs and asked me how I was doing in a very serene only-Chairman-Meow-can-do-it-in-such-a-way way. He proved instrumental in evicting me from the sinister headspace I had crossed. I slowly emerged from my brief experiment in bathroom stall monasticism, and within ten minutes of talking to him, I readied myself to rejoin the earth again. Our talk was inspiring to say the least. He told me to follow my heart and just ask a league to let me goof-off for them. "You look like you're ready to go," he added. He was right. Dressing like a banana was pointless if I wasn't going to mascot for anyone.

Good 'ole Chairman Meow.

I ended up growing a pair of balls to ask Charm City if I might mascot for them during their bout against the Rhode Island Riveters. They said yes! Knowing it was an odd question, I asked several Charmfolk if any of them had pompoms. *Some mascot I am, I had forgotten mine at home.* They didn't, but a

---

[7] Nirvana, "Territorial Pissings," *Nevermind*, Geffen Records, 1991.

Charm Citier[8] said she would buy a pair for me the next morning before the bout.

By the time we reached the Sportsplex the following morning, I was a wreck. Sober now, I thought more clearly about the situation. *Did I dare cheer for such an accomplished team like the Charm City All Stars? What if I got in the way? It'd happened two years earlier with Lady Quebeaum. What if it happens again? What if Captain got mad at me for doing it? What if I got mad at me for doing it? Did I really need to be here? I mean, other than to guard Statisfire's burritos? And now that that's done, what business did I have even asking Charm City in the first place?* Fearful symptoms from the day before started to bubble up inside again. Roller derby was quickly becoming a panic trigger. I couldn't bear the thought of it any longer. I was going to vomit. *Air. I need air.* I exited the rinks still feeling nauseous. All I wanted to do was spread a little bit of silliness, and now I had stepped on the toe-stops of the Charm Cityfolk. *I can't do this. I gotta go*! I scurried away to ... well, I didn't know where I was going. I was just trying to get away from everything and everyone. And lo! I ran right into the Charm Citier. She had a small red plastic bag.

Shit.

"Here's your stuff," she said, handing me the bag.

"Oh ... okay, thanks," I replied. Inside the bag were two orange colored pompoms and a small yellow plastic bullhorn.

"Thank you. How much was it?" I asked as I reached into my inner pocket to pull out my loot.

---

[8] Up until 2010, I had been under the impression that the unnamed "Charm Citier" was Holly GoHardly. When I brought the story to her attention, she swore it hadn't been she who bought me the pompoms and bullhorn. You'll have to excuse me for this one ... I wasn't "all there." Thank you, Mystery Charm City Girl!

"Whatever. Like 2 bucks or something. Don't worry about it."

I didn't know what to say. She had just made my decision for me; I was to mascot for Charm City. I did thankfully assume a bit of easiness when I learned that I wouldn't be mascoting alone. Chairman Meow agreed to take on the role of "Dirty Frank," the Charm City All Stars' hot dog mascot, and Charm City founding member Marzipain's son, Monsieur Doom (who mascoted one of Charm's home teams), also emboldened our roller ramparts. Death, should her arctic whispers beckon the Charm City girls home, would not swallow them without a fight from their mascots!

The Charm City girls were on their game that bout. The day before, they quashed Houston (the point spread had been near 200 points in Charm City's favor) but apparently hadn't satisfied their hunger. They were now going to take out their frustrations on Rhode Island. They needed to roll out hard, to show Rhode Island that they weren't fucking around. As evidence, Charm City sent Pistol Whip over to the jammer line first. Assisting Pistol was an impenetrable wall of yellow and black. Capping off the pack, Dolly Rocket and Holly GoHardly's two-woman human barricade assured that Rhode Island's own jammer-extraordinaire, Hysterica (showing that Rhode Island, too, wasn't fucking around), would experience turbulence in her flight path. But the Riveters were no easy targets. Indeed, they too had come off not only a good win but also an unbelievable comeback the day before; thirty points down against Atlanta, the Riveters made up the differential in the final squeeze.

I looked beside me. Chairman Meow and Monsieur Doom waited in anticipation. At the first whistle, the pack took off, followed by Pistol and Hysterica at the sound of the second. Pistol shot through the pack, leaving smoke-rings on her

Roller Derby: The Sensation That Caused A Book!

opponents, but Hysterica ran into the Rocket/GoHardly obstruction. Chairman, Doom, and I hooted and jumped as Pistol scored the first Charm City points I ever cheered for as a mascot. I wanted to be the loudest, happiest, cheeringist mascotingest mascot that Charm City had ever known—no easy task as Chairman and Doom were as fevered as I was. I wanted to show Charm that I could keep up with them from the sidelines. But I was ahead of myself. Still reeling from my maddening episode, I exhausted myself quickly. I grabbed my bottle of water and emptied it into my mouth fast—too fast. I started to hiccup as Lady Quebeaum approached the jam line. Penalties had left only Joy Collision and Dolly Rocket on the track to assist her; that was all she needed. I held my breath, trying to suppress the hiccups and backed up an extra few steps to ensure I wouldn't be in her way. The jam erupted with Quebeaum taking lead quickly. I tried to scream for her, but every word started and ended with a glitch in my delivery.

"Que-beaum-*hic*!"
"Que-*hic*!-beaum!"
"Que-beaum-*hic*!"

But my, did penalties continue to abound! I had never seen anything like it. At one point, Charm blocker Mibbs Breakin' Ribs stood in the pack all alone, surrounded by a sea of red (both wearing and seeing) Riveters. Behind her, Hysteria took position against Flo Shizzle. Flo glittered in her gold bootyshorts, looking like she had just starred in a sequel to *Saturday Night Fever: The Roller Derby Edition*. With an iron fist full of confetti, she would rule the track—her dance floor—like Stalin at a disco. I had seen Flo playfully shake her moneymaker on the jam line in past bouts and eagerly awaited it. But her head was in the game, looking deadeye at the wall of red before her. Something had to be done! I started to scream, "Flo! Flo! Shake that thang! Flo! Flo! Shake that thang!"

Chairman and Doom got in on it, and together, the three of us amplified the sidelines with our mantra. The call to arms spread through the crowd. Flo heard us, looked over, smiled, and started to bounce her rump up and down. The audience went ape-Shizzle!

I quickly ran into some problems. The Charm City All Stars was just that—*all stars*. At first this made my job easy; then boring. They revved the crowd up so much that I realized I was once again going to have to step up my mascot game.

The second half grew more bizarre than the first. I watched as penalties accumulated and thinned-out the two opposing teams. Chairman, Doom, and I ran around the sidelines trying to build up the trackside energy. Then finally, a turnaround—a revolving door of unstoppable, indestructible Charm jammers sent the point spread from a controllable thirty-point gap for the Riveters to an insurmountable seventy-point one. I cheered the jams on, despite such a routine pushing me to exhaustion. Round and round they went; down and down I went.

After a solid win for Charm City, I took my dilemma to Rink 3 and joined those already assembled for the Windy City Rollers/Carolina Rollergirls bout. It occurred to me that between several panic attacks and mascoting for Charm City, I hadn't spoken with a single league representative about my mascot tour—and it was the last day of ECDX! I saw a girl wearing a Texas Rollergirls Texecutioner shirt.

"I want to go on a mascot tour," I said. "I'd love to put the founders of the sport's revolution on my list."

Belle Star was amicable indeed. She gave me her number and told me to call her when I had a better idea as to what my mascot schedule would look like. Nothing was promised, but I hoped that I would at least be able to make it that summer to Austin—to the revolutionary roots of modern derby.

V

THERE AND BACK AGAIN: A MASCOT'S TALE

*Sometimes the river don't know which way to turn,
just that there's an ocean to catch ...*
TOSHI REAGAN[1]

'Twould be a lie if I claimed to have inherited my lust for adventure from anyone but my father. Unfortunately, the likelihood of my steadily approaching would-be mascot tour actually coming to fruition grew bleaker by the day. And I needed this trip—times were fraught with uncertainty. Years from now, I imagine posterity looking back at this time the way we look back at the 80s. *What the fuck were they thinking?*

Masters degree complete, I exhausted my psyche nightly; as if on cue, every morning at 3:30 am, a lump of neuro-chemical anxiety materialized in my brain jangling every corner of my mind from my innate whimsy to the cold realization that one decade and two degrees later, I was still unqualified to enter the workforce. But I guess that's an American education for you. I originally planned to pinball my yellow ass around the country that summer, starting with a bout between the Roller Rebels and Virginia's Cape Fear Roller Girls that July 4th

---

[1] Toshi Reagon, "?," *I Be Your Water* (2004).

weekend. We had to cancel though, as not enough Roller Rebels could make the trip. Furthermore, I still hadn't heard back from Belle Star from Texas Rollergirls or my B.ay A.rea D.erby contact Miss Moxxxie, whom I spoke to shortly after ECDX. One by one, I envisioned the pending bouts falling by the wayside. *Okay. I'll just postpone my trip until August.* I checked various league schedules and was disheartened to discover that there wouldn't be many bouts occurring in August at all. *Think man, think.*

I did what I always do when my head is awash with thoughts. I grabbed my journal and started to write: "...And lo! Synchronicity! I shit you not. Belle just called as I finished writing that last sentence about how I couldn't get in touch with her!"[2] Oh, happy day! The gods must see it fit that I make it to Austin. Belle invited me to mascot for her team, the Honky Tonk Heartbreakers at the Texas Rollergirls championship bout that August 3rd. Later that day, I heard back from Pixie Rocket from Charm City. I'd be mascoting their July 26th bout. Two days later, Miss Moxxxie emailed me. I also heard back from Chairman Meow in Chicago and Killer Tofu in Arizona. I was finally hearing back from everybody! But there was still a problem: only four leagues and no RollerCon? I decided to add Madison, Wisconsin and Portland, Oregon, to the trip—where Regionals and Nationals would be held respectively. As I mascoted around the country, I'd feel out leagues to possibly guest mascot for at those events. The journey would end with me, somehow, shaking my pompoms for a team in Portland, Oregon at WFTDA's 2000Great Championship, Northwest Knockdown.

---

[2] Bane-ana, "Where have all the cowgirls gone?" *My Journal,* July 10th, 2000Great.

Gasoline had reached a record high that summer, nearing $5 a gallon. The lectures kept coming from family and friends: "Have you seen the price of gas?"

Of course I had, but why did one's life have to revolve around the price of oil? I would simply take a few weeks breather after San Francisco to work odd jobs, save up, and continue on to Madison and then to Portland, my *Oz*. Eventually, anytime someone asked, "Have you seen the price of gas?" I'd just say, "Gas?"

The GPS lectures followed. "Across the US? Without a cell phone? What if there's an emergency? You'll need a GPS!"

"GPS?" I gasped. "And kill the adventure?" Was it not that great commentator of American road trips, Clark W. Griswold, who remarked, "Getting there is half the fun"?[3]

Only there was no *there*. Granted, I wanted to reach Baltimore, Dallas, Austin, Phoenix, San Francisco, Chicago, Madison, and Portland but I wasn't really trying to get to those states, per se; rather, I wanted to get to the heart of what has been dubbed by some as "Derbylove"[4]—one word. For the derbyists of the world, "derbylove" is self-explanatory. Every single skater, ref, announcer, NSO, volunteer, and mascot knows exactly what I mean; for those who don't, I offer this unofficial definition: Derbylove is the notion that the common struggle of building a new sport from the ground up as experienced by derbyists the world over has manifested invisible glue, uniting us all in our efforts. Therefore, my trip would determine if:

---

[3] Yes. See John Hughes, "National Lampoon's Vacation," *Warner Brothers* (1983).
[4] Sometimes spelled "derbyluv."

a) Derbylove actually existed and was not just a myth?

And, if the affirmative upholds:

b) What does it look like and could I capture it?

I would conduct interviews with derbyists from across the country and find out what exactly it was about roller derby that had us all so addicted. I spent the next few weeks altering my costume, sewing different patterns of yellow over the original banana with large "X's" crossed with black yarn. I also sewed an inner-pocket into the costume to carry money, fliers, and other small necessities. At the bottom, I stitched a blue cloth that featured bananas and monkeys in homage to Furious George. He wouldn't be coming, but he'd be with me.

The Fortune I Almost Didn't Earn by Not Eating the Cookie

Since I would be gone for a while, I desired one last trip to Mr. Beery's, my favorite local watering hole. I called my friend Tara and we went out that Wednesday night before I left. After several drinks and feeble poetic attempts, I saw a fortune lying on the bar. I eagerly picked it up and read: "You are one of those people who goes places in life." As fortune cookies tend to only espouse good news, it probably meant, "You will be successful." Ignoring such a bullshit fortune, I took it to mean that I was about to embark upon a road trip, substituting the "places," which really meant "end results" with the various cities I would visit. I wanted the fortune to be true. This alternate interpretation gave the fortune more meaning than most other fortunes I have received. I usually get fortunes that are chockfull of useless lines of kismet crap, which read something to the tune of, "An old love will come back to you."

But there was a problem: I couldn't find the cookie itself. For it is written on a scroll[5] that unless the fortune candidate eats the cookie itself, s/he will never become the cosmic incumbent of stated fate. The fortune would have been wasted, a wistful thought from an unprepared applicant.

I grew edgy. I needed to secure that cookie and ingest its magical properties. But how? What if the cookie had already been eaten? *Nah ... I'm the only one in the world who eats those things.* But I couldn't take the risk. If the cookie had been eaten, I'd either be completely fucked or have to take that person with me on the road—two halves of the same destiny. Tara had gone out to smoke and could not assist me in my quest. I scanned the bar area for signs of Chinese food refuse: containers, duck sauce packets, chopsticks, noodles, something! A soy sauce stained shirt; a smile that only appears after eating Chinese food—anything! I ran to the bathroom hoping to find some guy blowing up the toilet with preternaturally liquefied shit—the ultimate sign. *Wait-a-minute! Back by the bar where I found the fortune in the first place. If the cookie is still somewhat intact, it shouldn't be too far a distance from its textual counterpart*! I rushed back to where I was sitting and had first stumbled upon this growing hemorrhoid of a fortune. There on the floor under the bar stool was the displaced cookie, waiting patiently for me. Well, not all of it. Maybe 70% of the fortune's flesh remained—enough to affect sorcery. I didn't want to eat it but had to; just not there, not then. I asked Brando, the bartender, for a plastic bag to transport the crumbs in, but she didn't have one. So I took a napkin and wrapped the remaining crumbs up for safekeeping.

---

[5] Not really.

I went home that night and washed the cookie off. Still not satisfied with its presumed cleanliness, I decided to boil the fucker—kill any and all bacteria that could have accumulated on the cookie before I found it. I filled a metal pot with water and set the stove temperature on "high." I contemplated the encroaching trip. By and by, the water boiled; I pulled the liquefied flakes out, gave praise to the goddess of sweets and fortunes, and swallowed them. Crisis averted. 'Twas all coming together nicely. The gods had seen it fit that I leave for Baltimore in two days. Cookie and fortune intact.

VI

MODS AND DOLLS! JUST A BUNCHA CRAZY MODS AND DOLLS!

*You spill into the streets with
the phenomenon and the anointed.*[1]
MIKE MILAZZO

26, July 2000Great, just past noon; I began my journey. My gas was near empty. I hadn't filled up because gas was cheaper in New Jersey. I had driven the Jersey Turnpike many times over the past few years, what with roller derby constantly destroying and improving my life and all. As the heat and stench hit my car that sunny afternoon, I thought about what I always think about while driving down the Jersey Turnpike—*what the fuck is that smell?* I followed I-95 down to Baltimore. Charm City was my first stop—a familiar segue into the unknown. I'd grown to love the Charm City girls as a league and their warm and welcoming "hellos" gave me an impression that, despite the hundred plus miles between my house and car, I hadn't really left home.

---

[1] Mike Milazzo, "The Show," *The Show* (2010).

Bane-ana

The Charm City All Stars pool girls from its four home teams: The Speed Regime, The Night Terrors, The Mobtown Mods, and the Junkyard Dolls. That day, at their "Saturday Evening Roast" home game, the girls played a double-header intra-league bout. The fiery-red draped Mobtown Mod girls allowed me to mascot for them against the pretty in pink Junkyard Dolls. The Mod mascot, for one reason or another, couldn't make it to the bout. I felt conflicted.

As I sat in traffic on the damn Jersey Turnpike, I wondered about my ability to rightfully cheer on one team over the other. It was different with the Rebels. I came up with them. I knew the personalities, quirks, dynamics, and vendettas of the girls. I only knew Charm City as the All Stars. Even before mascoting for them at ECDX, I had watched them as a collective when I traveled. How do I split the group? Cheering for Lady Quebeaum, Duchess of Torque, and Joy Collision was easy (Mods)—I had done it only a month prior; but how do I ignore my conscience when, for example, at that same bout, I rooted for Dolly Rocket and Flo Shizzle as All Stars, and now I had to cheer against them as Junkyard Dolls? I prefer inter-league bouts because then I'm cheering for the league as a whole, not just the team whose mascot couldn't make the game. I can't just cheer for any team; I gotta *feel* it.

Passing from Jersey into Delaware, I also devised a little mind game to play with myself at bouts—joke jamming. With joke jamming, I would approach a roller derbyfan (or several) and tell joke after joke without giving the poor individual(s) a chance to say a word. Since I never got to skate, I wanted to use jokes as a way to make up the difference. Externally, I would look like a banana mascot telling stale jokes. Internally—and with every victim's laugh—I would pass her or him as a blocker, mentally mimicking the masterful moves of the matrons I marveled at. If I made everyone laugh, I got lead jammer. But if a person said that a joke was dumb or gave me a look of disdain, they would take lead and effectively "call off the jam."

I arrived at "Du" Burns Arena about an hour and a half before the bout ready to deal with the multitude of undertakings (some small, some large) that needed to be met before the bout could commence. Charm City used Sport Court, a track comprised of giant portable plastic puzzle panels perfect for a plethora of playing particulars. We laid wooden boards over the soccer-friendly Astroturf floor, then covered them with Sport Court, hammered the pieces into place, swept the track, and mopped. After the bout, we would do the whole thing in reverse.

When it came time to section off the skateway, I partnered up with Matt De Capitator, who had over the last year become my unofficial track laying buddy in various states. With roller derby, one develops relationships with people one never would have known otherwise. Derbyfolk will often tell stories about how s/he used to do some specific job with "this guy or that girl." For me, De Capitator was "that guy." We went right to work, employing our secret tape laying system. So secret, in fact, that we didn't even know what it was. We just sort of *did it*. De Capitator was a statistician, and his statis-position in the middle of the track—an area that I do not tread—left few opportunities for interaction with me during bouts. In fact, there was none at all. As was the situation every time I arrived in Baltimore, Matt De Capitator was happy to team up to lay track tape.

Bout time neared, and soon I was lining up with the Mobtown Mods, wishing each girl a good game. My initial confusion about being able to cheer presented itself that very first jam when Dolly Rocket took position beside Duchess of Torque. The whistle blew, and I didn't know what to do. Dolly

Rocket took the lead, and my muscle memory said, "Cheer!" Only I couldn't. I was back at my first bout at Skate Safe again; I blanked, releasing an odorless brain-fart. The jam went right by me. It didn't get any easier. The second jam matched Flo Shizzle against Joy Collision. Although I flipped my shit as Joy took the lead, a mere thirty seconds earlier a part of me was wishing I could scream "Flo! Flo! Shake that thang!" again.

    I finally snapped myself out of it. *You are here to cheer for the Mods.* As I readied myself to finally give 'em hell, a loud "Oh!" from the crowd turned to a hush. Junkyard Doll blocker Coach Ballbricker had taken a bad fall to the knee. I couldn't give her a knee, so I took one instead and thought about a comment a friend had recently made: "Roller derby? Everyone knows that shit is fake." *Yeah, right.*

    Ballbricker was able to walk away on her own, but the injury took her out of the bout. Several jams later, while cheering for Thumper Good over Flo Shizzle (which still felt a little awkward), I cart-wheeled for the crowd. As my right hand came down over my left, I felt a sharp pain fire from my pointer finger to my brain, which proceeded to tell my legs and hands to fall over and grab my finger. The crowd laughed. I didn't. There was a damn splinter lodged in my skin. It must have broken off from one of the wooden planks under the Sport Court that the large push brooms and mops had either missed or moved. I walked over to the EMTs. By the time I exchanged the tweezers for a band-aid, we were in the half-time.

    Wanting to test out joke jamming in friendly Charm City waters, I waited like a silly sniper for the right group of folks to assail with hilarity. Outside the merch area, where fans generally accumulated to smoke cigarettes, I heard the call—laughter! I responded. I walked over to a group—three guys and two girls. "Hey, it's Banana Man!" one of the guys yelled. *Perfect.* I confidently swaggered over to them and wasted not but a second to blow the whistle and start the joke jam. *Bane-ana approaches the pack*: "With enough Monet, an art forger and a mechanic can make a Van Gogh." They stared blankly at me. "Obesity should not be taken lightly ... as fat people tend to be heavy handed."

"I, uh, just wanted a picture with you?" said one of the girls. *Doppelgänger Bane-ana enters the pack.*

"Did you see the show about vocabulary? ..."

More blank stares.

"... it was a play on words."

"Are these jokes?" asked the girl. *Bane-ana's blockers can't stop him*!

"If your sink will not work willingly, then faucet," I said with a rising inflection.

"Ohhhhhhhh! I get it," the girl said. "Like 'faucet,'—'force it.'" *Bane-ana enters the pack just behind Doppelgänger Bane-ana.* She started to chuckle. *Yes, keep it up old man*!

"Foolishly not wearing a watch is counter clock wise," I continued. "Tensions at the elevator factory have escalated."

Now several of them started laughing. *The nonsense was spreading. I was breaking through the pack, my blockers having built a defensive wall against Doppelgänger Bane-ana.* I tailored my next funny to a girl smoking a cigarette by herself. She was dressed in all black with black and green hair, knee-high combat boots, a black and red plaid skirt, and a band shirt whose name was so "metal" that I couldn't make out the spelling behind all the cobwebs and blood that was strung throughout the letters.

I called out, "Goth is my favorite oxymoron; it's death as a lifestyle!"

The group laughed and the goth girl even let out a small snicker as if she thought the joke was funny but was too goth to admit it—*and Bane-ana takes the lead*! After my onslaught of jovial bullshit, I asked my victims if they knew any jokes.

"Yeah, I got one for you," said one of the guys. "What do you call a ..."

"Good, please tell my friend here," I interrupted. I pulled a random person into the conversation and then walked away. I heard them still laughing behind me as I approached a group of three guys. I stopped before them.

"My ice skates ... melted!"

"Huh?"

"I threw paint on a canvas for my art test ... I passed with flying colors!"

"Seriously guy, piss the fuck off."

"Easy fella, they're just jok .."

"Now, asshole!" *Doppelgänger Bane-ana takes the lead, scores a million points, and fucks Bane-ana's future wife in the ass.*

Undeterred, I ran up to a third group of folks near the bathroom entrance: "A barefoot bear bared left on the Bering Straits to get his bearings but could barely bare the bareness of his environment and the embarrassment of being bare-naked," I said with a laugh in hopes that I was contagious. I was; they laughed back.

"I know a guy who said he could make an alligator out of poop ... personally I think it's a crock of shit!" They laughed louder and asked for more.

One girl with a particularly endearing laugh screamed "more!" in between giggles. *Bane-ana passes the pack again! He can't be stopped!* An EMT walked by us, and I grabbed her shoulders saying histrionically: "What do you call two EMTs in an ambulance?" She looked at me in anticipation. "Pair 'a medics!" She balled over laughing. I quickly turned around and darted away, right hand on right hip, left arm stretched into the air with my pointer finger aimed skyward a la Peter Pan.

I began the second half in good spirits. The audience had eaten my baloney (for the most part). After two bouts of rousing derby exceptionalism, the Mods took the win over the Dolls, as did the Terrors over the Regime.

Afterwards, we of the Charm City volunteer squadron spent a good hour or so deconstructing the track. Happily, there were PBRs and burritos handy for all who served diligently in the post-bout (Ch)army. A dude known only to me as Hal (who I interchangeably referred to as "Hal A. Burton" or "Bat Outta Hal") and I tried to set a record for ourselves by lifting every plank of wood and every slice of Sport Court and stacking them in a neat pile behind the playing area. Roller derby would take a tremendous leap backwards if it ever lost the hundreds of volunteers like Hal who donate their time and energy to the sport.

The after-party was at a bar within walking distance from "Du" Burns so I left my car at the arena. I could smell the damp waters of the Patapsco River as I walked down the road. I wandered inside to grab a beer and then back outside to write some thoughts down.

After enjoying the sweet hop and barely nectars, I ran into Mobtown Mod, Essie Ecks. As had become customary every time I visited Baltimore, Essie Ecks and I changed clothes. We then made our way out to the dance floor. There was, at least for me, something unnerving about dancing with her while dressed like her ... to The Cure, no less. I don't know if she felt it too. Not that I have anything against dressing like Essie or even The Cure for that matter, but both at the same time? My sexual orientation felt a tiny strain.

Mobtown Mod Penaltyna—who would host me that night—and I left the bar, walked back to "Du" Burns to get our cars, and I followed her out of the parking lot. When we pulled up to her house, I ran to the bathroom and unloaded the whole of the Atlantic Ocean into the toilet ... and I think some of the Pacific too. I went to sleep on Penaltyna's couch that night staring at a lighter that sat on her coffee table. The lighter 'twas all white with a stripe of red and blue; between the red and blue stripes were little stars and a warning, "Don't Mess With Texas."

We'll see. After all, I'd be there in two days.

Before I set off for Texas the following morning, Penaltyna asked if I'd ever heard of one of the Texas girls, Melicious, and her book *Rollergirl: Totally True Tales from the Track*. I told her that I wasn't familiar with either.

"Here," she said. "Take this with you for company." She handed me the book.

"Are you sure? I mean, I am going across the country. Shit might happen. There's a chance I might lose it."

Penaltyna, always chill, always hospitable, insisted that I take the book anyway.

"You'll love it," she assured me. "I sure as hell did."

Interlude ...

The 440 or so miles from the eastern tip of Tennessee to its western border into Arkansas is actually longer than it sounds. But the freedom of the open road, the fresh smell of summer foliage, and the cool breeze through my cracked windows made the trip tolerable, albeit lonely. The only thing on the highway that really stood out among the endless tree line was a giant metallic cross set beside a small church—the biggest cross I'd ever seen. The planning involved in constructing such a *state of the art, art of the state* was the first indication that I had officially crossed the invisible border into the South.

As night slowly enveloped my car, I realized that I would not make it through the whole state in one day. Moreover, after passing one-too-many closed gas stations, I figured that it 'twould be better to just pull over and bed down for the night. This I did on the side of the highway, hoping that a state trooper wouldn't drive by anytime soon to bother me. I didn't have to worry; the highway was desolate. So desolate, in fact, that I started to feel uneasy. So uneasy, that I started to hope a state trooper would drive by sometime soon to bother me.

My sleep was broken and shallow. Every roll of wind stirred not only the trees but also me. I grew more and more scared by the minute. *What was that noise? Is that a person walking by me?* At one point, I dozed off and dreamed that three men were standing right outside the driver's side window. A flash of lightning behind them illuminated their diabolical faces—cliché, I know, but it happened. I woke and panicked. Realizing how vulnerable I was out there by myself, miles from anyone who could possibly help me, and with no cell phone to even call a friend for company, I grabbed my ice scraper out of the trunk, exited the car, and smashed it on the side of the road. Using my lighter to brighten a sphere a foot or so around me, I picked up the biggest, sharpest, piece of plastic and cleaned the remaining shards off the highway, placing them back in the trunk. I laid back in the driver's seat holding the shank over my heart. Not that it would have mattered if a stranger approached me with a gun, but at close range, I definitely could jab the sharp plastic into someone's face if necessary. If anyone was going to rob me, kill me, and wear my skin around his house, I was at least taking one of his eyeballs with me to Hell.

Thankfully, no one disturbed me that night—only my imagination. I awoke the next morning at roughly 5 am and continued my drive through Arkansas into Texas. I was on my way to Austin but would first stop over in Dallas to visit two old friends. I passed Hope, Arkansas and saw signs bragging that that was Bill Clinton's hometown. It brought me back to one of my short and interrupted dreams from the night before. It involved Bill and me taking bong hits beside my friend's pool. He inhaled, only to lie about it later.

I passed through Arkansas, where a lot of places are butcherings of two or more names of other states ("Texarkana" for example), into Texas. I was warned several times about the strict laws of the Lone Star State—a place that I imagined still had pockets of uncivilized redneck towns where the only law was mob justice. The state is red, which, when coupled with rigid borders that funnel south, results in a shape like dried blood over a bullet wound. It right-angles on the western end creating a jaw-like border that seems to be swallowing New Mexico. If God is to bless America, it is conditional; it depends on Texas, where lunatics are supplied with crusading propaganda. And ammo. Growing up in New York, I was alerted to my city's murderous reputation since childhood. I never thought the stereotype fit though. Among the shitty subway service, traffic, taxes, and the general rat-race of metropolitan living, New Yorkers simply don't have time to kill anyone anymore ... but Texans do. *Proceed with caution.*

About fifty or so miles outside Dallas, I came upon a litter of highway billboards. One in particular caught my eye—a friendly reminder to "Drive Safely, Jesus Loves You"; just below the sign, I saw one of the most horrific car crashes since the advent of driving like an asshole. Paramedics pushed a black bag laying atop a gurney into an ambulance. Onlookers prayed, never once, it would seem, aware of the divine irony shining down from above.

I arrived in Dallas just in time to catch my breath and witness my two friends breaking up after a long-term relationship. They were busily moving into different apartments. *Just what I needed after driving a thousand or so miles.* I promised myself that I was not going to take sides. After the long drive through Tennessee and Arkansas, I just wanted to sit back, drink a beer, and pass out.

The gods had other plans. When I finally did make it to my friend Tyler's development, I sat by the entrance gate reading *Rollergirl* until he arrived. We spent the next few hours moving his furniture from the old apartment into the new one. RollerCon kicked off the next day and I griped incessantly to my very tolerant buddy about how I wished I could go.

"Why can't you?" asked Tyler as we lifted his dresser into the moving truck (which had no side or rearview mirrors).

"Because I have to be in Austin on Sunday, and there simply isn't enough time to drive up north to Vegas and then back to Austin. I'm dying to mascot for Texas. It's going to be the high point of my trip—a return to the pre-Cambrian roller derby revolutionary mud ... where it all began a few years ago. Those girls are brutal from what I hear. And before I left my friend Penaltyna gave me a book written by one of the Austin girls." I held up *Rollergirl*. "A sign!"

"Oh, you know her??" he asked.

"Actually no. The only one I sorta know is Belle Star. But then, I guess I don't really know her at all. We met last month at another derby gathering. I have been amped for the Austin bout ever since! But still ..."

" ... you wanna go to RollerCon?"

"Yep ..." I answered with a sigh.

At about 2:00 or 3:00 in the morning, we finally tired of moving, and at about 4ish, I fell into a sound sleep. I wasn't used to having a floor—a superior stage with which to rest my tired soul when compared to a car seat.

VII

V<u>AGUE</u> A<u>S</u>

> *She tried to put a dead*
> *chicken on my chest!*
> ESTRO JEN

Fuck it.

My first thought when I woke the next morning. I hadn't planned on attending RollerCon, but at around 9 p.m. later that night, I sat at the Dallas/Fort Worth International Airport awaiting my flight to Vegas. On TV, CNN ran a "news" (and I use that term softly) story about a family from Indiana (if I remember correctly) who made the rather bold (and probably untrue) statement that the Shroud of Turin had manifested itself on their cat. I watched but for a moment before I decided that Melicious' book was far more interesting than newscast sophisms.

Sitting there, I began to feel uneasy about my own scribblings. Other derbywriters handled their prose like pros, so apropos for our pro-skater progenitors. I reminded myself that I was an adventurer, not a writer (more of a wronger). My impromptu decision to hop a flight to RollerCon, with no place to stay and no one even aware of my pending appearance, meant that although my prose may be semipro, at least I can never be accused of not being proactive. This was my chance to test the theory (some might say "legend") of roller derby camaraderie.

On boarding the plane, I quickly found my seat up front—just where I like it, so I can quickly exit after landing. I took the aisle, an elderly lady took the middle, and a flamboyant cello player took the window seat. The three of us spoke briefly about this and that, exchanging origins stories like comic book superheroes. Maxine, the elderly lady, wore her wrinkles with pride—the sign of a person who had experienced a lifetime of love and loss. I told her of my travels along the roller derby circuit.

"Oh! I remember roller derby from the 40s. They were tough women."

"Yes," I agreed. "For sure, but I think there is something a little more to it these days. Some call it 'Derbylove'."

"Derby ... love?"

"The theory is that we are all united in a common task to build an old sport that keeps disappearing into something new and lasting. I've heard stories about the camaraderie of derbyfolk; how strangers can show up anywhere and find a league to skate and crash with. I'm on my way to Vegas to see if it's true."

Maxine was on her own journey, doggedly trying to visit every state capital in this great land of ours before she expired. She hailed from Idaho and boasted about how often she ate potatoes right out of the dirt—"they are that good," she assured me. A fellow adventurer, Maxine was ambitious and sweet with a taste for the raw. She reminded me of many of the derbygirls I'd met along my travels. I couldn't help but feel that in another time and place she would have been a derby queen. Lance, the gay cellist, wasn't familiar with derby, but I could tell he was intrigued.

Bane-ana

To an onlooker, the scene was calm. Inside ... inside I frantically kicked around the mess I'd made in my head. I don't like airplanes and would have preferred a train, no matter how long that would have taken. Take off and landing are the worst and usually end with me so nauseated that I can barely hold onto the barf bag. I looked in the seat pocket in front of me. No barf bag—just a bunch of useless magazines that nobody reads. *Fuck.* A child in 1st class started screaming, vocalizing the feeling in my guts.

"Well this'll be good," Maxine commented, momentarily snapping me out of my inner turmoil. "I'll be here to give you boys' motherly care."

I didn't respond. I wanted to ask Maxine for a favor and spent the next few minutes agonizing over how one goes about asking a stranger for a favor of savior type behavior meant to stave off the aches of danger—the danger echoed by that little shit in 1st class. Finally, I couldn't wait any longer. I started to panic. The plane was about to take off into the sky and I needed assistance.

"Ma'am, I know you don't know me very well, but may I trouble you for a small gesture of goodwill?"

"Okay!" She answered in such an assuring tone that made me feel like I could have asked her anything.

"Well, I'm not very good with planes, especially the take-off. Usually, when I get on a plane, I have my little sister hold my hand during take-off, which, admittedly, makes me feel like a total puss ..."—I caught myself—" ... wimp. Can I put your 'motherly care' to the test? ... Would you mind holding my hand during take-off?" I finally beseeched her with much embarrassment. Lance looked over at me. The lift of his right eyebrow said, "Man. I thought *I* was gay."

Maxine mustered an endearing smile. "Oh sweet child, no, I wouldn't mind at all." She extended her hand to me. I clasped her veteran palm and felt a rush through my body like chicken soup on a December evening. Her tranquility emitted through her fingertips, slowing my heart rate from a Manhattan pace to a gently rocking hammock, swinging only a beat or two behind an Idahoan sunset.

"You hold it for as long as you'd like ..." she whispered to me as we took off into the night. She laid her head back and closed her eyes. I followed.

Thank you, Maxine.

Sugar's Sweetness

I exited the plane and boarded a shuttle to take me to the hotel where the Roller Rebels had stayed the year before. I hoped that trend would repeat itself. Last year, I couldn't get through the doors of the hotel without bumping into rollerfolk the world over. Now, as I entered, I didn't see anyone. *Shit.* Perhaps derbyfolk were here, but I hadn't run into them yet. I decided to check way over in the back of the casino by the Maui Bar. That's where we all hung around the year prior, and I assumed that that's where everyone would be. Success! I ran into ex-Charm City blockers Mercy Less and Cindy Lop-her, and Derby News Network host Hurt Reynolds.

"Hey!" said Cindy. "What's up? Where's your outfit?"

"In my bag."

"Well go put it on, now!"

Lop-her felt (somehow) that getting into mascot mode would help my chances of finding crash space. I ran to the bathroom and got into myself. As I exited, a man came up to me.

"You on crack, boy?"

"No. Potassium. But I don't have time to play with you right now, sir. Sorry." I still didn't know where I was staying and couldn't lose a second.

By the time I ordered my first beer, I had already received several offers for places to crash with different derbyists at the hotel. But I couldn't accept any of the offers—they were all people I knew. Indeed, Cindy Lop-her, Mercy Less, and Cherrylicious all kindly presented me with lodgings. Not that that was a bad thing—I appreciated them dearly. But I was there on a mission. Accepting offers from friends would be cheating. Cherrylicious mentioned that the next day she and Flo Shizzle would be skating on the challenge team, Team Party, against Team Straight Edge (sXe) at Fremont Street.

"Know any mascots?" she asked.

I eagerly accepted her mascot offer. Finally, a Fremont Street bout!

Good 'ole Cherrylicious.

I continued to look for a place to crash when some girl sitting on a barstool started screaming that she hated me. I didn't know what league she was from, but I guess I must have offended her in some way in the past—or she was just an asshole. "I fucking hate you Banana Man!" she kept yelling. "I fucking HATE you!" *So much for the camaraderie amongst all derbyfolk.* Somehow I had incurred a nemesis during my travels.

I quickly forgot her, and introduced myself to Estro Jen and Sugar N. Spikes, both from the Angel City Derby Girls league in Los Angeles. I tried my best to strike up a conversation with them without sounding like an idiot. *No easy task.* Just when I thought I might actually start making sense in my drunken rants to the two Angel Citiers, someone grabbed my ass from behind. The Angels laughed—with me or at me, I couldn't tell. I turned to face the culprit, but there were derbyists everywhere and I couldn't pinpoint who had violated my ass space. Not that I minded, I am Greek after all.

At about 4 in the morning, Sugar N. Spikes wanted to go to sleep; Estro Jen wanted to do back-flips and busied herself tackling everyone in sight.

"I'm hungry! I want food!" she suddenly blurted out.

"I'm going up to bed," said Sugar. "Get food and be back in the room in twenty minutes. We have a long day tomorrow." With that, Estro ran off yelling loudly, flailing her arms through the casino; she was kneepad deep in late-night RollerCon madness.

"You! Banana!" Sugar called to me. "Watch Estro! We have a busy day tomorrow! Make sure she's back upstairs in twenty minutes!" With that, Sugar walked on to the elevator. I turned towards Estro. She was gone.

"Bu ... but ... I ... who?"

Fuck.

Sugar N. Spikes had decided that it was my responsibility to ensure Estro Jen's safe return to their room—and not too late either. *Mission.* I ran out of the casino screaming loudly for Estro through the thick, whore-riddled strip.

"Looking for a good time, banana-boy?" asked a random harlot.

"Yes." I hurried on by.

I finally caught up to Estro, who was surrounded by several other derbygirls.

"Estro! Estro! Please! I know I don't know you, but your friend is going to be mad at me if I don't get you back to the room safely! You have a busy day tomorrow!"

"Shut up Banana Man!" yelled one of the girls in the group. "Don't suck!!"

Shit. Whoever shouted that out was right; I was sucking—fucking with their good 'ole RollerCon time. I decided to just keep my mouth shut and only intervene if my banana sense started to tingle.

Estro and several others went to a restaurant down the road from the hotel for late night munchies. Although Estro had a steadily encroaching busy day and Sugar's warning hung over my head like a rusty guillotine, I felt quite well for some reason. I had made it to RollerCon, and I couldn't help but continuously smile at that fact alone.

The waitress tried to avoid us for as long as she could. I can't say I blame her. We were loud, really loud. Like, "the sun is coming up, what are these assholes screaming about?" kind of loud. She must have thought we were natural predators, cruising the strip for whatever cheap thrills we could find. She obviously had dealt with the likes of our circus before and learned to ignore it. There we sat, derbyists from various corners of the country, collected in the one decadent enclave amidst the larger God-fearing American interior. We were tired, drunk, drugged, and fucked from travel. I missed the opening statements from both Daddy's Girl (known affectionately as "Deej") and Estro Jen, but heard the tuning up of usual 5 am conversation slowly crescendo into Tchaikousky's 1812 Overture. Deej was a Sacred City skater who once famously broke a girl's nose during a bout. At the after-party, she pulled out the bloody tissue stuffed up her victim's nostril and ate it. She was rather outspoken about how important derby was to her. It seemed to be the air in her breath, the food that she ate.

Estro felt differently. Roller Derby was just for fun, nothing more. In a way, they were both right; although I fall more on the Deej side of opinions, in my travels I have learned that roller derby means different things to different people. Some saw it as a lifestyle; others saw it as a pastime. I broke my silence, adding that derby *is* all about fun, but that at times, the commitment to the sport overshadowed that fun. Before the talk slid into bedlam, Althea N. Hell recommended that we lambs slide into bed. I agreed; only, I had no bed.

We paid the bill and left. "Stay with us!" yelled Estro. "I don't mind!"

"Well, is it *your* room? I wouldn't want to impose …"

"It's all good! Sugar won't mind! She's sweet! Please, stay with us."

Estro had completely avoided my question, but I didn't need any more encouragement. I smiled. "Sure."

"Yeah! Banana Man is staying with us!"

"I have a name, you know."

"What is it?"

I turned around and pointed to my cape. She grabbed it and stretched it out like a scroll.

"Yeah! Bun anal is staying with us!"

Bun anal?

"Ummmm … I think it says 'Bane-ana,'" I snickered. But it was too late—Estro had lit her own fuse. She didn't care what the cape said and ran down the street towards the hotel, thrashing her arms about just as she'd done an hour ago when she ran out. *Fuck. An hour ago?*

"Bun anal is staying with us! Bun anal! Bunny anal is staying with us! Bunny anal! Bunny anal! Yeahhhh!"

I ran up to her, passing smut dealers that drooled as she ran by. Just outside the hotel, she turned to me. "C'mon, hurry up! Let's get to bed! I got a busy day tomorrow!"

I could only smile at this point. *God, I love this gig …*

We stopped at the Maui Bar for a nightcap, then up the elevator to Estro and Sugar's floor. As we walked closer to Estro's room, things began to look familiar to her. A few twists and turns through the hallways, and we finally stood outside her door. No keycard in hand, she simply pushed the door open, seemingly unaware that she needed one to get in. *Remarkable.* I stepped into the grandest hotel room I'd ever seen. Used to sleazy, smelly places on the sides of highways, I was not ready for the large bathtub that sat beside the bed (yes, there *was* a bathtub next to the bed). How convenient—easy for either early morning accessibility and/or late-night stink eradication. Estro jumped right into bed, joining Sugar and a mystery body.

"Good night funny bunny anal!" she called over to me.

"Good night."

The Vegas sun was fully bloomed, but the air conditioner had turned the room into an igloo. Banana costumes offer no protection from either the heat or the cold. The felt is heavy and sticky on hot days and nowhere near thick enough on cold nights. Shivering, I started to unhook the shower curtain from the bathtub. Unfortunately, the last rung was secured to the wall. *Bastards knew I was coming.* I pulled it down as far as I could and lay awake spooning the tub. My body began to feel the first stages of dehydration. *I shouldn't have had that last shot at the Maui.* I forced down a disgusting cup of water from the bathroom sink. I should have taken a second, but the taste was so terrible, I convinced myself that one would be enough. I got back down on the floor and thought about that girl who screamed that she hated me earlier. Had she single-handedly proved the Derbylove theory false? *Couldn't have.* She was offset by Sugar's sweetness. There I was, lying on the floor of a stranger's hotel room—*mission accomplished*! I was immediately seized by a new question: Just how deep does the Derbylove go?

Expanding the Circle of Sentiments

The next morning, I woke up to a whirlwind of need-to-do's. Estro had launched her skate business *Via Derby* and there were myriad tasks that demanded her and Sugar's attention.

I, too, had business besides mascoting. Before boarding the plane to Vegas, I had phoned Belle Star to let her know that, despite my flightiness, I would make the Texas bout—no matter what. As we said our goodbyes, Belle conscripted me to a mission:

"Oh, one last thing! Find J. Crush and tell her I love her!"

"J. Crush?"

"From B.ay A.rea D.erby. She'll definitely be at RollerCon."

"I don't know her."

"Find her!"

"How?"

"Look!"

I didn't want to look for anyone or anything except a toilet. J. Crush would have to wait. *Should have had that second glass of shitty water.* Eardrum elves slammed hammers into my brain, each strike reverberating throughout my muscles. *What did I have to do today? Oh, yes ... Peam Tarty ... bananasomething ... Streetmont Freet.*

But how?

I couldn't disappoint Team Party—Cherrylicious had personally asked me to mascot. Having absorbed her, Sugar, and Estro's hospitality, it was now my duty to expand the circle of sentiments. *One receiveth Derbylove, one passeth Derbylove along.*

But moving was tricky. Nausea usually led to vomiting, vomiting to self-deprecation, and self-deprecation ... well, that is mascot fuel. It was all I had. I couldn't unload in the bathroom and stink it up—what kind of good turn would that be to Sugar N. Spikes? Forcing myself up and out of the room, I puked in the lobby bathroom (after a close call on the elevator). Fully purged and with a stomach that began to feast on itself, I staggered aboard the Fremont Street shuttle. *I ... will not ... let you ... down ... Team Party*!

When I arrived at Fremont Street, Team Party and Team sXe were gearing up. Several dudes tried to give me flyers for strip clubs and whore hotlines. Dirty Marty and Rhode Island announcer Reverend Al Mighty joked into the microphones. My stomach twisted. Both teams and refs were situated in the middle of the track—an area I had learned to never tread. My bench area was the whole of the outside track line. I was free—so long as I could move, which actually grew more difficult. At least it would be easy to stay clear of the skaters and refs ...

"Move it, asshole!"

... but not of the bout photographers.

I moved over to the fist turn of the track and looked towards the middle. Cherrylicious wasn't the only Charm City Roller Girl skating for Team Party. Flo Shizzle and Dolly Rocket joined the celebration on skates as well. *Perfect.* Cheering for them would make up for my treason back at the Mod vs. Dolls bout a week earlier.

Dolly Rocket always gave me a lot of material to work with. Her skating style was that of a *wisenheimer*—always staying one turn of a skate key ahead of her opponents. She bolted. Stopped short. Tap danced, taunted, and took off again, gliding on a burning cushion of air like cigarette ashes flickered into the breeze. I waited anxiously for the climax, like awaiting the refrain during a barroom sing-along. It hit; the crowd was swept up in a frenzy, and I silently hoped that the needle would stick, as I never tired of begging her for an encore. But unlike that barroom record, we couldn't rewind Dolly. A blink, a sneeze—even these tiny eye diversions could have caused me to miss the masterful nuance of her footwork. But it didn't matter; I needed only wait for the next time Dolly lined up along others on the track and remember not to blink. She was a provocateur—she looked like she wanted her opponents to hit her; she needed the laugh. I recalled a quote from Winston Churchill: "Nothing in life is so exhilarating as to be shot at without result." Such was Dolly Rocket; for it was as if the gods suspended the laws of gravity with every hit, nudge, or rollergirl battering ram committed against her. WHAM! BAM! She took the shots ... without result. She slid here, she swirled there, but never fell. She mocked her opponents' best efforts with wiseass wobbles, pretending to teeter, all the while having total control of her movements. Her skating became an addiction, another vice to add to my list of personal poisons: coffee, beer, burritos, Dolly Rocket, blunts.

Despite my nausea, I had come too far to miss a slice of her magic. I grabbed my bullhorn and started screaming at Team sXe, "Dolly Rocket don't fall down! Dolly Rocket don't fall down!!" I wouldn't have been surprised if my obnoxious antics caused a straight-edger to kick me in the face with an Earth Crises-stickered Doc Martin boot, but it never came. I ran around the track waving my orange pompoms as Team Party skated Team sXe under the table.

My enthusiasm didn't go unnoticed. After the Party/sXe bout, Cherrylicious asked if I wouldn't mind also cheering for Team Caulk Sucker the next day. The truth was she and the rest of Team Party had been my inspiration in the first place. The Derbylove was recycling itself! The Caulk Suckers were the straight rollergirl team—the "strictly dicklys"—and had challenged (or been challenged by) the queer team, The Vagine Regime (The VR).

I took a few photos with some folks, and ran into Miss Moxxxie—my B.A.D. connect. *Wait! B.ay A.rea D.erby! Something about San Francisco? Mascoting ... no, not yet. Jay Belle's ring? Wedding ring? Belle Crush? No! Belle's crush on J. Crush! I must deliver Belle's endearments!*

Bane-ana

Between the new Caulk Sucker assignment and the hangover that had redoubled its ferocity from all my jumping and running, I had forgotten all about Belle's assignment. What would I do if I arrived in Texas without having given J. Crush her message? A skate to the face perhaps? Who knew? I surely didn't and surely didn't want to find out the hard way. *The circle of sentiments must expand*! I asked Moxxxie if she was aware of Crush's whereabouts.

"Yeah, she's over there." Moxxxie pointed to a girl standing in front of a small stage set beside the track area. "She's wearing the Sacred City hat."

I stumbled over to J. Crush and on bended knee, hid my face in my forearm.

"I request an audience," I slurred.

"Uh, sure."

"Belle Star says she loves you."

"Awww! You know Belle?"

"Well sort of ... not really."

"How do you sort of not really know someone?"

"Uh, well we met at E.C.E and all she told me was to give you the message. But I'm mascoting for Texas this Sunday."

"Really? That must be exciting! You know they were the first league, right?"

"Yeah, we owe all them a debt of gratitude. The bout is going to be the highlight of my trip ..." I caught myself "... except for B.A.D. of course!"

"Nice save. Tell Belle I miss her."

Fuck. Another mission. But it was my charge and must be done. What would happen if I now showed up in San Francisco without having delivered the message to Belle? 'Twould displease the goddesses of all things Derbylove, for certain. I hadn't the audacity for that.

The Chicago Outfit vs. Pure Asshole: The Final Verdict

A quick nap and shower, and I headed back at the Maui Bar with Sugar N. Spikes to share drinks and wait for a friend of hers to arrive. Sugar had a delightful radiance about her, accompanied by a mellifluous tone in her voice. Clever and witty, she mastered artful conversation with a grace that can only be called angelic. Indeed, her deep sapphire eyes could excise demons with a single enchanted glare. I felt consecrated simply by staring into them, awkwardly tripping over irises and slipping on pupils.

"Are you passing through L.A. on your way to San Francisco?" she inquired.

"I wasn't planning on it, but I think I'd really like to," I said with a smile. "Now that I know you and Estro ... and Cherrylicious just moved out there too?"

"You'll also meet my friend tonight. She is beautiful. You should talk to her."

We didn't wait long. Sugar's friend arrived at the hotel not too much later and was, indeed, stunning. Hair like an autumn sun, Friend had an ironic beauty. She worked as a makeup artist but she didn't need any; her own careful blush and eyelash strokes besieged the work of the gods' sculpting perfection. Yet, I couldn't help but notice that beyond the clinging lights and noise of the casino, her dolled-up features roused my baser instincts. *No, old bean*! *No repeats from last year*! She went up to the room to drop her stuff off, and my heartbeat regained a semblance of normalcy. *My god, is every Angel City girl a knockout*?

A commotion behind me knocked me back into reality. Some rollergirl who had drunk about ten too many started to act belligerently. Sugar and Estro ran over and grabbed her. The last thing I saw was the belligerent girl yelling and resisting her captivity as Sugar and Estro pulled her into the elevator.

Suddenly, I was by myself and walked around the casino to see if I could find anyone. Just outside the bathroom entrance, Mortician Murphy of River City Roller Girls was receiving a spanking from one of her teammates. As her league mate disciplined her, I stupidly got too close. One strike chopped across Mortician's bottom so savagely that, as she fell forward, she instinctually tried to grab onto something. End result? She punched me right in the dick. I fell to my knees in pain. The girls erupted into uproarious laughter as I rolled on the floor next to Mortician. I spent about a moment being the butt—or rather, the dick—of every joke, and after much effort, I managed to stand up. Mizz Monstah, another River City girl, gave me a pin that read "I Love Mizz Monstah!" and ordered me to remove all the other pins I had fixed to my costume. As I wobbled away clenching banana jr's luggage, a girl with a Chicago Outfit midriff pulled me over. "With me, Banana Man."

She led me across the casino to a group of girls, most of whom wore either a Chicago Outfit shirt or a Vagine Regime one.[1] A rowdy bunch of rollergirls, they looked like a small contingent of Richard Hell cherubs, guarding all that was punk in the Garden of Derb-Eden. Soccer moms quickly dragged their husbands passed them. The Joan Ranger fixed an Outfit sticker on my media pass; Suzie Crotchrot stuck another onto my bullhorn. I belonged to them now, but I didn't want to ditch Sugar and Estro while they dealt with Belligerent. I figured I'd walk over to the Maui, and if they weren't back yet, grab a drink and return to The Outfit.

"Hey, where you going?" Suzie Crotchrot called out.

---

[1] Many, it turned out, skated for both.

"Oh, just to get another drink."

"You're coming back though, right?" asked The Joan Ranger.

I smiled. "Yes, I'll be right back. Anyone need a beer?" The girls lifted their drinks; they were all set. *Cool fucking girls, dem Chicarga Outfitz.*

Sugar and Estro still hadn't returned so I purchased another overpriced beer from the Maui, and as I headed back to The Outfit, some girl asked me if she could wear my cape.

"Sorry, but it's what gives me my magical powers." I said jocularly. "I can't fly without it."

"I don't want to have to fight you for it. Now hand it over!"

Was she serious? *Couldn't be, could she?* I should have just walked away, but instead I did what I always do in confusing situations like this: I took a deep breath and promoted roller derby.

"You don't have to. Fighting won't be necessary off the track." *What do I mean "off the track?"*

"Off the track? What track?"

Gotcha.

"What the hell are you talking about? Should I go upstairs? Do you want me to leave?"

I was startled. *No, I don't want anything from you. You, my dear, stopped me.* And now I wished she hadn't.

"Never mind." I turned to walk away. *The Outfit is far more interesting than this thing.*

The girl pushed me from behind. "Hey! I'm not done with you, asshole! Should we fight upstairs?"

Fight upstairs? I kept my cool and joked about the force of her shove. "Damn, you got a strong push. Are you sure you're not a rollergirl? We could probably use you on the track."

"Use me? What's a rollergirl? Use ME?! Should I get my boyfriend? He's big and he'll definitely kick your scrawny little banana ass!"

I couldn't tell if she meant it or not, but I really didn't want to find out. Her words reeked of pure asshole. Rollergirls have free reign to give me a good pummeling whenever they desire. Stupid meatheads, like the one this specimen probably dated, don't.

"I'd rather just enjoy myself. I told The Outfit that I wouldn't stray too far," I said as if The Outfit would register to her as easily as The Yankees. "They possess me now," I added, displaying The Outfit decal on my badge as proof. "One banana: bought and sold for the price of a sticker."

Pure Asshole put her hand on her hip and shifted her weight to one leg. "Who? What the fuck is an Outfit?" she said snidely.

I couldn't resist: "Well, an 'outfit' is any combination of clothing usually including but not limited to a shirt, pants, socks, and sneakers. The Chicago Outfit, however, is that group over there." I pointed to arguably one of the easiest derby leagues to pick out of a lineup.

"Them?! You're going back to them?" She pointed in disgust at two Outfitters, who were busily grinding on each other.

Pure Asshole gasped. Her eyes widened. "You suck! You're sick! Go fuck yourselves, Banana Man!"

She really had a way with words. "I don't think I can. I'm not their type ..." I finally said. I knew I was pushing Pure Asshole's buttons. I stopped caring.

"You disgust me! Fuck off!" She pushed me rather hard in my chest and stormed off. I took two steps back but caught myself.

Bitch!

I returned to The Outfit girls; they struck me as antithetical to Pure Asshole; they were everything she wasn't. Final Verdict? The Chicago Outfit trumped Pure Asshole!

Good 'ole Chicago Outfit.

"So, you're the banana?" asked Gaygan, another Outfit/Regime skater. "What league you with?"

"Well, as of tomorrow, I'm a Calk Sucker."

"Why not The VR?"

She must have sensed something about me was awry.

"Truth is, I wanted to mascot for you guys, but a friend of mine already asked me to root for the Suckers. I don't suck caulk and prefer what you guys are dishing up."

I've often heard (usually from morons not too unlike Pure Asshole) that *all* rollerfolk are queers. In point of fact, the opposite is true, and "many times ... queer identified sisters are left looking for a community that better understands them." The Vagine Regime sought a loose federation for any "bisexual, pansexual, genderqueer, transsexual, swinger, kink, etc. identified person who is involved with derby." [2] Straights were also invited to join as Vagine supporters. I wanted the full story and asked Outfitter and Regimeist Althea N. Hell if I could interview her about The VR's origins. Not there and then (as she was ... ahem, busy at the time) but at some point that weekend. She handed me an itinerary-style pass to all forthcoming Vagine Regime events: after-parties, bouts, and what-have-yous. It featured a picture of Althea holding a rainbow flag while sporting a shirt that read: "Gay As Fuck."

---

[2] Switchblade Siouxsie, "The Vagine Regime: Fracture Interview with Injure Rogers aka The Matron of Muff," *Fractured Magazine*, (Dec. 6, 2008). Accessed via: www.fracturemag.com/derby/features/the-vagine-regime. See also: Jennifer "Kasey Bomber" Barbee, "The Vagine Regime: Queer Pride and a Raucous Good Time," *Blood and Thunder Magazine*, 12, (Summer, 2009), pgs. 30-5.

"Catch up with me at any of these places," she said.

Interviews aside, I was about to ask her how one goes about mascoting for The Vagine Regime in the future when someone pinched my ass. I turned around and saw two girls walking away, laughing.

I turned back. "So, how does one ..." A scream behind me severed my sentence.

Estro Jen came running wildly through the casino, stopping with a frantic grab of my costume. "Let's get food, Banana Man!"

I said half-assed goodbyes to The Outfit/Regimers as Estro pulled me away to one of the hotel restaurants.

"So, whatever happened with that ... that belligerent girl?"

"We brought her back to the room. She started pounding on the bathtub and screaming obscenities at us. But after ten minutes of struggle, she tired herself out and fell asleep."

We ate nachos with fries and went back to the room, once again opening the door and stepping into an icebox. The floor was empty; Belligerent had gone. We walked around the room getting ourselves together to bed down for the nigh ... morning. After taking her shoes off, Estro stepped in something wet right over where Belligerent had collapsed.

"Shit, someone spilled beer on the floor!" she said. I walked over, also stepping on moist carpet. I pulled back; the saturation was firmly attached to my feet, making every step squishy.

"What's that smell?" I asked.

"Oh God, don't tell me ..."

I leaned down to the wet spot and sniffed. *Yep. Piss.*

"EEWWWWW!" Estro whisper-screamed. "Belligerent peed on the fucking floor?!"

We ran to the bathroom and frantically scrubbed the bottoms of our feet. Soap, water, rinse, repeat! Then we used about seven bath towels to sop up the urine. *There go my blankets for the night.*

We left the towels outside for room service, wrapping the wet ones with one large dry one. The bed had several covers on it. They looked so warm and cozy. Carefully, and with the most exquisite grace I have ever seen produced by a person as intoxicated as she, Estro removed the extra blanket that covered the three girls lying in the bed, disturbing no one. She then maternally tucked the girls back under the remaining blankets. We lay down beside the bed, right next to the door that led out to the balcony. I decided to give her the blanket, as I felt it bad form to lay beside her under it. *No repeats from last year.* I lay there wishing I could sleep in a glacier—it would have been warmer. My head pounded. But when I looked over and saw that Estro had warmly lulled off to sleep, it made the whole thing worth the trouble. I, on the other hand, froze my cock 'n balls off that night. Somehow, I managed a chuckle over this comedy of errors. Fucking Belligerent ...

Holy Wars on Fremont Street

We woke up at noon the next day late for the Caulk Suckers/Vagine Regime bout. With no time for coffee or food, Sugar, Estro, Friend, and I jumped into Sugar's rent-a-car and gunned it to Fremont Street. By the time we got there and found parking, the bout was near over.

"Get in there!" yelled Reverend Al Mighty at me in all his raspy, sandpaper-voiced glory. I was so discombobulated and ran around the outside of the track in a half daze waving my pompoms in everyone's face. I scarcely remember more than Cherrylicious employing her impenetrable booty block on the Regimers—much to some of their delight.

Among the crowd, I saw a tousled man holding up a billboard, looking like he had been up all night mainlining Jesus with a wooden syringe—a relic desperately seeking escape from the final judgment come the End Times. He wielded his sign like a battle-axe, proclaiming that we were all going to Hell.

"Sodomizers! Adulterers! Thieves! Liars!" he called out to us, letting it be known to all witnesses where he stood on each issue. Although he didn't just scream at derbyists, but random

Cherrylicious stopping Lola Blow with an enticing booty block.

gamblers and whores, there was no question that The Vagine Regime incurred the bulk of his Old Testament wrath.

"Faggots burn! Faggots burn!" he screamed, pointing to Gaygan, Althea, and several others who had been so chill the night before.

I couldn't let him get away with it. True, I wasn't mascoting for The VR, but fuck did I Derbylove them! Bout allegiances were brushed aside in favor of the larger derby picture. I ran up to God's Warrior and asked him if he liked jokes.

"This is no joke! Repent!"
"What do you call killing people in church?" I asked.
He looked cockeyed at me.
"Mass murder."
"How dare ..." he started.
"What did Jesus do after his bumpy airplane ride?" I interrupted.
His eyes widened. " ... The Son of God commands you!"
"Punch-his pilot," I smiled.
"Someone else might need a punch!"
"How many holy women are allowed to get pregnant? ... why, Nun, of course."
"Don't test me, Banana Man!" He raised his sign again and waved it over my head.
"Lemme ask you something, asshole: Which of The Vagine Regime do you think Jesus would do?"
"He'd send them all to Hell!"

A Brit who had overheard the exchange asked me to kindly just walk away. "Look, mate. He has his beliefs, you have yours. Let it be." I was about to walk away anyway. People that disillusioned cannot be reasoned with. Besides, the bout was over, and I wanted to get to the track for the last challenge bout of the weekend.[3] I was somewhat vindicated, though, when I saw Althea N. Hell posing for pictures in front of God's Warrior, seductively grabbing her crotch. I laughed my ass off.

Good 'ole Althea N. Hell.

---

[3] See Appendix 8: The Saga of Team DoucheBag.

Quite Contrary:
Or How Team Dance Party Saved the 'Nanner

After the bouts, Sugar and Estro dropped Friend and me off at the hotel, as they had *Via Derby* business to attend to. I passed out in the room with Friend. When I woke up, she had left—gone to the Flamingo Banks scrimmages with Sugar and Estro. I went out to face my last night at RollerCon 2000Great. I was on my way to the Black and Blue Ball, a semiformal dance/drinkfest that had become a tradition of RollerCondom (get your head out of the gutter; you know what I mean). Only thing was I had nothing to wear other than shorts and a black shirt. I got dressed, grabbed the room key that Sugar had left for me, and hopped an elevator downstairs. When I eventually did make it to the party, I didn't know that one needed a Rollercon pass to get in.

"How much are the passes?" I asked.

"Can't get 'em here."

"But I'm writing a book about roller derby!"

"Title it, 'The Security Guard Doesn't Give a Fuck.'"

Beaten, I walked all the way back to Sugar's room, got into my banana costume, and moseyed back down to the casino. One rather loud fellow caused a stir at a craps table. He had apparently just made a financial comeback. Two ladies cheered him on. He got quite the kick out of me when I walked by and called me over to the table. I paused momentarily, but only that. I mean, he was certainly loud, but didn't strike me as dangerous—just obnoxious. Maybe I could work out new material on him? Try out some of my bits?

I walked over to the table. One of the ladies, Joyce, lived in Vegas and bartended at the same bar her parents had conceived her at twenty some-odd years earlier. This was a point of pride. "Full circle!" she reckoned. The other one, Lisa, came with the ramblin' gamblin' man, Dave, and almost eclipsed his boisterousness with a bravado all her own. I asked if she was from Long Island.

Dave cut in, "Credit analyst. Minneapolis. Where you from?" Apparently, what I did was be a banana, because he didn't ask.

"New York."

Dave was passionate about finances and wasted not a moment explaining the banking world to me—a topic I know as well as I know Sanskrit. I asked Dave if I could bother him with a sensitive financial question.

"You got it, Banana Man," he said throwing the dice on the table. Craps. "Fuck!"

"I dunno ... it's kind of embarrassing."

"Whatever, I've heard it all. What'd you do, blow all your savings here? Need a second mortgage? What?"

"Well, it's just ... I don't know what those numbers floating by at the bottom of television screens mean during news broadcasts. Can you help me out?"

Dave turned and looked at me. "You serious?"

"As surely as I am dressed like an apple."

Lisa and Joyce laughed.

"Wiseass, huh?"

"Actually, the only thing my ass can do is fart and shit. It's my brain that is so wise."

Lisa and Joyce laughed again. Dave was about to yell at me when Lisa swatted his back.

"Relax, Dave. Kids just messing around." She ordered three whiskeys from one of the waitresses that wandered about the casino. When the waitress returned, Lisa handed Dave one of the glasses, me another, and kept one for herself.

"Cheers!" We clinked glasses.

"You've been to a bachelor party, haven't you?" Dave asked, eyes still glued to the table.

"Yes, once. My friends and I rented a boat and went fishing on a stormy night and I threw up."

"That's not a bachelor party," he scolded. He almost seemed pissed that I would liken fishing with my good buddies to a bachelor party.

"What about a strip club?" Still looking at the table.

"Once, and I hated it." I remembered that time in Myrtle Beach with some friends of mine. I had wasted five dollars at that "gentleman's" club stuffing three tacos worth of singles into some whore's panties. *No thanks.*

"So, what are you doing tonight?" asked Lisa.

"Nothing really. Just wandering around, I guess. Everyone I know is at a dance that I can't get into."

"Wanna go to a bachelor party? We need entertainment," said Dave.

I gasped. *I'm not your entertainment. I'm their ...* but when I looked around, there were no derbyfolk about. I swallowed my last sentence. "I don't know that it would be such a good idea."

"Nonsense! Come with us; I'm done here."

"It's all good people," Lisa assured me.

Joyce declined the invite. Dave gave her the room number in the event that she felt like stopping by and fucking him. He was, after all, a financial genius.

Lisa and Dave left the table; he chattered on, unaware that I stood where they'd left me, contemplating my next move. Truth be told, I was curious. I figured before Dave noticed that he was walking and talking to essentially himself, I'd dash over and catch up.

"... so, bachelor parties, if done right, are like strip clubs," he continued, never missing a vocal beat. "If you have money, like me, you can throw a killer bachelor party. And ... we left the wives at home." He elbowed me for emphasis. Lisa smacked him lightly in the chest.

"Oh, are you two married?"

"No," said Lisa. "He's engaged to some slut back home." The pair bickered back and forth for several minutes over the details of the rest of Dave's life with his bride-to-be. We arrived at the elevator and Dave (somewhat duplicitously) reasoned that he wasn't married yet and was still allowed to have fun. And it didn't sound like Lisa would rat. We took the elevator up to the fourth floor.

"Where's the room again?" he mumbled to himself. When we did find the room, he opened the door. *Holy shit! No wonder they left the wives at home!* The room was actually a suite complete with women in miniature dresses sprawled about all over the place. Smoke clogged up the air, drinks passed from person to person. Every girl, a Paris and Lindsey wannabe who wouldn't make it passed the second turn on a flat track, pointed and giggled at me. Almost every guy was either balding or had a shinny spiked haircut. Those who were balding tended to wear facial hair to make up the difference. I watched two gentlemen (a hedgehogger and balder, respectively) and a lady sniff lines of what I took to be cocaine off the nightstand. Shitty club music mixed in the air with an array of putrid perfumes and colognes. To my pleasure, it also reeked of the Lord's plant.

"What the fuck is that?!" asked a balder in black slacks and a shinny blue shirt. He held a shabby blunt between his chubby fingers as he pointed at me. I froze. *What the fuck am I doing here? This is really stupid.* I could just see the headlines: "Guy in Banana Suit Beaten to Death in Hotel Suite."

I shifted into an authoritative mode and quipped, "I'm here to make sure things don't get too out of hand. I'm security."

The guy laughed. "Security? Really? That's funny because we don't want security in here, do we?" He took a large sip of the blunt and passed it on to a hedgehogger next to him.

Shit. Poor choice of words. He's right. Why would they want security in the room?

But I did not give up. "No, no, you have me mistaken," I replied. "I'm here to make sure that everyone's *fun* is nice and secure." The ruse worked. His friend laughed and passed the smoking hickory over to me. Taking two tremendous tokes, I passed it along to the balder next to me.

A girl approached. "Okay. What is this?" she said laughing and pulling on my costume.

I took a deep breath: "I'm a roller derby mascot and I'm currently touring the United States mascoting for different leagues in an attempt to find out what it is exactly that is so different about roller derby this time around based off a theory I have about the traditional demeanor of athletes, and how derbygirls and Derbylove transcend that, and show that to the rest of the country so that everyone knows that it's the best sport in the world." I started to huff and puff. I looked over at guido #1, adding, "… and I'm also hotel security."

She laughed. "I have no idea what you just said."

"You're writing a book?" asked another hedgehogger. "Am I in it?"

"No, this is a serious book, full of serious things," I gaffed in such a way as to palliate the insult.

He brushed it off. "You look like a clown. You juggle, boss?"

I hate when people call me "boss" or "chief" or any of that other insufferable nonsense. It's so arrogant, so pretentious—*so Long Island*. I brushed it off and focused on the juggle request.

"I'm the best juggler since Stalin!" I ripped. I didn't have any balls to juggle so I ran into the bathroom and came out with three small hotel bottles of shampoo, body wash, and conditioner. I couldn't juggle for shit, but then neither could Joseph Stalin. My bumbling and overly serious attempts to juggle caused a clamor from some of the guests.

"E E E Enough of this!" yelled a girl whose name I hadn't been furnished with yet. She swam through the crowd, grabbed her purse—a thin black bag that I couldn't imagine fit anything inside it—my arm, and walked towards the door. The copper tint to her skin told me that, despite visiting a desert, she had purchased her tan in a salon. She wore a short red dress with black spaghetti straps. She clumsily teetered over due to her high heels and quickly yanked them off her feet.

"Take ... taaaake these!" she said, pushing them into me.

"Mary! Where you going? Don't leave!" said the only dude there that wasn't a balder or a hedgehogger, opting instead for a Julius Caesar straight hair dipping-over-the-forehead look.

"Yes," I added eyeing the size of his muscles, "perhaps you should stay here."

"No! Come, come with mmm m me me!" She opened the door and threw me out, following close behind. I didn't get to say good-bye to Dave or Lisa. As we walked down the hall, something struck me about the way Mary moved her jaw to speak. She chewed her words like she had ten wads of bubble gum in her mouth. I've seen that look in a person's face before. She had to be on some kind of upper. Meth? Cocaine? Poppers?

"Ecssssstasy. You ever done it?"

"Where are we going?" I asked ignoring her, still somewhat intimidated by thoughts of Caesar's shiny black shoe crunched over my face.

"Mmmmmmm ... doesn't it feel soooooo good?" Mary started rubbing her hands up and down my arm. "Mu ... my roooom ... just help help mmme to my roooom ...."

She would have made a real easy target for a masher. I conceded and entered the elevator with her. *Maybe she really does just want a safe escort back to her digs. Mission! Get her back to her room safely!* She pressed several floor buttons on the elevator.

"Don't buttons feel sooooooo good?" she asked again.

"Sure do," I replied standoffishly looking at the ascending floor numbers. "What floor are you on?"

"Mmm … 15? 17? Ahhhhh yeeesssssssssss, 16! You ever done E? Do you know what I feeeeeel like? I want you to feel like meeeEEEE."

I could feel the weed creeping up on me, and her rising inflections were growing irksome. I quickly pressed the button for the 16th floor—one number she hadn't pushed. Mary flopped her head over, taking her body down with her. I caught her and held her up. The elevator stopped at the 10th floor. A middle-aged couple got in. Mary lifted her head up, "Issss this my my floor?" Her eyes rolled into the back of her head.

"I hear the pre-frontal lobes are quite scenic this time of year," I joked. I couldn't imagine what that couple thought about the two of us.

The guy grinned at me. He caught my reference. His wife looked at Mary in ill repute. And at me, in even iller repute. I could tell she was thinking, "You did this to her, you sicko!"

When the elevator stopped on the 16th floor, I threw us out into the hallway. I turned and gave a desperate smile to the couple as the doors closed. *If only I could have just gotten into that damn Black and Blue Ball …*

"Good luck," the man wordlessly lipped to me. His wife turned and gave him a cold stare as the doors closed.

"Mmmmmmmmm ….. carry me," said Mary as she let her body go limp on the floor.

"No! No! Please get up!" I glanced around the hallway to see if anyone was coming. It was clear, but I had had enough. "Please!" I begged.

She just laid there smiling. *Fucking non-violent resistance.*

I picked her up, securing my left arm under her knees just below the reach of her dress. I placed her shoes in the crevasse between her belly button and breasts, and walked down the carpeted green mile.

Turned out her fucking room was conveniently on the other side of the fucking hotel from where we got off of the fucking elevator in the first fucking place! So I lugged her around the fucking hallways. I was pissed. Frustrated. I wanted derbyfolk. It wasn't until we reached the door that I realized this idiot might not have her room key on her. Thank the gods, she did. She pulled the keycard out of her tiny black purse. I let us into the room and plopped her onto the bed. She squirmed around the sheets in sheer, well, ecstasy. I sat at the table to unwind for a moment.

Mary jumped off the bed and lunged towards me.

"What the fuck are you doing?!!" I screamed.

"Where wh where is is it?!" she said fumbling around my costume. She lifted the bottom half up, and pushed her hand down my yellow boxers.

"We can't do this!" I yelled. She pulled my yellow boxers down my thighs and slammed her face into my groin. She started to breathe heavily and licked my penis with her tongue. I shot up, the chair falling to the floor behind me. Mary, too, fell over on her back.

"MMMMmmmmm, I'm ready!" she said squirming on the floor.

Now's my chance! I ran to the door, thrust it open, and darted down the hall. *There's no way I'm taking advantage of a drugged woman. Mom taught me better.* I had no particular flight path but zigzagged my way through the corridors lest she pick up my scent. My only destination was as far away from Mary as I could possibly get.

I reached an ice/vending machine outpost and stopped to cool off. A man filling his ice bucket looked up at this panting, apple-faced banana in full-blown panic attack mode. I hadn't even noticed him at first, not until the ice started pouring into his bucket. My heart pulled itself from my chest; I didn't think it could take any more strain. A serotonin-battle erupted between my primitive fight and flight mechanisms. I couldn't decide which to go with. I was faint. I needed air. I felt trapped in that vending machine confessional and sat against the wall for a second. I needed to catch my breath. And my sanity.

The gods showed no mercy. Indeed, they never do. I thought I was dying. I wanted to be home with my kitty cat. My eyes swelled up. I knew I had reached the Ninth Circle of Hell when meter-maids and rubberneckers[4] started flashing before my psyche.

"Are you alright?" asked the man. He startled me. I looked up, trying not to look directly into his eyes—the "head under the sand" trick.

"I ... I," I started to explain. *I just ran away from an ecstasied-up whore who was trying to blow me. I'm now having a panic attack. Nice to meet you!* "Never mind," I managed to get out.

The man left me. I needed derbyfolk! I needed good people. I couldn't deal with these nut job club-girl whores by myself. And Caesar? Maybe he hadn't forgotten about me and was at that very moment hunting me down! It's not like I could disappear in a crowd wearing a banana costume. I didn't want to be the banana or the person under it. I was lost, unsure of

---

[4] No politicians, though—even Satan has standards.

every decision I had ever made. Oh, what was I doing out there? Oh, that's right, *the book*. This book. *Fuck this book.*

This was exactly where teachers, bullies, and the clergy had told me that I'd end up my whole life: alone and distressed. In fact, back home in New York, on that very night, my high school graduating class was celebrating its ten year reunion. I'm sure I wasn't mentioned, but what would have been said if I had been? "Oh, Tom?" one of my old classmates might ask. "I don't know. I heard a rumor that he's in Vegas dressed like a banana with a bunch of crazy broads that roller skate." To which the only reply by one of my other ex-classmates would have been, "Figures."

Then it struck me. My fellow alums were correct. That's where I *should* be—amongst the good, the bad, the derby! *Maybe the Black and Blue Ball is over?* With great trepidation, I snuck back down to the casino, ducking around corners and dodging tourists. My brain pounded the big bang from beneath my skull. I felt jagged stones fermenting in my throat. I made it to the casino, inches from cracking ...

It was here, in my oubliette, that a friendly face found me. Justice Feelgood Marshall was dancing in the middle of the casino with a horde of rollergirls. He pulled me deep into the dance floor. I didn't move at first. I was so shook up. After I stood there for a minute, derbydancers started shaking my hips for me. Before I knew it, I was shaking them myself.

Good 'ole Justice Feelgood Marshall.

Some mystery girl threw me to the floor and started riding up my back. She then stood up and started to spank my bottom blue. Then it was Cherrylicious' turn. When I finally lifted my head up, I was surrounded in mirth and merriment. Derbyfolk had commandeered the casino, turning it into one big dance party. Another mystery girl handed me a bottle of something. I took a nice drag off it. "Take another!" she said with a large, inviting smile. I did. *The Fear* slowly receded; the rubberneckers and meter maids were dissipating—dying! *Hooray for dying meter maids*! A security guard rushed over to us.

"Look! I've told you all a hundred times already! The casino isn't a dance hall! Take it somewhere else!"

The dancing stopped, only to be resumed after the guard walked away. This would happen several times throughout the night in what was the founding weekend of Team Dance Party. I put the whole weird night behind me, forgot about Mary and Caesar, and danced myself into roller derby bliss. *It was alllll good.*

And that is how Team Dance Party saved the 'Nanner.

Good 'ole Team Dance Party.

A girl tapped me on my shoulder. I recognized her. I had seen her earlier at the Caulk/Vagine bout.

"Hey, you're the guy staying with Sugar and Estro, right?" she asked.

"Yes," I said in a winded voice. "They went to The Flamingo Ban ..." *that was hours ago* "... I think they may be upstairs."

"Are you heading up there now?"

"No. Yes. I don't know. I don't know what I'm doing. I don't even know who I am anymore."

"Of course you do! You're the banana!"

I didn't say anything back to this very sweet person, but she saw in my face everything I kept from her.

"Why don't we go upstairs? You look like you've had a long night."

I agreed, and we went upstairs. When we arrived at the room, I grabbed the extra blanket that Sugar had left loose for me and threw it on the floor. We both got under it. My plane left in three hours.

Roller Derby: The Sensation That Caused A Book!

"You know, I still don't even know your name," I said.

"Oh, it's ▓▓▓. And you're Banana Man, right?" She stretched her strong derbygirl legs underneath the blanket.

"Actually, it's 'Bane-ana,' but nobody calls me that."

"Really? What do they call you?"

I smiled. "Banana Man."

She set her alarm for me and went to sleep. When I had first joined the Long Island Roller Rebels, Butterscotch remarked to me that every new derbyist spends about a week or so coming up with a zillion different derbynames. She was right; I remember that *month* well. One of the names I came up with back then, coincidentally, was the derbyname of the girl who I lay beside. The gods had seen it fit that I meet her one day, I reasoned. I loved being sandwiched next to her. I didn't want to sleep, just drown in the sheer beauty of the moment. I never wanted to leave, but endlessly feel her warm inhalation; let her pulsing heart cool my soul like a kitten's purr.

I had spent the whole time at RollerCon in the care of wonderful people like Sugar, Estro, Friend, those crazy Chicago Outfitters, and now this lovely. Pure platonic Derbylove—the legends were true!

When ▓▓▓'s alarm went off, I contemplated not getting up—"over sleeping" my flight, dealing with it later. But I couldn't. I had to get back to Texas. I promised Belle; more importantly, I had to return J. Crush's sentiments to her. Only, I couldn't move. ▓▓▓ had pulled the blanket over her body and mummified me inside. I struggled to get up. Finally, after much effort—and paradoxically, reservation—I inched my way out the bottom. I grabbed my bags and wished the still sleeping Sugar, Friend, and Estro farewells. I turned back to ▓▓▓, leaned down, gave her a small kiss on the cheek, and said "thanks." Eyes tightly shut, she smiled a "so long."

Good 'ole ▓▓▓.

I crawled outside into the early desert sun. My ton of bricks almost felt like a head. I somehow remained awake by the time I arrived at DFW airport. Trying to keep up with my thoughts and events had been futile. *Did I really think I would be able to write ev-ery-thing down?* I kept thinking about Pure Asshole, God's Warrior, and Mary. Every bit of their insanity had been deflected by one rollerfolk or another. Pure Asshole and Mary, especially. They were the kind of girls my parents probably would have urged me to consider settling down with. And yet I would have given anything to be back next to ███. *How quite contrary.*

As I rode the shuttle to the airport, it occurred to me that I never interviewed Althea N. Hell about The Vagine Regime that weekend. Some writer I was. I got a good taste of it spending quality time with The Chicago Outfit, but I wanted the full story. My only chance to quell such feelings of failure would be to make it a mission. Such missions were non-negotiable; I'd *have* to find her. Reluctant as I was, I swore a silent oath to myself that I would not rest until I got Althea N. Hell's interview. I wouldn't have to wait long, as I'd be in Chicago in a week. 'Twould be the perfect opportunity.

VIII

LONE STAR SKATE

I've never had a bad day. Just great days where shitty things happened.
ME

On the return flight home, I didn't have a Maxine to sit next to and was a queasy wreck by the time I landed in Dallas. My friend Summer picked me up from the airport, and I threw up on the car ride back to Tyler's apartment. We parted ways, and not too long after, I fell asleep.

I woke up the next morning and readied myself for a personal milestone. I hated leaving RollerCon and leaving the warm house that ▓▓▓ built, but I had a fully blossomed bluebonnet masturbating in my tummy that even the cold breeze of a Norwegian winter couldn't wither. For on that day, in just a few short hours, I, Bane-ana, would be mascoting for the league that started it all. I felt so ... important? *Elated* is the word! The Texas Rollergirls had unwittingly united every derbyist and every league the globe over under a common bond. And now, I was going to share in their magic. Only a mere five-hour drive from Dallas to Austin separated me from this climax—worth every mile! But a small misunderstanding of the state's slogan "Don't Mess with Texas" caused some shenanigans on my way.

Minimal Criminal

The slogan was—as it is to most New Yorkers—foreign to me. I mistakenly mused that the "mess" was more akin to the colloquial "messing" or "fucking" with a person. The phrase means no such thing and was born out of a "don't litter" campaign back in 1986. Signs spread across the vast—holy shit are they vast!—highways urging all people not to litter. From what I understand, the campaign reduced litter by a significant amount. Since I give a hoot, those in Texas didn't have to worry about me discarding rubbish out my window. But I didn't know the true meaning of the slogan at the time and wanted to colloquially "mess" with ya'll. If I was going to mascot for the Texas Rollergirls, I wanted to do it righteously—as an outlaw.

On that long stretch of highway I-35 South, among the former plantation sized mansions and randomly placed shacks, locals sell small trinkets and souvenirs out of their houses. At one stop, I bought a beer tanker; at another, a plate that pictures all the U.S. presidents from Washington to J.F.K. Folks also sold gasoline out of small red gas cans—like the kind people use to fill up their lawnmowers. Perhaps to those living in the Midwest and South, a typical reaction to these "house stores" will be a "no shit," but to me, it was an otherworldly experience.

At one point on my trip, all the coffee, canned espressos, and water got to me and I had to pee ... no, I mean, really pee! I crossed another house store, parked my car in the dirt driveway, and walked to the front door. The house had a certain bumpkin appeal to it. Automotive parts spread across the front yard of dead grass; so rusted, in fact, that I couldn't tell a transmission from a steering wheel. All were for sale. Those blades of grass that still had life were tipped off with yellow, lying in a state of *in extremis*. Outside the front door sat an old, gutted soda machine priced at $50. I opened the door and was charmed by the sound of a bell that hanged on the inside, strung up with what looked like fishing line. How quaint! I stood by the door for a moment to take it all in, including the pervasive dust. A tickle formed in my nose, and a sneeze hung over the precipice of my nostrils. Random knick-knacks, new and old, littered the floors and shelves. Some of these things might have been antiques if not for the shabby condition they were in. The floors creaked an old wood panel twang with every step I took. I tried feverishly to tiptoe across the floor and see how far I could get without making a sound. I didn't get an inch.

The proprietor, Pa, sat behind a makeshift half-wall counter. Obese and dirty, Pa wore clothes that smelled worse than a derby team after a bout. An oil stain (I think) had crusted onto his forehead to the point that it looked natural. He seemed suspended in a state of permanent sloth, slouching in his rickety wooden chair the way he did, you betcha! I could barely see his mouth, hidden behind a beard of loose wire and coarse wool. When he coughed, I caught small glimpses of his teeth. They were so jagged I was surprised he didn't cut the innards of his mouth open with every wheeze. On a positive note, his Appalachian dentures momentarily took my mind off the smell emitting from his breath. Beside him sat a nearly finished bottle of whiskey. His mannerisms and slurred speech told me that only a few hours ago the bottle had been significantly fuller.

In the great debate between so-called "cat people" and "dog people" (although I like both animals), I fall on the side of the kitties. However, there is such a thing as having *too* many kitty cats; Pa didn't seem to understand that concept and let his cats breed like rabbits or, worse yet, Alaskans. He also kept dogs. I didn't see them but could hear barking and chains rustling in the backyard. It sounded like two were tied up, but I suppose there could have been more. In fact, I cannot be sure if Pa didn't have a whole host of animals tied to stakes or rotting in milk crate cages somewhere in the nooks of his house. He had also adopted the local insects. A considerable amount of flies, mosquitoes, gnats, and spiders had populated every crevice of worn furniture (all for sale) that I saw. The mere thought of bugs scurrying around the couches and chairs made my skin itch. But I did have to pee and asked where I could find the toilet. With what seemed like a significant amount of effort, Pa lifted his finger and pointed to a small door towards the back of the house. I walked through the back door, which was peppered with shotgun-sized holes. The "bayffe' throom" (his words) more closely resembled a coffin with a toilet, lacking basic restroom accoutrements like the seat on said toilet (maybe it was once for sale?). No sink either. In fact, I didn't see a sink anywhere in the house at all. I finished peeing as quickly as I could; my arms grew tired from swatting flies and mosquitoes away from my balls. I tried not to breathe and even used my aiming hand to plug my nose shut—not so much to block the smell as to stop the insects from flying up my nostrils. Back outside in the "store room," which was really a converted living room, I saw a dirty, red cooler. Curious of its contents, I opened it up. Among near completely liquefied ice floated sodas, waters, and beers.

An outlaw opportunity presented itself. I would mess with Texas by purchasing beer on a Sunday, when such terrible and immoral things were against the law. I would be a "minimal criminal" of the Old West.[1]

"How much are the brews?" I asked, hoping that Pa would be too drunk to realize that it was indeed Sunday. I was wrong.

---

[1] The Warped Weeble Wobbles, "Minimal Criminal," *Enemania*! Self Released (1993).

"Caynt seal ya bea una Sundu," he said, meshing each word into one long one. "S'gainst a low."

It seemed somewhat like a double-standard that this man wouldn't sell me beer when he himself was fully sauced on The Lord's Day. Technically, he was within his legal rights, though; such is the hypocritical stupidity of the law. However, it also led me to a good—okay, not a *good*—idea, but an idea nonetheless.

"Um, can I use your phone?" I asked.

"Dun work."

Perfect. If I could somehow get his last bit of whiskey, he wouldn't be able to call the cops. I don't steal—never have, never will—so I reached into my pockets and fumbled for some money. I found a ten and a five. Separating the bills from my license, lint, and loose papers, I crumbled them up into a little ball. Judging by the amount of whiskey left in the bottle, I sized it up as fewer than fifteen dollars—so he'd be getting a tip too. Cojones intact, I threw the wad of money at Pa's face. It hit his oil stain and fell to the floor.

"Whas is fo?" he asked and bent over to pick the money up. When he was fully bowed, I leaned over him—he smelled worse up close!—grabbed the bottle and skedaddled out of his house. I jumped into my car and roared away, dirt from the driveway flying everywhere. I kept peering into my rearview mirror. Pa never came running out of the house. I was pissed. I had so hoped that he'd complete the scene by waving his fist in the air and calling me a "whippersnapper" as I drove away. He didn't. But still, I was thrilled! I had bought alcohol on a Sunday in Texas and rolled into Austin as a watered-down frontier bandit.

I arrived at the fabled Playland in an even better mood. The bout would be a double header: The Hustlers battling the Honky Tonk Heartbreakers for half a bouts length; then the Hell Marys would play the Hotrod Honeys, then The Hustlers and Honkey

Tonks would finish their business, followed by the Hell Marys and the Hotrod Honeys again. It was like two bouts for the price of one. And since I'd never mascoted for Texas, I didn't feel torn about cheering for one team over the other like with the Mods and Dolls the week prior. I couldn't wait!

I parked my car in a shady area in the parking lot and walked through the front doors of Playland. You know the following scene well:

An out-of-town cowboy saunters into a small mining town on the edge of the known frontier. His horse is tired and thirsty; he is tired and thirsty. Ignoring ownership of the trough, the stranger leads his horse to the bucket of water. It is filthy, but both care not. He sticks his head in with her, and washes his

face as she drinks. After a few drags of the water, he pats his horse on the back of the neck and turns towards the entrance of the saloon. He pushes the two vested wooden doors apart, unsure of what he will find on the other side. The creak in the rusty hinges causes an uneasy stir amongst the locals. A dozen or so ten-gallon hats turn towards him. A man, about to take a shot of bourbon, lowers his glass so as to better examine the outsider. Their eyes speak volumes: "*Who's this stranger?*" *Walking up to the bar, the exhausted visitor tips his hat to the barkeep.* "*What'll ya have, stranger?*" *the barkeep asks, as he sizes up his customer. He doesn't really care what will ale the stranger. He wants information.*

Of Potassium and Poison

My entrance into Playland went something like that. Heeding all these caveats, I quickly tried to make myself useful. I asked a girl if Belle Star had arrived. Instead of an answer, I got an examination.

"Who ah ya?" she asked.

Frozen. "No … nobody. Just a friend." I was taken aback. That meager answer was the best one I could come up with at that moment.

"Belle ain't hea yet. Fans ain't 'lowed in. Ou'syyde." She pointed to the door.

Okay, so I'm not exactly a friend. I clarified who I was and that I was there to help, not ignoring a single detail, lest she restart the interrogation. This was Texas; there was no telling who had a gun. She told me to lay track tape with a young man from Houston named Sum Jung Kid.

He was easy to find: "Jus' loogh for the onl' kid in he'ya layin' tape," she told me.

At the center of the track, some young kid had already started measuring out the proper regulation depths of rope. He was a member of The Derby Brothers, a "crack commando unit" that had been wrongfully accused of various crimes. They toured the derby underground, setting up tracks, doing the hard labor of derby work, and living off of beer.[2] I told Sum Jung Kid that I had been assigned to him, and he to me.

"Whereya' frum?" Jung Kid asked. Ignoring social convention, he wanted to know where I was from before he even knew my name.

"Me'all is from New York."

"Yeah, ya' soun' lie ya' from Nuh Yor'. Eye'm frum Hous'in," he replied in an affable southern plunk.

"Well you sound like you are from Houston, so we are even."

As we lay the track, little crooked wrinkles of uneven tape stuck together, forming little bubble-streams along the track line. This happens sometimes; the corners usually take the brunt of it. Most volunteers (myself included) typically ignored these flaws unless they were grossly unattractive to the overall aesthetic of the track itself. Sum Jung Kid felt differently. His experience far surpassed his youthful age, and he remained unwaveringly militant about not allowing any creases in the tape. The job took triple the amount of time it normally takes to complete, as he made sure that *every* millimeter of tape looked perfect. By the time we finished, I could not locate a single breach in the integrity of the track outline. Not one.

After the most brutal track tape session I ever endured, Belle finally arrived. *Mission*! I ran up to her. "I have delivered your message to J. Crush. She loves you in return."

"Oh, tell her I said 'Thank You'."

---

[2] For the full lowdown, visit www.derbybrothers.com

AAAhhhhhhhh!!!!!!!
"Sure."

I then asked her for the names of those in charge so that I may introduce myself. Before every bout, I liked to meet all the refs—especially the outside refs—and let them know that I will always be cognizant of their movements. As such, they never had to fret about me. *Just go along with your reffing and never worry that I'll do a tumble into you or anything. I will never be in your way. I know my place, I'm a professional ... sort of.* Belle told me to find a specific person and introduce myself. I didn't know who this specific person was and started to ask around. Everyone seemed to know Specific, but nobody wanted to introduce us. The buck—i.e. me—was passed from an announcer to a skater, from a skater to a ref, from a ref to a skater again, until I ceased being a mascot and became a pinball. I found this rather odd.

Finally Ozzy Zion, dressed in a curly pink wig and tutu (and also the first person I'd met to ever successfully fuse mascoting and announcing into one entity), agreed to introduce me to Specific. When we found Specific, he outright dismissed me, clearly peeved at Ozzy for introducing us in the first place. He spoke to me as if I didn't know the rules; as if I'd never set up/broken down a track before; as if I hadn't just driven halfway across the country mascoting and learning new things at each bout; as if I'd never set up sound equipment or done any of the other jillion things that need to be done before a bout. I wanted to defend myself, but my throat choked between my thoughts and my words. I was a guest so I kept quiet during the snap session that Specific hammered upon me. The bout hadn't started and I already wanted to hightail it out of Playland. I wasn't an outlaw; I was an outcast, a poison. I had brought bad karma into Austin, and now it was biting me in the ass. Specific could smell it all over me.

Not everyone acted so dismissively. Sometimes the urinal station is a momentary meeting ground for friendly chaps, and I saddled up next to announcer Jimmy "Kool Aid" Jones, a rather warm and welcoming fellow. Echoing Pee Wee Hurt 'em from my first bout, Kool Aid kept telling me to go out and have fun.

"Don't worry about Specific," he said as he flushed the lever. "If he doesn't like you, you'll know."

"I think I already know."

"Nah, man. It's cool; just get out there!" Kool Aid kept encouraging me to mascot, but I felt so empty that not even his booming encouragement could get me out of my lost headspace.

"I'd really love to get out there," I finally managed to say. "But except for you, Belle, and a few others, I feel wholly unwelcome here." *Like a stranger in a frontier town.*

"So then, for me, get out there and do your thing!" he responded cheerfully.

I perked up, determined to go strut my stuff and just stay as far away from Specific as I could. I walked outside the bathroom and stood by the Honky Tonk Heartbreakers'—Belle Star's team—bench area. I even decided to try some funnies. I turned to a girl eating a banana.

"You're breaking my heart," I said as she took bite after bite. "Now, I'm going to have to go find a rollergirl to eat." I smiled at her, anticipating a reflection. She didn't say a word; she just looked at me and continued eating the banana. Her eyes said, "Keep talking ... you're next."

Okay, so that didn't work. With the bout minutes away, I pulled my pompoms out of my bag.

"Those better not be pompoms!" yelled Specific as he skated over to me. "We don't need those strings breaking off and making a mess in here! I don't need anyone slipping on them either!" There was a serious and annoyed tone in his voice that locked my mouth shut. It's hard to talk when your stomach is in your throat. Every heartening breath of wind that Kool Aid had blown into my sails petered out and died. I put the pompoms back in my bag. Belle Star skated over and handed me two squares of blue and white tablecloth—a fan's symbol of Honky Tonk Heartbreaker support. Then she skated back over to the entranceway, where the rest of her team waited to roll out for the first bout. The National Anthem played. During the last few bars, the girls stomped their skates on the floor in rhythm.

The Honky Tonk Heartbreakers came out to a square dance number on their skates, momentarily cheering me up. I liked seeing the different regions' take on derby, each with its own little ditties. At the sound of the whistle, I did my best to flip my shit for the Heartbreakers, but it was difficult. I hadn't felt so awkward since my first season. I didn't hang by the team's bench long and opted instead to stand behind them—barely visible. I jumped, I cheered, I waved my pieces of tablecloth but felt no real sensation from doing it. My moves were merely mechanical representations of a fun I remembered having at every bout I ever cheered at. No heart, no soul. I couldn't even fake a smile. I didn't know what to do—that had never happened before.

Just then, Belle Star came skating off the rink towards me.

"Get a garbage!" She yelled as she threw her helmet off.

A large can sat on the floor to my left. I went to grab it, but another fellow got there first. Belle blew chunks of whatever she last ate into the pail. Then, in a move worthy of Spartacus, she wiped the puke off her chin with her wrist guard, crunched her helmet back on her head, and rejoined the pack just as the next jam started. I was speechless—eyes wide open; jaw firmly entrenched in the floor. *This girl is hard-Fucking-core.*

The first period for the Honky Tonks and The Hustlers ended. The Hotrod vs. Mary bout was about to begin. I don't remember much of that bout, as my mind struggled to reconcile the positivity and negativity. One thing, or should I say *one person*, I do remember was Rice Rocket, a Hotrod.

I grabbed my pen and notebook out of my sports bag. *How does one describe this phenomenon? This Rice Rocket?* She danced around the Hell Mary blockers with all the gentle motion of Bach's baton, massaging each note—each blocker—down to a shiny finish. Her gyrations presented a paradox in themselves, probing gulfs deeper than any bass while simultaneously soaring over any soprano. The sturdy pulse of an entire brass section pumped in her wheels; the agility of the woodwinds glided her down the track and exhaling *en masse*, shone through her confident stride. Every turn of her skates were tastes of the delicate score, and I licked my lips anticipating the crescendo. It seemed odd to compare such a raw aggression with a harmonious sonata. But no other standard of comparison sufficed. She controlled the jam; Rice Rocket controlled the music.

The crowd was equally fantastic. When Rocket took the lead, the constant screams of "Faster! Faster! Kill! Kill! Kill!" weren't mere words—they were true calls for dismemberment. When one girl literally skated with one foot on the track (the other over the back of a fallen girl), the crowd went ballistic. The Texas derbyfans seemed in tune with every elbow, every foul, every lead jam of the Hotrods. This is *their* sport.

At halftime, I wrestled between laying low or saying *fuck it* and letting loose. Belle's little puke brigade and Rice Rocket's symphonic movements livened me up. The second half of the Honky Tonk/Hustler bout was due in five minutes or so. I went to the bathroom and decided that I would give talking to Specific one more chance. I would simply tell him that although I knew that I looked like a doofus in a peel running around aimlessly, my moves were actually premeditated. Just as there is a lot of athleticism and precision involved in playing roller derby, there is a lot of calculation, at least for me, with mascoting. We mascots *cannot* interfere with the sport! Maybe then he'd lighten up on me. Everyone else had been really cool. If I could just cinch Specific, it'd all be swell. I didn't want a repeat of the first period. I wanted to enjoy myself. But first, I had to relieve myself.

I exited the bathroom (yes, I pee a lot at bouts) and bumped into a dude who towered over me in both height and weight. His arms were covered in skulls, and death, and killing, and guns, and America, and bombing, and guns, and death. His beer spilled on me. He said nothing; just stared grimly at me. *Ho. Lee. Shit.*

"Buh-naw-naaaa …. hehehe …" he said with the creepiest voice I've ever heard and the creepiest smile I've ever seen. Okay, I'm just going to say it: *He was the creepiest dude in the entire history of creepy people*!

"Uh … uh …, I'll g …get you another … b …b ..beer … sir!" I said, creeping away.

I ran to my sports bag, got money, and bought a beer. On my way to deliver the beer, Specific rolled by me. He looked at me, then at the beer, and then at me again. He skated back to the track.

God! Damn! It!

The whistle blew and the bout exploded into play. Ozzy Zion kept calling me out trackside, but I couldn't go now. Even the slightest mess-up would have Specific accusing me of being drunk during a bout. I finished out the Honky Tonk/Hustler bout, staying behind the bench, dreaming of joining Ozzy along the track lines. I hadn't had someone to mascot with since Furious George. Ozzy was hilarious as a mascot, on-point as an announcer, and the crowd loved him. Who wouldn't?

The Honky Tonks lost but put up a tremendous fight, thrilling the crowd. As the second half of the Hotrods and the

Marys' mêlée kicked off, a very beautiful girl approached me. Dottie Karate almost seemed happy to see me. She asked me if I had ever heard of Melicious. I told her that my nose currently resided in her book.

"Would you like to meet her?" Dottie asked.

Would I? "Oh, yes! I'd love to!" I grabbed my bag not mentioning that I had Melicious's book in it. Across the room, Dottie shouted a "there she is!" and we made our way to the other side of Playland. We walked up to her, and Dottie introduced us. I pulled her book out of my bag and asked if she wouldn't mind slaughter-graphing it.

"Of course not!" she exclaimed. She wrote on the first page: "To Bane-ana, where would the fans and Rollergirls be without the mascots?" She capped off the slaughter-graph with her trademark craps dice.

As we walked to put my bag back with the rest of my crap, Dottie Karate asked me if I planned on attending the after-party or if I intended to just haul on out.

"I'll have to think about it."

As the audience dispersed, talking about this and that favorite moment of the bouts, I helped clean up. I remembered a story about an old woman and a scorpion, although where I heard it escapes me. Nonetheless, it goes something in this wise: *An elderly lady spotted a scorpion yelling for help as it clung to a branch that hung over a raging river. If the scorpion let go, it surely would have drowned in the violent rapids. It asked the lady for help and she obliged. The lady picked up the scorpion, which stung her hand without hesitation. Quietly taking the stings, she placed the scorpion on dry land. A man had watched the whole deed unfold and asked the lady why she would help such a vile creature that only stung its rescuer. To this, the lady replied, "It is in the scorpion's nature to sting. But it is in my nature to help it regardless."* My nature is to be happy and useful. I had already felt robbed of half this axiom—to have fun; I wasn't going to be robbed of the other half. As I stacked chairs, moved barricades, and pulled tape, Dottie Karate again found me and asked if I would attend the after-party. I had decided I would. Truth was, I had nowhere else to go.

How the Announcers Saved the 'Nanner

A long caravan 'a cars 'n vans pulled out of the Playland parking lot. I arrived in downtown Austin and found a parking spot around the block from The Jackalope, the bar that hosted the after-party. I parked and sat for a moment trying to decide if I dare go inside. I looked at the passenger seat and saw the whiskey I had bought from Pa underneath my notebook, loose papers, and a shirt or two. I was about to drink it when I remembered the jagged dentures of the bottle's previous owner. I got out of my car, found a garbage pail, threw out the bottle, and headed for the bar. *Whatever's going to happen is going to happen.*

I walked in, bought a Lone Star beer, found a lone table, and by the lone light of a lone candle, started to write my lone thoughts. I rested my head against the clumsily laid brick walls that gave the place a cavernous feel. Among the red-tinted air and the high ceilings, a devil girl hanged bearing a sign that read: "Damn Good Food."

I started to crash. I wanted my bed and my kitty. I still hadn't secured anywhere to sleep and started to feel uneasy. Lost. Was this all a mistake?

Ozzy Zion sat down next to me.

"Good job," he said.

"What good job?" I cracked. "I didn't do anything."

"If we had known you were coming, maybe you and I could have worked out a routine or something ..." He was trying to make me feel better, justifying the bout with ipso facto hand motions in an attempt to spin my mood. 'Twas a nice gesture. I could see the sincerity in his eyes. But he didn't need to justify anything. He had been friendly to me the whole time. A great announcer/mascot and something told me, an even greater person. I was being difficult, letting the bout hang over me. I guess every derbyist has a shitty bout. I had already sobered up from the high hopes I had dosed myself with before the bout. Zion eventually gave up and went to find more uplifting things—this I don't blame him for, as I was very bad company.

Where was my Captain to consol me? I missed her laugh. And Butterscotch? Always ready to give me the biggest hugs and say, "Love me some banana!" And Fiesta? My buddy at 4 am. Heidi Ho-bag, to laugh at my jokes? My Killer Tofu? My league? My heart? I had been up too long, driven too many miles. The room turned into a reddish haze. I couldn't believe that I had driven all that way only to have it end so unceremoniously. My head began to rock back and forth. Eyelids turned as damp as soggy laundry sitting in a dryer. I started to fade. I was giving up ...

NO! Stop this maudlin shit, and get up you asshole! All this self-pity crap! You were so taken back by Specific that you've overlooked how wonderful everyone else has been! You sound like an unappreciative prick from Long Island! Now get the fuck up and find what it is you came all the way here looking for. This is 2000Great; don't let it get to you. Get up and find your Derbylove!

And I did just that.

I slide over to the bar where the Texans enjoyed some post-bout tacos. *See? Tacos! Oh happy day, blessed tacos!* Desi Cration, a Honky Tonk Heartbreaker, greeted me and handed me a Lone Star.

"No thanks," I said smiling. "I'll get my own. That's yours."

"No! Take this one. I want to buy you a beer! I didn't sip from it, so don't worry."

"It wouldn't matter if you did. I'm not a germaphobe."

"Perfect!" she said, licking the mouthpiece of the can. "Here!" She pushed the beer into my hand and walked away. I looked at the spittle-covered mouth of the beer. My smile grew even bigger, curing my face.

Good 'ole Desi Cration.

Another derbineer made her way over to me through the dense crowd and asked if I was the banana from ECDX.

"Would anyone else in the world hate himself so much that he felt the need to do this?"

She laughed. "Ya' funnah! Wan'a beeah?"

Funny? Me? Ladies and Gentlemen, the lady thinks I'm funny! I blushed and then raised my can up to show her that I already had one. I smiled to let her know I appreciated her offer.

I *will* make it. I felt so much better. *Change of mind ... that's all it took.*

Kool Aid approached me and asked if I had a place to crash. Before I could even respond in the negative, he offered me his couch provided I assured him I wasn't a psycho. *What, like the kind of person who dresses up like a banana and drives across America?* Kool Aid had been part of a roving band of comics that, much like the roller derby circuit, met up all over the US performing standup comedy routines. As such, he held empathy for those like me. "I've crashed on so many couches in my day that it would be the height of hypocrisy to not let you crash at my house," he said. I toasted Ozzy and Kool Aid and thanked them very much for their hospitality. It was finally time to enjoy myself. And so it came to pass that the announcers saved the 'Nanner.

After a long conversation with Kool Aid about the impact roller derby had on younger girls[3] (his daughter was a Derby Brat), Jackalope's closed for the night. The after-party leftovers were invited to the after-after-party back at Spitfire's apartment complex, a U-shaped building with a pool in the middle of the structure. Kool Aid and Desi hopped in with me, and we drove to Spitfire's digs. We walked through the gates with several others that carried a large cooler's worth of beer and set it beside the pool. I took the banana over-cover off and asked where I could finish undressing without making a scene.

"No way man! You gotta leave the banana leggings on!" yelled Zion from across the way. I jumped into the pool, yellow from the waist down.

I didn't plan on drinking much because I still had to drive Desi, Kool Aid, and myself back to their house. But that would be in a few hours, so I cracked a beer open and nursed it. I sat next to Ozzy Zion on the edge of the pool.

"Blind regional hatred," said Zion. "That's what this sport needs. We need more 'fuck you! My team is better than yours for no other reason than we are from different cities.'" Then to emphasize the point, he said it again, each word its own sentence: **Blind**. *Regional*. Hatred.

"Well Gotham is 2nd in the nation. New York is better than Texas," I chimed in at once agreeing with his statement and baiting him in the same breath.

"Oh, you're Gotham?" he quipped back at me.

"No. Long Island Roller Rebels. But still New York. Still my *region* ... jealous?"

"Hardly! We'll destroy you guys!"

---

[3] See Appendix 9: The Heavy Kids.

Fanning the flames further, I resorted to history: "I'm sorry, but wasn't it Gotham that wiped the track with you guys at E.C.E?"

"Fuck you! We'll kick your New York asses any day!"

"...Except for last month."

"Hey!" yelled one of the girls. "Calm down you two! Neither of you were on the track that day!"

Touché.

"No, it's all good," said Zion. "We're still cool over here!" And to prove it, he grabbed me in a headlock and kissed the crown of my head. "See? That's what's needed in our sport. Friendly competition. But it's all love." Then he pushed me into the pool.

At sometime o' clock in the wee hours of morning, Desi, Kool Aid, and I collected our clothes to head out. I had my costume folded in my arms. As we walked towards the gate that led onto the street, one of the Texas Rollergirls in the pool yelled out to me, "Lemme see your banana!"

Zion stood next to me. "Dude, do it!" he whispered. "She'll do it if you go first!" I knew she was referring to my—*ya know*—but played dumb. I unfurled my banana outfit and confusingly said, "Here it is ... what?"

"No!" she snapped. "Let me see your *banana.*"

"Just do it, man! Seriously!" whispered Zion.

Again, I unfurled the costume. This time I made the extra effort to smooth it out. "Look ... here it is," I said perplexedly. It took every muscle in my body not to crack up.

"No! Your ba-na-na! Let me see it! Pull it out!"

I just stood there mustering up the most stupefied look I could.

She eventually gave up. "Forget it! Man! You're stupid!"

Yeah, realllly stupid.

The next morning I woke up before Desi and Kool Aid. I was happy to leave Texas on a high note and even happier knowing that in a few days I would be in Arizona to see Killer Tofu. She and Thor, her husband, had moved out to Arizona when Thor joined the Army. I missed everything about the two of them. Though I wouldn't see Thor, who still attended basic training in Georgia, it would be so wonderful to see Tofu again.

I don't want to end this chapter without an honest "thank you" to Specific. He taught me a lesson that I remember learning long ago, but had forgotten all about: You cannot let one storm cloud determine the totality of your sky. I've never had a bad day; just great days where shitty things happened. Just when the sport of roller derby had all but destroyed me, that culture (and its innate camaraderie) saved me. I drove out of Austin feeling what I had felt on my drive into Austin: Nothing but love, nothing but respect, for the Texas Rollergirls.

The sun, indeed, still shone brightly on the open road before me. *I'm coming, Tofu.*

IX

How the West was Fun

> *We got a banana and we're gonna use it!*
> *ShEvil Dead's got a banana and*
> *we're gonna fuck you in the*
> *ass with our Banana Man!*
> Terra NüOne

> *I get by with a little help*
> *from my friends.*[1]
> John Lennon

Just Deserts

I stopped over in Las Cruces to crash with an old friend, Paul, before continuing on my way to Tofu. With a good night's sleep, a belly full of burritos, and a twelve pack of beers in my trunk, I rolled out of Las Cruces excited for our reunion. Just outside the city limits, a policeman pulled me over for "speeding"; I was driving 70 in a 65—Heaven forbid! When asked as to my business in Las Cruces, I explained that I was a wandering mascot for women's flat track roller derby. I offered

---

[1] The Beatles, "With a Little Help From My Friends," *Sgt. Pepper's Lonely Hearts Club Band*, (Parlophone, 1967).

to show him my banana outfit, but I think he was so bewildered by my answer that he just let me go.

Somewhere in the middle of the vast desert that separates New Mexico from Arizona, the first puffs of smoke started to creep up through the lining of my car's hood. *Idiot! You forgot to refill the engine coolant back in New Mexico!* I pulled over to the side of the highway, got out, and looked all around me. Nothing around for miles—just deserts. I waited for almost an hour for someone to stop. A few cars passed but did just that. With the sun slowly descending, I decided that my only hope was to just wait out the night and hope for the best. I didn't have a phone to call Tofu, but I did have that twelve pack; they were piss-warm from sitting in my trunk all day. Nonetheless, I cracked open one after the other and decided to drown my sorrows with a drunken stagger around the desert—not straying too far from the highway, of course.

I strolled awhile westward, trying to savor as much of the sunset as I could, and happily crossed a sign that said that there was a service station fifteen miles further down the highway. I doubted that it would be open by the time I got there, and I was certainly too drunk to drive even if my engine had cooled down. When it finally hit me that I would be spending the night in the desert alone, I yearned for my guitar. Or my kitty. I wanted both. I wanted to lie back in a real bed and cuddle up with a woman. Instead, I walked back to my car, drank some more, and wrote lyrics to a song that I later titled *The Only Man that Jesus Never Loved*.

I sat on the hood of my car, beer in hand, and watched as billions of heaven's tiny nightlights slowly illuminated the darkened screen above me like lighters at a rock concert. I was smack in the middle of an all-star cast. I began to dance. And sing. Right there under the desert moon set within a bejeweled sky, I sung to whatever night prowling desert creatures came within earshot of my voice. On it went. As I danced on the edge of earth, spinning lyrical dreams and songs of the roller derby revolution, I excised all fears and screamed even louder into the night. I let go. I took my clothes off and ran around the desert highway stark raving naked for no reason other than to lay claim to having done so. I pulled Melicious' book out of my bag and tangoed with it down the empty highway in all my bare-assed glory. When we both tired, we climbed up on the windshield of my car and lay back staring at the sky. I got dressed, and we talked about the past and future of roller derby. When I felt that the thousands of desert insects had feasted enough on my flesh and blood, I slipped back into the driver's seat and crashed.

I woke up the next morning swimming in a pool of sweat. I peeled off my slimy shirt and boxer shorts and wiped my body down with a second shirt. After dressing with dry clothes, I drove slowly for about seven or eight miles down the road reasoning that the engine had cooled over the night. But I didn't want to push it, so I pulled over again, and walked the last few miles to the gas station to buy coolant. A friendly couple offered to drive me back to my car. Coolant now soothing the once overheated engine, I continued on my way to Arizona.

When I arrived in Phoenix, the Arizona Roller Girls were deeply focused on their practice. Coach Pauly yelled his drills and the girls executed them with the precision and dynamic of a flock of birds. As I watched them go round and round, I sparked up a conversation with some of the observers hanging around the bench area. Adam, a ref export from Florida, was rather friendly and we spoke briefly about my role as a mascot. I explained that during the long drives between states and leagues, I had time to think of jokes and gags to play on audience members and other mascots. He paid me a compliment saying in effect that it is a good thing that mascots who know the rules grow their routines and bits around the sport as it evolves. "You are ahead of the times my friend," he said. *Maybe I hadn't made a mistake embarking on this trip.* The feeling that accompanied that compliment was cut abruptly short when another onlooker said not a minute later, "So you're a mascot? Don't you know that stuff is getting old? Man, you are behind the times." I found myself suspended over a chasm, each of my feet standing either side of the discussion. Either way, I wasn't *with* the times at all. But then the Second Commentator unwittingly gave me an idea when he asked me to perform the "Peanut Butter and Jelly Dance."[2] I would have my revenge ...

After practice ended, I gave Tofu the biggest hug I have ever given anyone in my life. She returned the hug in kind. I didn't get to meet the Arizona Roller Girls, as when practice ended I just wanted to go back to Tofu's and pass out. I hadn't slept or ate much of anything. Driving all day and night through three time zones had started to catch up with me too. The car breaking down had set me back a day. I was weak, and time was limited. I really didn't want to leave, but I had to be in San Francisco in a few days to mascot a B.ay A.rea. D.erby bout.

Trumpets Resounding in the City of Angels

When Cherrylicious moved from Baltimore to Los Angeles, she joined forces with the Angel City Derby Girls (ACDG), the flat track counterpart of the L.A. Derby Dolls banked track league. Before the split, there was only the Derby Dolls whose humble beginnings, like most leagues around the world, had "more ups and downs than Lindsey Lohan's blood alcohol

---

[2] See Appendix 10: Peanut Butter Silly Time!

level."[3] *It was exactly these sobriety tests that caused such long stretches of time between bouts for the Dolls. During one of the Derby Dolls' hiatuses, two girls from Seattle's Rat City Rollergirls, Billie Boilermaker and Joan Jetta, had moved to L.A. Anxious to get back into the swing of roller derby, they started Angel City Derby Girls. Several Derby Dolls, including Estro Jen, Sugar N. Spikes, and Vida Loca joined them. At first, there was some tension between the two leagues. But, as Sugar N. Spikes commented, "We're cool now; one big happy derby family. It took a minute. It's like a break-up—you can be friends, you know; just not right away. You have to get a little distance from each other, have time to heal, and see the other person's perspective before you can really come back together and be friends and understand what happened." "Though," she assured me, "some girls have been cool with it the whole time. Tara Armov [of L.A. Derby Dolls] has been a wonderful and intense supporter of Angel City from the beginning."*[4]

Traffic sucks in L.A. Really sucks. My soul could only take so much abuse. Tired of wasting and rotting away with the other corpses, I got off the next exit and used my banana sense to find Cherrylicious organically (by which I mean I drove around aimlessly until coincidence brought me to her street). When I finally found her place, we hugged, I settled in, and then we went out for dinner. After surviving on tacos and energy bars, I whet my appetite for a different kind of delicacy. Eating raw meat is barbaric, yet eating raw fish is high class. Cherrylicious is classy, so we ate sushi.

Somewhere over the rainbow roll, Cherrylicious invited me to skate with some members of her league that night. "Just a

---

[3] Kasey Bomber, "L.A. Derby Dolls in Three Acts," *Blood and Thunder: Women's Roller Derby Magazine*, 9, (Fall 2008), pg. 14.
[4] Bane-ana, *Interview with Sugar N. Spikes*, 8, January, 2000TenOutOfTen.

bunch of us, skating through the streets," she said. It sounded perfect. After dinner, we took off to ACDG skater Hard Cora's apartment.

When we arrived, Sugar N. Spikes and Friend were already inside attaching street wheels to their skates. Sugar introduced me to the girls: Dolce Dolore, Shiv, Hard Cora, Mia, and Ms. D' fiant. Estro Jen made an appearance in the form of her fedora that Sugar wore. I told her that she looked "fedorable."

I didn't have skates, but Hard Cora happened to have an extra pair in her car. I took my sneakers off and after the girls were ready, we made our way downstairs: sixty-four wheels, two black socks.

The ground had run dry of sweet moments; there was no place left to go but up. I felt myself lifted into the air, a high like no other I'd felt before. As we skated over the freshly paved clouds and passed the granite stars, the girls guided my novice feet through every serenade in the dreamscape. All the loneliness of the road I left under me—back on the road, back on earth. My insecurities dripped their pollutants out from the bottom of the wheels. The air swallowed them up whole and recycled the once tainted remains throughout the heavens. The Angels glided steadily over the soft ether, and I found myself intoxicated in the kaleidoscopic trails invoked in their wake. My feet, not used to such heights, gave way once or twice to gravity. The girls were there to catch and right me, keep me balanced, baptize me in the chalice that is their sky. Sugar floated over and smiled, dousing my skates with pixie dust; I never lost my balance again.

Angels on all sides, I fixed my eyes on Friend's long pig tails swaying gently in the breeze before me, tempting me to faithfully follow her experienced pace. I mirrored her movements so that I too could share in the moment. Tasting the opiates emitting from her deep breaths, I skated unafraid, jonesing for her addiction. Her wings hummed in the airstream with all the symphonic beauty of a harp plucked in paradise. As feathers pulled off, floated towards me and showered my face, I felt like a child playing in snow for the first time.

"Just let go," they whispered with every kiss. No mortal lips had ever tasted so satisfying.

I thought about the drive, the breakdown, the long walk through the blisters of the Arizona desert; how I couldn't see the light. And now here, despite the balmy blanket of night, among the cherubs of Angel City, I had finally curved towards the sun.

The experience breathed fresh wind into my sails. Everything would be okay. I pocketed Sugar's pixie dust for safe keeping.

After we descended back to earth, Cherrylicious asked if I wouldn't mind giving B.ay A.rea D.erby girl Demanda Riot an "I love you message." *Yep. Another one.* I asked her how I would be able to tell who Demanda was. Ms. Licious didn't give me any details other than, "Trust me, you'll know her when you see her." *Okay, so that's two messages for Bay Area girls. The new mission.* She said goodbye and left to waitress. The rest of us climbed up to Hard Cora's rooftop, had a few more beers, and polished off the night with Apples for Apples.

I left the next morning for San Francisco. Another sunny day and I felt a lot lighter than I had felt on my drive into Los Angeles. For the first time during my trip, I no longer cared if the road ahead was bumpy. I would survive. I thought about Sugar and Friend, and how once again, our engagement was cut short because I had to be somewhere else. Such was derby, and as I took the Interstate 5 north, I reckoned that I still had a piece of ACDG's magic with me in the form of Sugar's pixie dust—her kindness. Indeed, I could still hear the sweet resonance of angelic trumpets guiding me down the highway—the mellifluous song of Derbylove.

San Fun!cisco

I pulled into the small dirt circle driveway of a liquor store that sat just outside the San Francisco city limits. Although I preferred Knob Creek or Johnnie Walker, I opted for a budget-friendly whiskey, some no-name brand. At the checkout counter, the clerk asked me just two questions:

"How old 'ah ya," and "'ah ya a liar?"

"28. No."

The gentleman in front of me, an old school scallywag biker-turned-hippie, turned towards me. "I got hemorrhoids olda than you, kid," he said, scratching the air with his voice.

The clerk looked at me and bobbed his head up and down. "Tha's true. He duus. Twenta-one fity fo' is ya total, but dun worry 'bout tha 'fo."

I paid him everything (including the 'fo) and continued on my way into San Francisco.

B.ay A.rea D.erby formed in 2005 by girls "taken by delusions of grandeur and one too many late-night cocktails."[5] When B.A.D. first started, the league only had two teams: The Oakland Outlaws and The ShEvil Dead. In 2006, the Richmond Wrecking Belles was added as a third team to the league. B.A.D.'s first bout had been at the Dry Ice Inline Hockey Arena in East Oakland, where a line of fans two blocks long didn't make it to the bout in time to get seating. Lacking announcers in those days, L.A. Derby Doll Suzy Snakeyes made the pilgrimage north to lend a hand to her west coast derby sisters, as did several Derby Dolls refs.[6] My contact, Miss Moxxxie, had in fact been named by Thora Zeen of the Dolls. "Thora and Demo[licious] started the L.A. Derby Dolls banked track league and she is the reason why I skate. ... I met her and she gave me a bottle of Moxie soda and decided that that was going to be my name," she told me.[7]

I arrived in San Francisco on one of those beautifully balmy summer days when the streets pulsed with jugglers, stunt-bikers, and a hearty aroma that reminded me of Captain's house after a Roller Rebel fundraiser. I was running out of gas and time so I stopped at a gas station to fill up and ask directions to Fort Mason, where the B.A.D. bout would take

---

[5] Author unnamed, "B.ay A.rea D.erby Girls: Short Skirts, Shorter Fuses," *WFTDA Dust Devil '07: Western Regional Tournament Event Program*, (February 16-18), p. 18.
[6] Lisa Hix, "Club Land," *SFGate* (October, 2005). Accessed via: www.sfgate.com.
[7] Bane-ana, *Interview with Miss Moxxxie*, 9, August, 2000Great.

place. An elderly woman who pumped gas beside me told me I could follow her to Fort Mason. When we arrived, she recommended that I park outside the fort because the parking prices inside were astronomical. She even offered to drive me into the complex towards the Herbst Pavilion, a hanger inside the fort. I accepted.

"So what are you doing all the way here from New York?"

I told her about the bout, this book, roller derby, and about the ShEvil Dead.

"ShEvil Dead? That's quite a name. Who are they?"

I told her the story as I knew it. Apparently, not too long ago, during the times of "disco and decent blow," a Christian roller derby team known back then as the San Francisco Saints met their fate in a horrible auto wreck. According to the official story, there was a mix-up in the afterlife because instead of taking their position at the Pearly Gates for review, the San Francisco Saints found themselves cast into the depths of Hell. At some point in an attempt to make up the difference, the televangelist Jim Jones and the Dark Lord struck a bargain that granted the girls permission to return to earth to skate until Armageddon. The price? Their very souls.[8]

"That's quite a story."

"Right?" I laughed. "I don't often believe so-called 'derby bios' and stories, but for some reason, I find that this one is plausible."

She dropped me off just inside the fort grounds. I wandered around the vast parking lot looking for someone to direct me to Herbst Pavilion. I didn't get far. The large "Herbst Pavilion" lettered across the front of one building was a (ShEvil) dead

---

[8] Author unnamed, "San Francisco ShEvil Dead: From the Cradle to the Grave and Back Again: A History of the ShEvil Dead," *B.ay A.rea D.erby Girls: War on Wheels*, (August 9th), p. 6.

giveaway. As I walked into the pavilion, B.A.Dblokes were already laying Sport Court. I merrily joined the brigade. I found J. Crush, delivered Belle's "thank you," and lost myself in volunteer work before she could send me back to Texas on another Derbylove assignment.

Granted that the legend of the ShEvil Dead was true, I had quite the task placed before me. I reached into my bag and pulled out Sugar N. Spike's pixie dust, holding it in my hand like a trench warfare soldier's last bullet under a blaze of overhead gunfire. I looked around the back changing area for Miss Moxxxie. No sign of her, only a handful of Richmond Wrecking Belles warming up. As I turned to walk back towards the track, something rolled by me and brushed my left shoulder. I turned my head as a military fatigued girl on wheels sulked in her skates past me. The back of her jersey read "Windago Jones." I ran up to her to ask her where I could find Miss Moxxxie. She turned her head and I gasped at the sight of her face—it was half missing. Her neck had been slit from ear to ear grinning with a hunger that only the flesh of rollergirls could sate. She said nothing, just pointed her boney finger towards the back of the pavilion. My heart raced as a small army of the skating dead materialized before me. They said nothing, just skated out towards the track. I quickly sprinkled Sugar's pixie dust all over me—practically bathing in it! I wished I had read that *Zombie Survival Guide* Anna Tramp had always been urging me to read.

Dead can Skate.

It would take a minute for the dust to have total coverage over me. So when B.A.D ref Hunter Stompson invited me into the ref changing room, I jumped at the chance. I couldn't believe it. There I was, changing with the refs in a real changing room, not in a bathroom! *I have come so far!* I used the opportunity to tell all the refs at the same time that I would never be in their way and not to worry about me at anytime. After we all went back out trackside, Hunter decided to test my spiel—the first and only ref ever to have done so. He raced around the track in the opposite direction of the one I faced. Just as he zeroed in on me, my banana-sense tingled and I turned and jumped back out of the way. He turned to me as he skated off with a "good job" nod and a thumbs-up. Not a half hour later, the starting whistle blew the bout into action.

The crowd was already pumped. I was overdue for a mascot-friendly audience, and I struck gold with San Francisco. They were, without a doubt, the funnest people I had encountered so far. Despite all the booze, I did not get heckled by one drunken asshole. I didn't have to once beg the crowd to cheer or to chant. They merely waited for my cue and then went nuts. Even the obligatory "get out of my shot" from a bout photographer was cordial: "Excuse me, Mr. Banana Man, I don't mean to bother you, but I want to take a picture of the girls and it would help me out a whole lot if you could move to the side"—said with a sunny smile. *Wow!*

But I also did have Cherrylicious' love message mission. I looked out to the track and saw a girl with a ghost-white face, serving as a haunting backdrop to her blackened eyes. Her partially shaved head was accompanied by long dark dreadlocks that hung out the back of her helmet like flogging whips. *That must be Demanda Riot.* It was. A torture chamber on wheels, she looked so Goth that she sacked Rome. She didn't skate, she pillaged. One by one, ShEvil Dead girls fell to her wrath. *Army of Darkness* hero Ash and his puny chainsaw had nothing on this girl. Demanda laid her daggers out before the ShEvil Dead, charitably allowing her victims to choose their fate. Then, slicing through the pack like her skates were serrated, she penetrated each incision as if her body were an extension of the blades themselves.

My amazement was cut short and redirected towards one of Richmond's extraordinary jammers, Brawllen Angel; she seized the opportunities that Demanda negotiated and rocketed through holes cut open for her. She skated so fast that at one point, she found enough space between her considerable lead and the pack to dance the robot for the audience, whipping them into fits of ovation.

After delivering Cherrylicious' sentiments to Demanda at halftime, I joked with a man in the crowd. He seemed like a merry enough chap (hell! they all did!). I stared into his eyes.

"I'm going to read your mind."

"Oh! Really?" he asked skeptically, albeit intrigued.

"You are thinking ... 'there is no way this idiot can possibly know what I'm thinking.'"

He crossed his eyes slightly. "Shit ... yeah. ... Cheers! Want a beer?"

"Now you're reading my mind!" We walked over to the beer stand. He purchased the brew, then rather oddly said, "Okay, well, bye!" and walked away as if he had constructed a mental obligation to me and then decided he had fulfilled it.

I still had about five minutes to kill before the start of the second half, so I walked out onto the pier that overlooked the San Francisco Bay. Several derbyfans smoked cigarettes and drank beers. *Perfect.* I didn't waste a second. "Nice bay," I said as I looked out towards the sky. I turned to a girl: "Do you know what kind of news you get from the bay? Only the current stuff; Why do crabs go to the beach on Christmas Eve? For sandy claws; Getting over my agoraphobia was a walk in the park." Some in the group chuckled, and I mentally skated passed them. Only the *Doppelgänger Bane-ana* pivot remained, so I pulled out the big puns: "I try to understand my penis ... but it just gets so hard sometimes!" Now they were all laughing. An elderly hippy-looking cat walked out onto the pier. I called him over and went for the grand slam: "With the way technology is moving, it seemed like only yesterday 'the revolution would be televised'— today 'the television is being revolutionized.'" I ended the bomb with: "What's the difference between a pot head and a politician? Pot heads inhale, politicians just suck."[9]

I was about to wrap the whole thing up and walk away victoriously in a gush of laughs when a few other folks approached us and asked what was so funny. I took a deep breath and went into my fun liners: "What's so funny? What's so funny? I'll tell ya what's so funny: I quit deli meats cold turkey; I laugh while I poop ... for shits and giggles; festive communists paint the town red." They ate it up. In between laughs, a girl in the group asked me if I knew any more. I was flattered and couldn't keep from blushing. I only had two and a half minutes before the second half began and I didn't want to get on the ShEvils' b.a.d side. I turned towards her and said, "Actually, I heard the funniest joke ever yesterday." Her eyes widened and she looked at me with happy anticipation. "Just thought you'd like to know that," I said and walked back inside the pavilion with a shit-eating grin on my face.

I realized how dependant I am on the audience for my general mental well-being. Since the crowd was such a delight, I mascoted the second half of that bout more confidentially than I had ever mascoted any bout before. I felt as though I had broken through a ceiling. If anyone ever heckled me in the future, I would always have that B.ay A.rea D.erby bout to remind me of how welcoming a crowd can be. The rest of the bout presented an odd dichotomy. The ShEvil Dead lost, but I had (probably) the best time at that bout cheering for them.

---

[9] I must admit this last one is not mine. A friend told it to me. Good one, though, no?

After the bout, we deconstructed the track and drove off to the after-party, where several B.A.D. girls bought me shots of Knob Creek—*yes*! I spoke with Miss Moxxxie and Brawllen Angel about the origins of B.ay A.rea D.erby, and what they saw in roller derby's future. I didn't spend much more time with the B.A.D. girls because two of my old friends were moving back to New York and I wanted to help them pack. On Monday morning, I dropped them off at the airport and then drove about an hour north to Stanford University, where I had an appointment with the special collections division. After spending the day mulling over the papers of George Hunter White, I left. I had a long ride home ahead of me (3,000 miles to be exact) and needed to fuel up my car and my belly. Outside Stanford, I found a small, up-scale town called Palo Alto.

Dinner with a Bum

As I looked for a place to eat, I felt that old sting of loneliness creep into me; I wanted company. I figured that the only person I could entice to have dinner with me would be a person who possibly hadn't eaten dinner in a very long time. On the sidewalks, begging for spare change, I saw a lady with long, almost crusted black hair. I walked up to her.

"Change?" she asked. "Got any change?"

"No ... well, yes," I said, "but I'd like to offer a different suggestion. "Would you like to have dinner with me?"

She was taken aback by my request.

"Oh! I get it!" she laughed. "Good joke. But, really, do you have any money on you?"

"No, no, I'm serious. I have a long drive ahead of me and will not have any company until Chicago. I'd really like to have dinner with you if you wouldn't mind."

"Really?" her eyes lit up. "Nos jokin' now. I'm so hungry. You jus' wan' have dinner wit me? I's haven't had dinner in a long time. And not never with nobody."

We found a burger joint on a corner street, ordered our food, and sat at a table outside. People walked by us, disgusted by her smell and appearance.

I didn't know much about banked track leagues or the tension between some of them and flat track leagues. Although most girls didn't get involved in that nonsense and some leagues like the San Diego Derby Dolls were hybrid banked/flat leagues, some skaters took issue with the banked or flat track differences. I didn't like the idea of all these competing derby bodies, and found the notion childish. Over my travels, I'd met several banked track girls, and they were all so cool towards me. It all didn't make any sense. And as a result, I was terrible company.

"I want us to be united," I blurted without reference to what I meant.

"The Lord wants that," she said thumbing a wooden crucifix necklace between her dirty fingertips. "The Lord want us all to be united."

"Exactly!" I blurted out. "It's the right to choose! Banked, flat, old school, new school—what does it matter? I'm sick of the internecine feuding. B.A.D and the Derby Dolls unified for the sake of the former, why can't everyone follow their example?"

"And so what if some leagues have excessive flair! So what if our sport is different from all the others! Is it not the right of the skaters to choose how the league is run? I like the boutfits and derbynames! I find them aesthetically pleasing! And there is an irony here anyway. Anyone who wants to tweak the flair aspect until it dissolves completely, while simultaneously sporting a 'derbyname,' is a hypocrite in the foulest of ways.

Turn around. The very name on the back of your jersey proves that there is at least some 'spectacle' involved in roller derby. What is the aversion to this?"

She turned her neck and pulled the tag out of the back collar of her moldy shirt. "Muh name's Linda."

"Yes! You are Linda! I have never argued that roller derby is not a serious sport. Never! It is a real sport comprised of real athletes who train really hard—that is understood by all. I just do not see how adding the other ingredients that makes roller derby stand out will destroy the integrity of what we are trying to build here. Think about it: was it not all these other things that attracted many of us to the sport in the first place? I have asked dozens of girls from across the country to explain to me why they loved roller derby more than any other sport they ever played. The overwhelming majority just says, 'I don't know ... I guess it's just ... everything.' That "everything" of roller derby, it seems, is simple: creative freedom. Individual expression. We aren't owned. One doesn't have to alter one's uniform, but the option remains nonetheless. In what other sport have you ever seen players tailor their uniforms to their own personalities? None. It is an artistic sport that every single individual is allowed to embrace or reject," I said pointing my freedom fry at Linda. "None of these things is found in any other sport. It is what makes it revolutionary! And it won't kill the sport! You know what will kill the sport?"[10]

"Not playing it?"

"Yes! But also shitty mascots, lousy refs, and lackadaisical rollergirls. That's what will kill us! Not derbynames! Not boutfits! If I interfere with the bout, that will destroy it! If refs and NSO's aren't trained properly, that will destroy it too! And mostly, if we aren't unified—that has cause to inflict the most

---

[10] See Appendix 11: Of Sports and Spectacles.

damage! Here I have spent the better part of three weeks searching for and finding Derbylove everywhere I went! It's real, for sure! What can I do to show it?!"

"They don't seen enough movies," Linda said very matter-of-factly.

I stopped complaining for a second. "What would you recommend?"

Linda put her hands over her face and started to cry loudly. "I don't know!" she sobbed. I don't know what books to tell 'em to read neither! I seen books an' movies. I seen movies! And I know I read a book about a lawyer a long time ago, but I wouldn't know what to tell 'em!" She grabbed her food tray and ran away. I was alone again. I managed to scare away the only person in Palo Alto more desperate for company than myself.

Fang Boner

I finished eating, feeling rather uneasy about what had just transpired. I had a long ride ahead of me to figure it out. But poor Linda! She's probably terrified of roller derby! *What have I done*? With a full tank of gas and belly (and a rattled soul), I jumped in my car and rolled out of Palo Alto to continue my mission: head eastbound on to New York and pick up Chairman Meow in Chicago along the way.

Althea N. Hell complicated matters. Maybe it was coincidence that she lived in Chicago? I didn't know, but the search to interview her was on. I left Palo Alto, heading south. With little money left for the return trip, I bought a loaf of bread at a supermarket just outside Sacramento.

After driving for hours, I pulled over at a truck stop on the eastern edge of Utah, nudged my car between two eighteen wheelers, and took out my plastic makeshift shank that had sat under my seat since Tennessee. I also stuffed my pillow underneath my blanket on the passenger seat like high school kids that fashion facsimile bodies when they sneak out at night. I figured that someone might be less inclined to fuck with me if they thought that I traveled with company. After about an hour or two of broken night terror sleep, I got up and drove into the rising eastern sun towards Chicago.

But that was still a day away. I looked out my windows wistfully watching wandering wildlife while wondering why Wyoming's wide wheat fields weren't whetting my wearisome wishing. It always ended up the same. *There is <u>nothing</u> out here.* I had been assured wonderful scenery by people who—I realized as I drove through Nebraska—had never been to the Midwest. They just assumed. They were wrong. *"They" often are.*

Books and movies, like the kind Linda "seen," rarely tell the return story—the protagonist magically ends up back where s/he started, sparing the audience the mundane details.

Not this banana.

I pulled over in Nebraska to take a huge coffee-shit. The whole mid-west has interesting gas stations—they're like mini shopping malls (I could have purchased a bust of Elvis for $200) that sell gas too. I proceeded to the bathroom (of equally impressive size) and performed my seat cleaning ritual. I grabbed some paper towels from the dispenser, ran to the sink, pumped the soap onto the towel, tip-toed into stall, wiped the seat down, folded the towel, washed the floor where my pants would lie, threw out the soiled towel, and placed dry towels on the seat and on the floor. I commenced defecation. Hours of lonely highway can wreak havoc on the mind; I needed something to do. I knew that my shit was going to be a big, loud one so I decided to use it to scare the local population. Leaning certain ways, I would get a range of pitches out of my butthole; crunching forward caused a "frap!" sound, while a slide to the left caused a godless noise (and noisome smell) that can only be described as a "prutz."[11] I played my stomach like an accordion. Between the "fraps" and "prutzs," I yelled random noises and phrases like, "AHHHHHHHHHH" and "OHHHHHHHH." The tiles made for wonderful acoustics. I echoed "Satan be praised!" off the walls in my best Dominican monk chant. "Frap! ... SaaATAN ... Ommmmniaaa ... be ...PRUTZ! ... Praised!! aaaAAAAHHHH!!!!!" My ass and mouth were in Apocalyptic harmony. I had gone banana-shit crazy! Under the stall door, I watched hordes of cowboy boots run out the door.

Success!

Not ten minutes later, I was back on the road. As the hours rolled by, the loaf of bread got shorter and shorter. Soon I was turning the paper bag upside down, sliding the crumbs down my throat. I couldn't spend any money on food until I reached Chicago; I simply didn't have the budget.

The highways were on loop and had long since become monotonous. Although, I owe Iowa an iota of itinerary interest; indeed, intrepidly inching into Illinois, inspiration incremented into instigating iterations! I screamed with glee when I saw a rusty tractor that was abandoned by the side of the highway. *Glory be! Something that isn't highway and air! A tractor!* The jubilation subsided only moments later when I was met with more highway and air.

After driving all day and night, I finally arrived at Chairman Meow's apartment at about 6 or 7 o'clock or so in the morning. Our "hellos" were short—he had stayed up all night to greet me, and when I finally arrived, we both just passed out. The next day, I woke up with a severe leg cramp and an even more severe hunger.

"I feel like I haven't eaten in days."

---

[11] You have to roll the "r."

"Rawk ever tell you about Kuma's Corner?" asked the Chairman after I finally showered.

"No. What's Kuma's Corner?"

Chairman smiled. "Get dressed."

On the way, I told Chairman of my Althea mission. "Kuma is pretty much staffed by rollergirls—both Windy City and Chicago Outfit."

A quick car ride found us on the corner of West Belmont and Francisco Aves—Kuma's corner. Beautiful rock 'n rollergirls poured drinks, took food orders, and navigated around the thin space between tables. Across the back wall, pictures of latex wrapped fetish girls kissed promises of hamburger superiority. *No! The mission! Find Althea or someone who knows how to.* Alas, Althea didn't work there, and no one knew of her whereabouts.

I got distracted; a whiff of cooking meat kissed my nose. *Smells perfect.* I was famished. I hadn't really eaten in two days and felt like I owed myself a treat. Chairman and I took our seats right up at the bar and I looked over the menu, free to choose between hamburgers with names like "Pantera," "Neurosis," and "Goblin Cock," to name but a few.[12] Mya Ssault, a recently inaugurated Windy City skater, took our orders.

Chairman and I clinked glasses. "To a good trip," he toasted.

Not fifteen minutes later, Mya brought us our food. I took a large bite into my burger.

"How is it?" she asked.

I wanted to tell her that the hamburger saved my soul; that it was the reason the universe unfolded itself billions of years ago; the reason that our species pulled itself out of the oceans

---

[12] Kuma's Corner "Burgers," *Menu*, 2000Great.

and evolved arms and legs: so that one day modern humans could enjoy a Kuma burger. But I was so enthralled by its juices—the elasticity of the mozzarella, the flavor of the shrooms, the caramelization of the onions, the consecration of the pretzel bun, the divination of the meat itself—that all I managed to get out was, "Bliss."

After we ate, we waited around for a little so that I might try to locate Althea N. Hell—or at least get her phone number. But it was all for naught. The traffic was only getting thicker on the highways out of Chicago. I gave up, and we left for the last haul of the trip.

Having another driver was relieving. I didn't fully appreciate how much so until, for a few hours at a clip, I got to exist in a twilight sleep as Chairman took the helm. By Indiana, I was already measuring the length of the trip in states. Hours meant nothing anymore; just passing state borders. Despite Ohio's flatland kinship with the rest of the Midwest, I didn't mind driving through it. Only a five hour trip—east end to west end. Pennsylvania was excruciatingly long to go through though. The scenery had finally changed to "not flat," but after three days on the road, one simply doesn't give a shit about scenery anymore. I just wanted to sleep in a bed. My own preferably, but any would do. At one point during our journey, we passed under a bridge that bore a sign: "Fangboner Road." For about two minutes, Chairman continued driving, neither of us saying a word; we were both unsure. *Nah ... couldn't be.* Finally, Chairman's inquisitive nature got the best of him. "Did that just say Fangboner?"

"Holy shit! I thought I was seeing things!"

"Sooo ... I'm not hallucinating? It really did say, 'Vampire Dick'?"

Maybe it was the long ride in a cramped car. Maybe it was the lack of sleep. But for some reason, we both started to laugh uncontrollably in the car. We sang about fangboners. Fangboner became the answer to the Theory of Everything: What caused the Big Bang? Fangboner. Who cooked the first Kuma burger? Fangboner. What is the meaning of life? And so on.

We drove and drove, and Chairman and I arrived at my place at 9 am that Saturday morning. I was home. Finally! My bed and my kitty!

Fan-eye-tickle Foe

The next weekend, I was back in Baltimore. Carolina Rollergirls' B Team, The Carolina Bootleggers, had moved its infantry north, crossing the Mason-Dixon, hungry. The Bootleggers consisted of a mixed team: 2 parts North Carolina, 2 parts South Carolina, and a whole lotta whoop ass. Supposedly, they had sent their "B" team to play Charm City. Though, when I saw such formidable skaters like Princess America and Kitty Crowbar among their ranks, I questioned just how "B" the team really was. Only Mob Town stood against them.

As the bout progressed, I realized how the trip had been worth it. I had a fairly solid mascot routine to fall back on. That bout was my first truly precise one—i.e. it was the first time I didn't question a thing I did. I played with my chatter ring, I joke jammed, I got people to do the Peanut Butter Jelly Dance, all while knowing when and where to position myself without interfering with the game. A timeout was called—*my turf*! On the spot, I grabbed a foldout chair and using my pompoms like oars, rowed around for the crowd. I ended the bit falling over backwards to loud laughs and applause. I had gone from conversational mascoting to fluency. I was on the verge of playing a "perfect" bout when it all went to shit. On one of my track runs during a timeout, I held my pompoms out and glazed them over fans' heads as I scooted by. I heard chuckles in my wake.

Not everyone, I found out, had been so amused. At halftime, a lady approached me. She was pissed. "My husband just had eye surgery! Don't hit your pompoms in his eyes, you nuisance!"

Cause I'm a psychic. I apologized and explained to her that there was no way I could have known about her husband's surgery. That wasn't good enough. She wanted to make me feel bad about it. To achieve this, she called me an idiot and a loser and whathaveyou.

She stormed off, and one of Charm City's fans—a girl about 19-20ish who had overheard the berating session—pulled out her ticket and showed it to me.

"That lady is an idiot," she said. "Look on the back of the ticket. It says that rink-side seating is done at the ticket holders' discretion."

She handed me her ticket, and I carefully scanned over the back of it looking for loopholes. Not finding any, I asked her if I could borrow it. "Of course," she smiled.

I found the lady and calmly made my case; people sit rink-side at their own risk. I further implied that perhaps, for the safety of her husbands' eyes, he shouldn't sit rink-side in the next half. She started to scream.

"Don't try to push this off on the girls! They didn't skate into my husband—you hit him with a pompom! You assaulted him!"

"Assaulted him?! With a fucking pompom?! Are you nuts?! I'm not trying to push this onto anybody! I'm just saying that in light of your husband's condition, it isn't a good idea to sit along the track—whether I'm here or not! I apologized for that already! I know no one skated into him; I'm talking about *preventing* that from happening!"

Her husband stepped in and pulled his cell phone off his belt holster like a six-shooter. *Real smooth, Dead Eye.*

"That's it! I'm calling the cops! Let's see how you like sitting in jail in that banana suit, asshole!"

"Call the cops, you Fangboner! The ticket says that you sit trackside at your own risk! If you just had surgery, you should be sitting in the stands anyway!"

I had never raised my voice to an audience member. I'd also never been threatened with arrest for the crime of assault with a "deadly" pompom.

I was done with these assholes. I had built something up in my mind, and they burst the bubble. Or maybe the bubble was an illusion to start with? I was still just that anonymous "Banana Man," there to deal with any and all crap from whoever needed someone to crap on. I contemplated ending my journey there, midway through it.

I only had two minutes to get back to the All Stars' bench. I found the derbyfan standing right where we had met, gave her back the ticket, and sulked away. I got about seven paces back to the bench when the girl called out, "That lady sucks! I think you're awesome, *Bane-ana!*"

I stopped in my tracks. My heart melted. Tiny diamonds dripped from my eyes.[13] I turned to her and smiled. I said only "thank you," but I meant so much more. Call it women's intuition, or the sacred feminine, or whatever, but the smile she returned told me she understood the depths of my appreciation. She just wanted to bestow me with some of that good stuff; nothing like a dose of delectable Derbylove from Charm Cityfans. I had the will to continue my quest.

Good 'ole Charm Cityfans.

---

[13] What?! I'm sensitive!

Leaving the Rebellion

Chairman stayed in Baltimore and would return shortly thereafter to Chicago by plane. Captain and I would drive back out, and pick him up again to go to Madison, Wisconsin, for Regionals. I drove back to New York and spent the next few weeks working odd jobs, saving money, and replenishing my soul to continue on with my journey into the heart of roller derby.

Some new members joined the Roller Rebels. We started to butt heads over how the league was run. Some of the girls agreed with me; others clashed over the issue. I decided to leave the league (amicably) and become a free-agent mascot.

Regionals crept up on me. I grew worried that I would have no one to cheer for. I would still have to go as part of the journey, but the mission had specifically called for mascoting at both Regionals and Nationals. I had to decide quickly what league I would ask to cheer for. During a conversation with Dolly Rocket, I confessed my desire to cheer for Charm City at WFTDA's 2008 Eastern Regional tournament, Derby in Dairyland. I would be a guest, of course, but Dolly's answer was a resounding "yes."

X

P<small>ISSING</small> E<small>XCELLENCE</small>

Be who you are according to every situation, each of which contains its own book of rules.
M<small>ICHELLE</small> E<small>FFRON</small>

"Sansleague." said Butterscotch Cripple.
"Sansleague?"
"Yes. You are going to Regionals sansleague."
"Don't follow."
"It's French."
Oh ... sans league. "Guess so. But it's all part of the journey; it must be done."
"Mascoting for anyone?"
"Charm."
"You've mascoted for them before, no?"
"Yeah, but always as a guest; even this weekend. But I think I might want to *be* the Charm City mascot—or at least one of them. Intra-league bouts and even inter-league bouts are one thing. Cheering for Charm at E.C.E felt great. I gotta see if there's chemistry on the regional frontlines. Gonna feel it out this weekend. Who knows? Maybe I'll even try to move to Baltimore if everything works and feels right. Derbyfolk move

all the time to try out different leagues. I mean, I'll have to see what kind of job situation there is in Baltimore, of course, but maybe it'll all work out his weekend."

"Good luck. See you out there."

Charmed, I'm Sure

Madison Wisconsin's Mad Rollin' Dolls hosted Eastern Regionals that year. Captain picked me up at 9 p.m. on Wednesday night before the 10th of October. After driving all night, we arrived at Chairman's new apartment just in time to help him move his last boxes into his room. We met up with Carnage Electra, who was visiting family in Chicago, and later that afternoon drove to Kuma's Corner. After feeding on chunks of Heaven's meat, we drove back to Chairman's place. He then went to work and Captain to sleep.[1] I couldn't sleep and lay in a daze on the common room floor, talking with WCR skater Chrissy Fiction. At 4 am, our Chairman Meow alarm went off. "Bane! Captain! Wake up!"

We cruised on up to Madison, Wisconsin. Chairman hadn't slept at all yet. Captain and I still shook the mental debris that accumulated in our dreams, having suppressed them for so many hours. I don't remember much of the voyage to Madison. Though, in the half daze I existed in, I could swear I heard Chairman Meow belting out Tina Turner's "What's Love Got to Do With It" somewhere along the seaway.

We arrived at the Alliant Energy Center in time to look like the living dead and dropped anchor in the first parking row near the front entrance. As we approached the stadium, I stopped for a moment and stood in awe at the size of the place. The Alliant Energy Center boasted over 10,000 seats! I fondly thought

---

[1] She slept for something like fifteen or sixteen hours.

about how far roller derby had come in such a short time. As we walked into the track area, I kept imagining that every seat would be filled. Although the crowd never grew large enough to cap the fire marshal's limit, a sizeable amount of fans would accumulate during several bouts over the course of the weekend.

I walked towards the back of the trackside area by the third turn, started to stretch, and did my warm up exercises. Little by little, derbyfolk the east coast over trickled into the arena. I knew some of them, but they didn't recognize me without the banana suit. When some Charm City girls showed up, I got nervous. I began to sweat. *What the fuck am I doing out here*? I ran to Captain, took her keys, and hid on her ship. A flask of whiskey sat in the back hull. To my knowledge, no one had taken so much as a drag off of it. I didn't want my confidence to be liquefied, but my nerves ached for deliverance. I imagined several different reasons to justify drinking from the flask, none of which actually result in a valid argument as I think back on them now. Nonetheless, the horizon in the flask slowly fell. By 10:30 am, I was drunk as a priest on Monday and still nervous. I called my buddy Rob and lamented my plight to him. "Just don't think about it," he said. "That's what I do." For a short while his words alleviated some of the strain, but in the back of my mind I couldn't help but think about it. Then some more Charm Cityfolk showed up; Mibbs Breakin Ribs, Psycho78, Radar Love, and Blind Banshee pulled into the next spot over from me.[2] *Do I ask them* now? *No. They just arrived. Relax. Start small*; *say "hi."*

I got out of the car. "I know that hair!" said Mibbs. She gave me a big hug—my favorite kind—and thanked me for showing up for Charm City. Radar, Psycho, and Banshee said

---

[2] Blocker, Jammer, Alternate, and Bench Coach.

"hello." The girls walked into the arena. I turned back to the car to take one last drag off the flask. Stopping midway, I realized how ridiculous I was. As I held the flask in my hand, I had a tiny but significant epiphany: *I don't need this. I think they like me. Now go bask in the radiant Derbylove of Charm City.* I twisted the cap back on, put the flask down, and opted for a bottle of water instead. It was near empty. So I put my costume on and headed back into the stadium.

I went to the bathroom and tried to urinate all of the alcohol out of my system. I knew that that wasn't possible, but I wanted my epiphany-induced ebullience to come from Charm City alone. I felt like I had tainted it by drinking.

Afterwards, still trying to detoxify myself, I grudgingly bought an overpriced bottle of water from the food stand. The lady handed me the water, but not before taking the cap off and placing it on the back counter top.

"Ummm … Why did you de-*cap*-itate my bottle," I asked in jovial confusion.

"Sorry, I can't let you leave with the cap."

I furrowed my brow. *I don't get it.* She must have been joking. After all, I *was* dressed like a banana. Perhaps the joker was becoming the jokee? Again, I asked her for the cap. Again, she said, "no."

"I don't understand," I finally said. "I really need to get back inside. Please may I have it back?"

"Look," she said pointing to a group of water-drinking derbyfolk. "They don't have caps either. I cannot give you the cap because of regulations."

"Regulations?" I asked. "But it's a bottle of water, not a nuke! *Water* you talking about? Have you kept these emotions *bottled* up for a long time? And if so …"—I glanced at the menu—"… I'm going to be *frank* for a moment. That is *nacho* cap! *So – duh!* I've been robbed! *Candy* manager please come to the counter? I might be a total *dud*, but you can't *milk* me for all I'm worth! I hope as you *snicker* about this to your friends, all *nestled* in your *jolly* mid-western *ranch*, you develop *butterfingers* and ... and drop something important! We, the *nerds*, will have our *payday*! Our revolution is growing by leaps and *mounds*! This is preposterous! That regulation is so convoluted ... so twisted like ..."

"A *pretzel*?"

"The game!" I took my water and stormed off.

An elderly man took me aside and told me that the vendors decapped the bottle because it is imagined that onlookers will throw the caps at the players. This didn't make sense to me. What's to stop someone from throwing the whole bottle—or any of the many other knick-knacks conveniently sold at The Alliant Energy Center—at the skaters? They were selling pretzels and hot dogs too. Both foods would probably fly further than a bottle cap.

"But why would someone throw a hotdog?" the man asked.

"For the same reason someone would throw a bottle cap," I said as I continued my journey back outside, huffing about how illogical the ridiculous cap-policy was.

Peeing out the alcohol had worked all right, but I figured if I really wanted to be safe, I should also sweat it out. I again returned to Captain's ship, changed back into street clothes, and ran around the Alliant Energy Center seven times like a pilgrim running around the *Ka'ba* in Mecca. True, I employed no ritualistic dances for each time around as pilgrims are instructed to do, but I still felt that in the very least my intentions might be noticed by the gods and they would ensure my sobriety. For Wisconsin in the fall, it sure was hot. The sultry day wrapped around my skin like a muggy banana peel. I must have sweat off five pounds running around that arena. But it didn't matter; I needed to sober up. Exhausted, I went back to Captain's ship.

Then back into fruit-form and into the bathroom for another marathon pissing session.

Heading back out to the track, I ran into Mad Rollin' Doll Fleur Tatious. We had never met, but she felt the need to give me a hug. I didn't mind; I would be lying if I said I didn't feel the need to hug her back.

The Charm City All Star girls laced up their skates and stretched their muscles in preparation for their first bout of the weekend against Ohio's all-star team, the Cincinnati Black Sheep. Mibbs Breakin Ribbs gave me a handful of black and yellow pompoms to hand out to audience members. I took up my position beside the bench area, feeling more important than I probably should have. *Yes ladies and gentlemen, I am here with Charm City.* I received an extra minute or so to compose myself due to a stopwatch malfunction. Flo Shizzle bumped her signature ass shake on the jammer line to keep the crowd screaming during the hiatus. I encouraged her with my own signature, "Flo! Flo! Shake that thang!" Black Sheep jammer Hannah Barbaric apparently couldn't resist the lure of Flo's flow and lightly smacked her rump. *It's all Derbylove until that whistle blows.*

Suddenly, a ref yelled at me, "Get away from that bench! Only two coaches are allowed!"

Apparently, I had positioned myself too close to the Charm City bench, and the ref imagined that I might feed information to my team about the Black Sheep. How a person can be both too close to his/her team's bench *and* close enough to eavesdrop on the opponent remains a mystery to me to this day. My enthusiasm dwindled. Even still, after several years of mascoting without a guidebook, I still had lessons to learn …

The teams lined up for the next jam. On the Black Sheep end, I had heard of several of the girls (as a cartoon enthusiast, I ranked Hannah Barbaric as one my favorite names) but had never seen them play as a unit. Ms. Barbaric handled her jam so smoothly that she seemed to buff the track to a glow. Dirty Marty jibed into the mic that Sadistic Sadie was "more famous on Youtube than Kimbo Slice." And from what I could see, he was right. I'd even heard before the bout that her moves rivaled those of Dolly Rocket. And how! Her razor sharp execution of every turn, block, and fall made it a more exciting bout for everyone watching. I started to feel nervous for my beloved Charm City.

Sadie's teammates were skating just as ferociously and knew how to take Charm's hits. Candy Kickass, for example, was no candy-ass. She took on a downpour of fire and brimstone rained on her by Charm City that didn't seem to faze her much at all. Gotham announcer Corndog also took note of her aggressive jamming and commented that Candy skated so forcefully that it was almost like the Black Sheep had "a fifth blocker out on the track."

To make matters worse for Charm City, Rosie the Rioter accidentally dropped the "F" bomb from when she contested a ref's call. She didn't say it to any official, per se, and used the word more as an additional exclamation point of emphasis than slander,[3] but it 'twas still considered cursing at the ref. She was ejected from the game and left Charm City short a formidable skater against a team of formidable Cinci skaters.

There was a problem. Drinking, jogging, and sobering up all before noon had tuckered me out. Through all the excitement, I didn't move. I was already bushed. I also felt intimidated. The arena was so big; the bout, too important. I couldn't tap into the energy of the crowd. There was no rhythm. Back on the track, the score never spread further than fifteen points—an exciting first half, yet it blew right by me.

---

[3] i.e., she didn't say "fuck you," to a ref, but rather "what the fuck did I do?"

At halftime, I stayed behind as the All Stars went off to discuss strategy in the locker room. I looked at the condition of the bench area. Half empty water bottles, band-aid wrappers, and crumbled sweat towels lay between the seats. I cleaned up the area and put fresh water bottles under the left front leg of every seat. A friendly ref approached me. "You're quite the roller derby fan!" she smiled.

It dawned on me that I was still referred to as a "fan" or "enthusiast," not as a "mascot." It didn't seem right. The ref hadn't meant anything disparaging by it, but it did make me wonder when people would stop referring to me as such. We were *all* enthusiasts and fans. I thought of Captain Morgan. She too was a roller derby enthusiast, yet when people looked at her they saw a rollergirl, not an enthusiast. No one called B.A.D. ref Sexy Beast a roller derby "fan" back in San Francisco, despite his roller derby fanship. Bonnie Thunders of Gotham was not a spectacular roller derby "fanatic"—she was a spectacular roller derby jammer. *Odd, no?*

The second period inched upon us. After receiving another hug from Fleur Tatious, I positioned myself next to Cindy Lop-her near the first turn. I had been so lazy during the first half that I decided to start my antics early in the second, taking off around the track a few jams deep. But, as I had grown accustomed to, the more visible one was (like, let's say if a person is wearing a banana costume), the easier a pie to the face becomes. One fan, who I imagine was either a diehard Cinci fan or just an asshole who didn't like bananas, extended his foot and tried to trip me between the first and second turns. *Fuck it.* I hoped he'd just leave me alone if I made him feel like he won. I ran up to him and "tripped" over his foot, exaggerating the fall as best I could. I rolled over. I played dead. Eventually, I got up and continued on my travels. When I came back the other way towards Cindy Lop-her, I stopped short right in front of the same douche. I looked down at his foot in anticipation—like I couldn't wait for him to do it again. He took the bait and stuck his foot out. I pretended to rev myself up in order to jump over his foot and still tripped over it anyway. I got up and in my best gangsta rapper voice said, "Damn boy! You trippin'!" It worked; he left me alone the rest of the bout. *Douche.*

As the second half progressed, I remembered Mibbs' pompoms. After passing out six to eager fans, I had one left. I noticed a girl sitting in the stands. She had one of the prettiest smiles I'd even seen. I didn't know her personally, but I recognized her from a previous bout. Her pristine jamming ability earlier that morning coupled with that smile was too much for me to resist; in roller derby, there are women of such immense beauty that one's defenses crumble at the mere sight of them. I wanted to give her the pompom. I ran over to the excellent jammer with the beautiful smile and handed her the pompom adding, "Next time this will be a bouquet of flowers." She smiled her beautiful smile—out of pity or flattery for me, I couldn't tell. Regardless, her mesmerizing grin (and good lord, those eyes!) swallowed me whole.

During one of the last jams, Dolly Rocket took the jam line beside Hannah Barbaric. They tapped asses for the crowd. Charm City came back strong in the second period and ended the bout with a solid win: 158-83. The girls from both teams hugged a "good game" to each other.

I darted for the bathroom and ran into Chicago Outfitters Sweet Mary Pain and Lola Blow. We said our hellos, and I asked if Althea N. Hell was with them. She wasn't but would arrive later that day. I figured I'd keep an eye out for her in hopes of getting that interview that I never got with her back at RollerCon or Chicago. But a new state offered a new chance. For the moment, though, I had someone else on my mind ...

One Rose; Two Kicks to the Nuts

I borrowed Captain's ship and set about finding the promised bouquet of flowers for the jammer with the beautiful smile. I wanted to make good on what Jammersmile might have taken as a joke. I first stopped at a convenience store that wasn't convenient at all; amongst all the candies, snacks, beers, and car ornaments, the humblest store-bought symbol of love was overlooked. I then tried a gas station. Nothing. The only thing I received there was a couple of rounds of "check this motherfucker out" by the locals as I walked about the service shop. I went back to the arena sans-bouquet. After a roller derby packed day, Captain, Chairman, and I went back to the hotel for some beers and some sleep.

The next morning, Captain and I stopped at a different gas station on our way to the arena. They didn't have any bouquets or any flowers at all. They did, however, sell fake plastic roses. There was one left—a sign! I bought the lone rose determined to win Jammersmile over with it. I grabbed a pen, tore a sheet of paper out of my notepad, and wrote: "It is often said that a rose by any other name would smell as sweet. I disagree. A rose called 'Jammersmile' would be infinitely sweeter."[4] I stabbed the paper through the stem of the rose in a pirate ship mast and flag fashion, hoping to anchor myself to a bountiful conversation later that night after the bouts.

We arrived at the arena around 9 am Charm City would take the track against Windy City in an hour. This bout was important to Charm City because a win would place them in the semi-finals with a spot in Nationals. Windy City showed up with the same idea in mind.

---

[4] Or something like that. And I think I spelled "infinitely" wrong to boot!

I got an excellent night's sleep, and my spirits ran high. I promised myself that I wouldn't be as lazy during the first half of this bout as I had been during the first half of the Black Sheep/Charm City bout. It didn't seem fair. Both Charm City and Cincinnati had put up a hell of a fight, and I just stood there sucking. *Well not today*! As Charm City and Windy City absorbed some last minute advice from their respective coaches, I started early by jumping into the stands and pulling out my bullhorn. Putting my lips to the mouthpiece, I pretended to yell into it and acted surprised when not a peep came out the other end. I turned to a girl sitting in the stands and asked her to "turn up" the volume for me. She looked at me confusedly. I climbed a few steps up and asked another girl. She got the joke. She reached her hand into the air and turned an imaginary dial. As she turned her hand, I ascended my "check ... check ... CHECK!" into the bullhorn. Eventually the volume leveled perfectly and I told her to hold onto the dial, lest I need her help later. She was a great sport—she opened her purse and dropped the invisible dial into it.

I heard Val Capone warming us all up for an intense game over the loud speaker. Her delivery was pure sports announcer: Quick and clever, she had the gift of gab; well-versed in roller derby history, she also had the gift of jab, harboring a *Matt Pinfieldian* knowledge of players' past performances.

Out on the track, Joy Collision stepped up to the line against Eva Dead. Both teams knew what a loss meant and didn't take any chances. The score remained roughly neck and neck a few jams into the bout with both leagues fighting for their spot in the forthcoming national tournament. Unfortunately for Charm City, one Windygirl, Varla Vendetta, scored a crowd-pleasing nineteen-point jam that first period. By halftime, Windy City held the high card: 87-29.

Charm City left to assemble in the locker room. Chairman Meow and I joined this time. Joy Collision, who always polished her wheels with positivity, told the team to smile every time they got up to skate—no matter what. "It'll affect your game," she promised the winded Windy City rivals. Chairman and I watched as the team went into a huddle for a loud "Pissing Excellence!" yell. Just before the shout, Joy turned to Chairman and me. "Get in here, you two." My heart jigged. I hadn't been in a team huddle since the Roller Rebels' second season. Every cell in my body jumped for Joy ... Collision's invitation. I felt like I had a league again—a sentiment I had forgotten.

Although Charm City ended up losing to Windy City, Joy's "smile strategy" seemed to have worked. For in that second half, despite a jaw-dropping twenty-four-point jam by Windy City's Shocka Conduit, the Chicagoans only scored three more points than the Baltimoreans.

Good 'ole Joy Collision.

After that bout, and with the stress of Nationals gone, Charm City skated splendidly against Detroit. We jokingly called it the "Murder Capital Bout," due to the high murder counts in those states (D.C. wasn't at Regionals). During the Murder Capital Bout, I saw a Detroit fan that had seized a parking cone from the parking lot and used it for bullhorn cheering purposes. The parking cone was at least double the size of my little yellow toy. He heckled the Charm City girls so much that during halftime Dolly Rocket made it a point to instruct the others to "just ignore that guy." When the halftime meeting adjourned (again, Chairman and I were invited into the huddle!), I lifted my small yellow bullhorn. "It's not the size of your bullhorn that matters ... it's how you use it. Don't worry about that guy; I'll take care of him."

During the second half, Bullhorn Man continued to jeer the girls as they passed him. He stood at the second turn with a gaggle of Detroit fans. Sniper senses at full alert, I waited for the opportune moment to present itself. Somewhere in the fleeting inches between the roar of the crowd and Dirty Marty hysterics, Bullhorn Man tired of yelling and placed the cone on the floor next to him (amateur!). I ran up from behind him in between jams. Then, as loudly as I could, I screamed "PISSING EXCELLENCE!" into the back of his head. It scared the shit out of him. *Mission accomplished.*

I was riding high. One long official timeout allowed me extra time for silliness. I saw Mouse from Mad Rollin' Dolls sitting in the audience near me. I grabbed her hand and pulled her out of the seat, tangoing with her along the track. I put one of Charm City's pompoms in my mouth like a flower and passed it along to her. The crowd cheered, and I felt that sense of masc-omplishment. I looked to the refs as they scrambled to interpret the admittedly difficult rules. For the first time in my derby career, I didn't mind not being one of them. While they discussed rules, I got to dance with Mouse. She reminded me of what made mascoting so special. What made derby so special: the Derbylove.

Good 'ole Mouse.

I had hurt my bottom during the Murder Capitol bout doing one of my signature cartwheel-land-on-my-rump moves that didn't work out so smoothly. After the bout, Butterscotch and I went back to her room for some rest and—thank the gods—an excellent ass rub courtesy of Ms. Cripple. Butter Cripple took care of my crippled butt.

By the time we walked back to the arena (and with Jammersmile still heavily on my mind), I opted to lower any discomfort she might feel by asking several girls in her league if she was available for conversation. She could have had a boyfriend, or a girlfriend, or both, and there was no sense in making her feel awkward by giving her a plastic rose. I saw a girl wearing Jammersmile's team uniform and asked her. She didn't know anything for certain. Not wholly satisfied with her answer, I asked a second girl. Her response practically mirrored the first one except she tailed the answer with an, "... but I don't think so." A third girl echoed the sentiments of the second verbatim. They encouraged me to just do it anyway. "At the very least, she'll think it's sweet," said number three.

I got the rose from my bag.

I saw Jammersmile sitting in the stands not too far from where I had first handed her the pompom. *Okay, I will be calm. I will be certain. I will hand Jammersmile this rose.* I raised my pointer finger into the air, declaring my intentions true! I floated over to her and handed her the rose. She smiled her beautiful smile. I got lost in it; I wanted to say something, but instead I froze. Saying nothing, I wandered away.

There are certain clues that will inform any planner that a plan didn't work. In this case, Jammersmile's answer came in two distinct ways. Firstly, she didn't try to talk to me, making her disinterest obvious. Secondly, later that day, some of the very league mates that encouraged me to give her the plastic flower made sure to avoid me at any cost, often changing their path if they saw me walking in the opposite direction. One rose; two kicks to the nuts.

Saturday Night's Alright (For Haikus)

With Butterscotch ensuring that my ass would be ready for dancing, I made my way to the after-party. Upon arrival, I realized that I had forgotten my notebook back at the hotel. I grabbed a few napkins off the bar to keep records. As I trotted around the bar, Minnesota Rollergirls skater CleoSPLATra induced me to switch clothes with her. I stood there in her little booty shorts, she in my banana costume. I was then traded off to her league mate Demora Liza, who handed me a beer without me asking for one. "Derby people got to take care of their own," she said, clinking her beer with mine. *Ahhhh ... Derbylove.* As Demora and I bullshat outside on the bar's patio, Carolina Rollergirls announcer Miss Treat asked me if I would write her a haiku. "Sure!" I said. *From Demora Liza to me; from me to Miss Treat.* Thus, my first haiku:

Announcers are great
Roller derby has the best
Miss Treat proves this true

From there, Minx, from Fort Wayne Derby Girls, pulled me into the bathroom.

"Is this your first time in a girls' bathroom?" she asked.

"It's my first time in a girl's bathroom dressed like a rollergirl."

After a quick outfit exchange back with CleoSPLATra, two other rollergirls took me outside for a smoke. At some point I got into a cab, made it back to the hotel, and crashed. Hard.

It's Always Phunny in Sillydelphia

I think it was that Sunday, just before the Windy City/Gotham bout that Olivia Face, a Philly Liberty Belle, injured her leg. Butterscotch and I decided to take control of the situation. I commandeered Captain's ship and we sailed to a pharmacy to buy a bandage. This was the first time I ever EMT'd a rollergirl to some kind of aid. Sometimes mascoting is like working as an office gopher; you are there to do whatever task is needed of you in that moment. Usually, the jobs are small like bringing girls' water or finding teammates. Other times, it will be bandaging up legs of fallen combatants regardless of what team they skate for.

We drove back to the Alliant Energy Center in time for the Gotham/Windy City bout. I couldn't help but notice the intimidation that Windy City captain Malice with Chains assaulted her opponents with. Before she destroyed them in play, she mentally lambasted them, hacking into their minds and scrambling their thoughts like a Y2K bug. The "With Chains" tag of her name was but a prelude to a deeper story. She, of course, didn't really bring chains onto the track; she embodied them. In the near-invisible space of curved metal between the links, I saw Malice's truest nature. A skater (link), a captain (link), a pivot (link), a blocker (link), a jammer (link), a leader (link)—she knew where and how to strike her opponents. Her crowd-pleasing movements weren't isolated incidents. She skated like she was needling the Gotham blockers with threads of chainmail; she kept their jammers at bay, all the while pulling the anvils of her malice in tow.

Still it wasn't enough, and with WCR jammer Varla Vendetta's eviction and a spectacular onslaught of roller derby Hell perpetrated by New York—I actually had difficulty breathing at certain moments—Gotham, the Beast from the East, reigned supreme.

Captain, Chairman, and I walked back over to Butterscotch's hotel. The whole of the Philly girls stood outside the front entrance laughing, cheering, and passing bottles of victory wine around, celebrating their third place seed in the East, and the now certain trip to Portland, Oregon for the WFTDA National Championship. In the mist of the merriment, Philly blocker Annie Christ and I started to talk about Nationals. She asked if I was going even though Charm City had been eliminated. I told her "yes." I already bought the plane ticket; I had to complete the journey. The prospect of mascoting for Philly at Nationals came up.

"Sure," I said. "I'd love to. Just post something on your leagues message board and get a general consensus from the rest of the girls."

"Message board?" Annie asked rhetorically. We don't need a message board!" She turned to the hoard of Philly girls and just blurted out, "Hey! Is it cool if Banana Man cheers for us at Nationals?"

The whole crowd of girls hollered and whooped. I turned red and hid behind Captain and Chairman. Not exactly what I had in mind, but it would do. This was roller derby; sometimes formalities were cast aside. Someone passed me the bottle of wine. I chugged down my initiation to mascot for Philly at Nationals. Butterscotch gave me a hug. She wouldn't be able to make it to Portland but was still happy that I would be cheering for her league. I thanked Annie Christ for her impromptu mascot support.

Good 'ole Annie Christ.

The dance party afterwards almost trumped the thrill of that last bout. Some girl kept asking me to break dance on the floor. I looked down at the filthy floor. "Not tonight," I kept saying. She tried to pull me down, but I evaded her and ran to the bar instead to grab a beer. Drink in hand, I ran into many Charm Citiers and about a hundred other rollergirls tearing up the dance floor like a flat track. I lost myself in them.

After the dance party, Chairman, a horde of Charm City Girls, the East Coast Jammersmilers league, a few stragglers, and I boarded a bus back to the hotel. In my obliterated state, I started trying to "fun up" the bus ride. My attempt to incite a riot of jokes didn't go well. I had passed the point of acceptable intoxication and into the annoying-dance-on-the-tables' kind of drunk. Loud. Boisterous. Teetering on obnoxious. I was full of an after-hours barroom sing along silliness that was not the sentiment of the tired majority. Finally, a girl from the East Coast Jammersmilers yelled out, "Oh why don't you shut up already and go write Jammersmile another love letter?!!"

Jammersmile sat across the aisle from her rather snappish league mate. She embarrassingly threw her hands over her face. I felt so terribly, sat down, and didn't say another word.

Sorry, Jammersmile.

We arrived at the hotel and sailed Captain's ship to the Gotham Girl after-after-party spot, a fine Paul Bunyan-esque bungalow cast deep in the Wisconsin woodlands. We spent the first half-hour or so schlepping hot water from the upstairs kitchen sink to the downstairs bathroom, transforming the bathtub into a Jacuzzi—or better yet, a "goth-tub," which is like a hot tub, but filled with the Eastern Regionals champions. Although I should have taken some precautions with relaying boiling water from the first floor to the basement, my merriment got the better of me and I spilled scolding water on my hands several times. Captain and Chairman crashed, and I stayed up to write some of the events of the weekend.

After the goth-tub party bath, some of the Gothamites went for a walk through the woods. They invited me to go along, but I declined their offer. I figured they probably wanted to celebrate as a team. I spent the rest of the night lying awake wondering if it would be insulting to Charm City to cheer for Philly at Nationals. After careful consideration, I determined it was not. I needed to end my journey cheering at Nationals. Indeed, I had made it a point to tell them as such. At the after-party they had given me the go-ahead, so they couldn't have minded. I still wasn't technically a permanent fixture with them anyway. That was enough to ease my mind—a perfect counter balance to the task that now plagued it. *Nationals?*

XI

Lit Up, Knocked Down

*That's a real chainsaw being used by the Texas mascot.
I'm sure this will end well.*
Justice Feelgood Marshall

Nationals was quickly approaching, and I decided that I wanted to add a new little absur-ditty to my mascot repertoire—magic! I bought a deck of cards. Not trick cards or anything like that, just a regular deck.

"Pick a caad, any caad," I would say in my best Las Vegas dealer voice. "Don't let me see it, but don't look at it either." The person would select the card and look back up at me.

"Thanks!" I'd exclaim. "I'll be rid of these in no time!" Then I'd walk away.

This would have a two-pronged effect. Firstly, it was a mind mess of a card game—more a joke than a trick. However, the "trick" had some real magic in it after all. If the person (out of nothing more than curiosity) were to look at the card, s/he would see that I had written something positive or complimentary on the face side. Such lines like: "Queen of the Track," on the queen card, "Ace of Skates," on the ace, "Ten out of Ten," on the ten card, and other small lines of optimistic reinforcement. It is no secret that mindset affects outlook. It's as simple as giving someone your bus seat. That is real magic. With a bit of luck, the card trick would have a similar effect.

I arrived in Minneapolis for a quick one-hour layover on my way to Portland. While boarding the next plane, I turned to a girl with small buttons and roughly stitched patches on her bag.

"What league you with?" I asked.

"League? What are you talking about?"

She wasn't with any league; I caught myself stereotyping someone—*not cool*. I explained Northwest Knockdown to her and watched a nearby gentleman smile. I recognized him ... faintly. "Are you going?" I asked.

"Yeah," he said. "Corndog ..."

From Gotham!

" ... from Gotham. And you're the banana guy, right?"

I was shocked. In that small hub of an airport, someone recognized me without my suit on for the first time.

Good 'ole Corndog.

After we boarded the plane, most of us quickly found our seats except for one guy about my age who paced back and forth in the aisle. When a steward asked if he needed any help finding his seat, the guy informed him that he was claustrophobic and as such, had requested an aisle seat. Claustrophobe was returning home from Poland after a brief teaching stint in Amsterdam. I couldn't imagine how he got all the way back to this side of the world on a plane without freaking out. A lady in his row, which was directly across from mine, offered him her aisle seat.

He still looked distraught. He needed comfort. I thought of Maxine. A flight attendant came by and closed the overhead storage bin just above my head. It didn't close quietly. The attendant again tried to slam it shut. It finally closed and locked, albeit haphazardly. I started to make cracks about how unsafe the steward had loaded the luggage. I pulled the safety manual out of the pouch in the seat in front of me and waved it at him. I flipped open to the picture that shows a chaotically placed suitcase falling out of the overhead bin and onto a passenger's noggin. There is a big red slash across the picture.

"See? See?" I pointed to the picture. "That's my head we're talking about here!"

Claustrophobe laughed. *Perfect.* Turning back to the attendant, I threatened that I would break out my pompoms if he didn't fix the luggage. He ignored me and continued making his rounds.

"You don't really have pompoms," said Claustrophobe.

Without responding, I opened the overhead bin, grabbed my bag, pulled my pompoms out, and tried to start a cheer on the plane.

"Who's going to Nationals?? WooooOOO!!!" I yelled, waving my pompoms about.

Corndog, a guy wearing a Texacutioners shirt, and a girl gave a low "yeah!" from a few rows behind me. I pulled out my bullhorn. Claustrophobe laughed some more.

Perfecter!

"This guy," I said pointing to Claustrophobe, "doesn't think we can rock this plane! "Woo Hoo! Lemme hear ya! Northwest Knockdown, where you at?!" Claustrophobe laughed even more. I felt a tap on my shoulder.

"In your seat sir," said a flight attendant. I sat down. Claustrophobe looked up at the steward and said, "I don't know this guy," still laughing.

I turned to him and blurted out loudly, "You promised you'd stop saying that after we were married!" He, and several others around us, cracked up. *Nationals was going to be fun ...*

Claustrophobe's flight went without incidence, but I got off the plane in Portland feeling sick. Not wanting to worry Rose

City skater Layla Smackdown, who would host me that weekend, I didn't mention the demons frantically churning butter in my stomach. We drove to her house, and I retired for the evening.

Nationals began at 5:00 p.m. Friday evening. Layla and I were picked up by her old Garden State Rollergirls teammate Choch, and together, we drove off to the Expo Center, a large venue that hosted several unrelated events that weekend. Nationals kicked off with the Last Regiment Syncopated Drummers percussion ensemble beating our senses into oblivion. As disco balls bounced off the flags waving to the beat of the drums, I rubbed my hands in anticipation. The flag holders juggled their flags between each other with such precision that I don't think they even noticed the standing ovation that they so rightly received from us, the audience. After the team introductions, The Texecutioners rolled over to the Carolina Rollergirls who sat around the fourth turn. I couldn't hear what the Texans said to the Carolinians, but after a long berating session, Belle Star sliced her pointer finger across her throat indicating her plans for Carolina. Soon after, the bout started.

Several jams in, Texas had a slowly mounting lead. A lead, though, that didn't come easily. Carolina's aggression was primeval; Kelly Clocks' em was sent to the box twice in one jam! But Texas refused to be messed with. After several stints in the penalty box, Rice Rocket was back in her natural habitat (the track) and made up for the damage Carolina had inflicted. When Texas' Sparkle Plenty faced off against Carolina's Princess America, she carefully navigated through the tiny explosions erupting between Carolina's blockers—holes that would not have existed without the support of blockers like Belle Star and Desi Cration. As I watched the blockers from both teams, I was reminded that a good jammer is only as good as her blockers. The Texas fans were just as ravenous as the skaters were. One Texas fan held a sign that she had personally evolved from the Hotrod Honey's "Faster! Faster! Kill! Kill! Kill!" to "Texas! Texas! Kill! Kill! Kill!" Their chants carried Texas into the first victory of Northwest Knockdown. Texas had rolled into Nationals strong—those girls weren't fucking around.

I wanted to supplement the great time I was already having with a burrito. As I looked for a stand near the front entrance of the Expo Center, some girl stopped me and placed a strap around my neck. It was a pass. It featured a pigtailed, axe-wielding girl decked out in a red shirt, short beige pants, skates, and kneepads. I had seen several kinds of passes that weekend, each of a different color and title: "competitor," "photo/media," and "talent." The girl had rung me with this last one. I had no idea who she was.[1] But I do know *why* she gave it to me—Derbylove. Feeling a little uncomfortable with a "talent" pass, I ran up to the main office and asked for whiteout, scribbling a "no" just above "talent." I darted back downstairs—the next bout between the Gotham Girls and Duke City was already underway.

Duke City had been the "Cinderella story" of the Northwest Knockdown weekend, having plowed its way to Nationals through a rough year.[2] The girls of Duke City lost their practice space (and because of that, a ton of skaters) and had to share practice space with other townspeople at a public basketball court. After (from what I was told) a nail-biting bout against 2007 WFTDA champions Kansas City Roller Warriors, Duke City came out victorious with a 132-117 win. The little league

---

[1] Still don't.
[2] Justice Feelgood Marshall, "2008 Nationals," in *Five on Five: The Official Magazine of the Women's Flat Track Derby Association (WFTDA)*, 1, 2 (Winter 2008), p. 34.

that could brought that same intensity to Nationals as they played Gotham. Scores didn't exactly mirror performance—a small truth that would follow every team that whole weekend.

The Texas/Carolina and Gotham/Duke bouts were the only two for the day. When we left, Layla and I got on the party bus that drove other derbyists and us around to different bars. The first bar was crowded—too crowded—and featured a scrawny white kid rapping about hard times in Spanish Harlem. Layla laughed. "This kid has never seen Spanish Harlem and if he did, he'd probably shit his pants!" We left for the second bar on the bus route. Derbyfolk abounded. We shared drinks and stories with many and not too much later, retired for the evening.

How the Mascots Saved the 'Nanner

Seattle's Rat City kicked off Saturday with a splendid bout against Windy City. As the Windy City and Rat City girls' spilled blood and love all over the floor, Dirty "Rat Man" Houllahan, revved up the crowd. With his neck full of jewelry, he resembled some kind of rodent gangster. *Or maybe a politician?* He carried a diamond-tipped cane, which caused roars from the crowd with every lift. I found his mascoting inspiring. I later learned that he placed third for "Most Energetic Mascot in Western Washington" in 2008.[3] I truly had my work cut out for me. I had heard of him and had hoped that I would bout against him, but after reviewing the weekend schedule, I realized that we would never come to blows on the trackside. *Shit.* I didn't want to be out there alone at Nationals.

The bout ended with Windy City taking the winning slot. B.A.D. and Philly would hit the track in a half hour. I went outside for air. Stories flourished about the melancholic weather

---

[3] Accessed via: http://best.king5.com/rocketman-houllahan/biz/138127.

conditions in the Pacific Northwest. Not that weekend, for it pleased the gods that we should enjoy what felt more like a spring day than a rainy autumn one. I spoke with "Rat Man" Houllahan outside and we took pictures for derbyfans. I congratulated him on his fine mascoting and gaffed that he needed to dust off his "A" material because the top banana had arrived. He joked about getting all of us mascots together for some secret meeting because, he assured me, *we* really controlled the outcome of the derby bouts.

For a rat, he had a good energy about him. It took some of the edge off of the slowly encroaching Philly/B.A.D. bout. I filled my lungs with the fresh Portland air and walked back inside. I wished Rat Man were walking back with me.

Just inside the main arena, I ran into a girl who looked strangely familiar, but I knew I had never met her. I looked down at my No Talent badge. *Ahhhh ... she was "Lumber Jill," the "logo girl" mascot on the Northwest Knockdown pass.* Lumber Jill skated for Rat City under the name "Sister Piston" but had volunteered to mascot at Nationals. She introduced herself, and I told her that I wanted to have someone to mascot against during the Philly/B.A.D. bout. She agreed to do it.

I happily darted towards the back of the arena, now free to move between "behind" and "the scenes" due to my No Talent badge. I put my bag down in Philly's locker room, which was really one in a series of tents lined up behind a large curtain. I began to warm up with some modest cartwheels and handsprings. Hell en Fuego, a ref for Eugene Oregon's Emerald City Roller Girls, saw me practicing and yelled, "Don't bust your leg out there!"

Shit! *I'm doomed*! I ran over to her and pleaded with her to recant. *That's just the kind of thing that causes an injury.* Hell en Fuego assured me that she did not possess magical powers. *Bullshit*! *I know a sorceress when I see one.* I asked her to please put a protection spell on me anyway. She grabbed my arm and shook it. But not believing she had invoked anything in the first place, only half-heartedly withdrew the curse.

At their respective sides on the track, the girls from Philly and B.A.D. soaked up last minute coaching advice. I didn't see Lumber Jill anywhere. *Shit! She's not coming.* My disappointment was cut short when I spotted a familiar pair of pants on the floor; the large, silver "Ozzy Zion" buckle on the belt shone like a mascot beacon. I looked up over to the B.A.D. side and saw him standing next to the girls. He wore shiny golden-scaled booty shorts, a gold bowtie, and a purple top. *Yes! Certainly he is mascoting for B.A.D.; he's wearing their colors!* I walked over to say my "hellos" and to thank him for his participation. I couldn't wait to bout against my favorite mascot.

After a brief but amicable greeting, a man in the audience asked us to stand next to each other for a picture. As the flash went off, I heard an unfamiliar yet distinguishable voice scream out from the stands, "I hate you Banana Man!" It was the mysterious girl from RollerCon. *My Nemesis! She's back! The one who screamed she hated me for no apparent reason at Maui Bar!* Excited that she had made it to Oregon, I wanted to find out who she was and what I had done to rouse such animosity. But not right then—I had work to do. I glanced over at her, mentally tabulating anything I could use to identify her later. I memorized her definitions—calculated the distance between her head and her feet. She was rather short and her friend fairly tall. I walked behind the stands and noticed she had what looked like a fanny pack on her backside. *Perfect. Remember to find the unevenly matched heights and fanny pack later.*

This time her taunts didn't faze me. I picked up Ozzy's pants and taunting him with them, ran around the track with them on my head. He chased me, and we got a few laughs. Ozzy made his way back to the B.A.D. side, and I to the Liberty Belles' side. I got the usual tap on the shoulder. *Another photographer.*

I turned to him. "Get out of my shot!"

He looked confusedly at me. "I ... I wanted you in the shot, jerk." He shuffled away.

Of ... fucking ... course!

I pulled out my bullhorn and moved on to the crowd, screaming, "Go Philly! Go Philly! Go Philly!" in as many peoples' faces that I could find. That line quickly turned into "Skill-a-delphia! Skill-a-delphia!" I was looking for reaction so that I could find my mascot "houses"—those small pockets in the crowd where fans of your team have collected. I hawked my eyes at the dense wall of screaming audience. At the second turn, I saw a group of folks in Gotham shirts taking up a large part of the stands; just below them, on the floor, I saw Heavy Flo and other Fillyphans. *Great.* That area would work.

After a few jams, I decided to get the Philly/Gotham stronghold cheering. Along the straightaway, Windy City girls sat and waited in anticipation for their bout. I hoped that it would be an Eastern Regional thing—*blind regional hatred*—and Windy City would root for Philly for no other reason than geographical proximity.

I recognized one of the Windy girls. We'd never met, but I'd heard of her before; she was an unruly troublemaker. The kind of girl I'd ask to help me steal Christmas if I were ever so inclined. I had heard rumors about a curse placed on her by some god. He was already fed up with her antics, but then she made a crucial mistake: she tampered with his tea. Such follies were too malicious to leave unpunished. With a blink of his eyes, and a chuckle in his soul, the god watched as wheels sprouted forth from the girl's shiny black hooves—turning her

Bane-ana

from a satyr to a skaytr. At least that is the story as passed down to me. I didn't usually believe skater "bios" but this one seemed plausible. As such, I approached Skaytr hoping she'd want to cause a ruckus and cheer with me. Aware of the breadth of her powers,[4] I approached her with much caution. I told Skaytr that Philly planned to grind me into a cheese steak if she didn't cheer.

Skaytr

---

[4] Supposedly, she once transformed her whole league into penguins and several rollergirl rivals into donkeys.

She looked up at me with an impish grin. "Cheering I be." Her pupils swayed back and forth from blue to purple and red waves; tiny red and yellow horns spiraled up from under her hair. A pointed tail waved from behind her with mischievous delight. *Fuck! She's sizing me up for a spell.* Hands shaking, I nervously reached into my inner-pocket to grab my bag of Sugar N. Spike's pixie dust. If Skaytr wanted a magical showdown, I was ready. But then I changed my mind and released the satchel from my hand. It would be unfair to all the skaters, refs, and spectators to put Nationals on hiatus while they decided what to do with two penguin/ass hybrids. I didn't have time for all that. I had a job to do. I moved on, turning once to make sure she didn't try to pull any trickery on me from behind my back. Her eyes returned to their normal color and her horns receded into her head. But she kept staring at me just as a warning. We were both safe. For the while …

I approached the Gotham/Philly stronghold at the second turn. The Phillypholk were already in an uproar; my "Bananas for Philly" sign got a lot of laughs. *If I can just get the Gothamites to join with the Phillypholk, we can make some magic happen here*! I jumped and screamed, "Go! Philly! East! Coast! Go! Philly! East! Coast!" at the horde of Gothamfolk. They responded tremendously!

Good 'ole Gothamfolk.

At halftime, I decided to find the "I hate you Banana Man" girl and interview her for this book. I went to the Phillypholk tent and grabbed my tape recorder and some money for a burrito. After wasting most of halftime wandering around, I burrito-lessly ran into my nemesis. She granted me the interview but wouldn't let me tape record it. Everything had to be written down. I didn't care, as I am a master at shorthand.

Her family had settled in the city of her league "400 years ago," as she claimed. It, of course, wasn't a city back then, but rather, a desert. Nemesis told me that roller derby helped her escape an abusive relationship and made her more of a feminist. She also told me that she never had any girls as friends, and now she was kneepad deep in them.

Finally I asked: "So why exactly do you hate my guts?"

"You don't remember me? From E.C.E this past spring? I told you that my team had a banana mascot and you acted like an asshole claiming, 'I am the one and only banana!' Well, you're not! We got one too!"[5]

As it turns out, her league formed the same year as the Roller Rebels so, technically, her banana and I donned banana costumes at the same time. I'd never heard of him, and I doubted he'd ever heard of me. I explained to Nemesis that my bombastic claim to be the only banana in roller derby back at ECDX was a joke, part of the act. She didn't care. Nemesis seemed to derive some sort of exhilaration from not liking me, and I wasn't going to beg her to reconsider. I shrugged off her explanation as easily as she had dismissed mine. It was quite obvious what happened between us. She had made a big mistake when we first met several months ago: she took a guy dressed like a banana seriously.[6]

My stomach still burrito-less, I kept moving. Shortly thereafter, the gods saw it fit that I should run into both Ozzy and Lumber Jill, who decided to join our mascot brigade for the second half. We put our heads together and decided that at the first timeout of the 2nd period, Ozzy and I would brawl trackside and Jill would run in and axe us both. "Don't worry, I won't hit you hard," said Jill.

---

[5] Bane-ana, *Interview with Nemesis*, 15, November, 2000Great.
[6] We have since become, as Kasey Bomber and Axles of Evil call it, "chummy adversaries." See Barbee and Cohen (2010), p. 172.

"You better hit me as hard as you can," I replied. Ozzy concurred.

Okay, so first timeout, we dance. Everyone got it? Perfect. Ready? Break ...

Once the bout restarted, it didn't take long for a timeout. I looked over at Ozzy, he at me. We ran between the two teams' bench areas and started to scuffle just under the announcer's high-rise. He took me down, but derby had readied me to be quite the scrapper myself, so I quickly got up on top. Lumber Jill skated over and started smacking us with her axe. Ozzy got the upper hand again, and I fell over. When I tried to get back up, I—and this is going to sound ridiculous, but it's true—slipped on myself. No, really. My foot caught the underside of my cape and I tripped. The officials called the timeout over, and I got up to run back to the Philly side. I took one step down with my right leg and felt a sharp pain in my knee. My run turned into a limp, and I just barely made it back to our side before the whistle blew the bout back into play. One of the officials asked if I was all right.

"What can I say, we bananas bruise easily," was the best thing I could come up with. But it really hurt. *It was that Hell en Fuego! She cursed me! What the hex?* I hobbled over to the EMT table where medics taped a large bag of ice to my knee; it constantly slipped with every limp to the trackside.

"So, I guess she really got you with that axe?" asked a fan sitting in the bleachers.

"Yeah, she made a banana split," I said back, knowing that it was a really bad joke. I finished out the bout, hobbling my "Bananas for Philly" sign across the audience line. *Twenty more minutes, then I can collapse.*

The bout was almost over, and B.A.D. was trailing behind by only a few points. The buzzer wrenchingly sounded. The final score undetermined. We all waited the refs' decision.

Finally, they reached a verdict: Philly had won. We all jumped for joy (okay, some of us staggered for joy) and went back to the Phillypholk tent. Olivia Face joked that this time it would be she driving me to the drug store for bandages.

"Does it hurt?" she asked.

Only when I wear yellow.

I met up with Ozzy and Jill. "Is your leg okay? Sorry about that, man," said Ozzy.

Lumber Jill, Dirty "Rat Man" Houllahan, Bane-ana, Ozzy Zion

"Are you kidding? That was great!" Hugs were dispersed, with the hopes that we would meet on the track again that weekend. Despite the aching in my knee, I had a smile on my face. Rat Man had inspired me, Zion was as on-point as always, and Jill was a riot! All had bestowed Derbylove of the highest order—resulting in a rare, but possible, outcome: mas-confidence! And lo! As had been foretold, the mascots saved the 'Nanner.

Gotham was next. The time between bouts ended sooner than I needed it to. My leg was still a gelatinous mess. When Philly and Gotham took the track, I hobbled around screaming into my bullhorn. My knee started to hurt—nothing serious, more uncomfortable than anything else. I ran back to Philly's bench. I wanted to sit but decided against it. If I couldn't run around the track, the very least I could do was stand in Philly's corner. So that's what I did. I just stood in their corner, waiting for the bout to end so that I could numb myself with goodies.

In the end, Gotham won. The Philly girls, tired from having skated such a physically and emotionally draining bout against the B.A.Dblokes, had given it their all. But a tired "all" was no match for the powerhouse that was Gotham.

The last bout of that day pit Windy City against Texas. Throughout, the point spread stayed pretty tight. Drooling with excitement, I sat right up to the track. With the clock steadily coming to a finish, the last few jams had us all on edge. After Malice with Chains' last jam against Lucille Brawl tied the score 91 to 91, all of Philly and Gotham stood together—every one of us in unison chanting, "East Coast! East Coast! East Coast!" The gods heard our cries for our Windy City sisters, who emerged victoriously.

Pants, Pants Revolution!

After going back to Layla's to shower, we drove to the after-party at the Jupiter Bar, which featured a small motel nestled beside it. The Jupiter was just a prelude; somewhere in that motel, Team Dance Party, in conjunction with The Vagine Regime, hosted a Pants Off Dance Off party. *Althea will surely be there.*

We had a problem. Not Layla, Terra, or I knew what room the Pants Off Dance Off Party was in. We found different groups of derbyfolk spread out across the bar/motel parking lot. With each group that we asked for directions to the Dance Party, our tribe grew larger. Eventually, we had mustered a small army of determined partygoers ready to take their pants off and dance ... off.

Up on one of the motel balconies, several girls in booty shorts danced along the railing. "There it is!" a person in the group yelled. We walked up the stairs and into the pants-less Sabbat on Bald Mountain. Dancing under the banner "Drink. Skate. Fuck," The Vagine Regime did not conceal its *raison d'etre* behind foggy language. The room tangoed booty shorts and fishnets, and smelled of stank kneepads, alcohol, and smoke. Everywhere I turned, lips kissed, asses shook, beer spilled, and gaiety thrived. Girls piled on top of others on tables, dressers, and on the bed. I walked in and cracked open a beer. Someone passed a burning joint to me. Then a camera came my way. I scanned the room for Althea N. Hell. Not seeing her anywhere, I decided to get the scoop on Team Dance Party. TDP had, after all, saved me from a complete mental breakdown back at RollerCon. One name kept coming back to me: "Cash Money."

"Oh, you're writing about Team Dance Party?" a girl would say. "Talk to Cash Money. She's pretty much the founder."

"Do you know where I can find her?"

One girl turned to me, "Yeah, I think she's over there," and vaguely pointed towards the back of the room. "Short girl, blonde hair."

I didn't know to whom she referred, but nonetheless started to squeeze through the densely packed rollergirl ocean when a friend grabbed me from behind and pulled me outside.

"Smoke with me!" She took her bowl out of her bag.

"Wait!" I protested. "I gotta find Cash Money!"

"How much you need?"

"No, no, not real cash money; Cash Money—the person."

"In a minute." She released her purse, fired up the bowl, and handed it to me. She then started grinding on the floor and took quite the spanking from her derbywife, ■. Suddenly someone seized someone else's ass, causing a loud shriek. The sound must have delighted us all because an ass-grabbing contest ensued—and for a short while, as Cherrylicious named us, "Team Ass-Grab" existed. After we pinched our bottoms rare, Team Ass-Grab disbanded,[7] and I went back inside the dance, still limping and looking for either Althea or Cash Money.

Someone danced into me, and my beer spilled down my leg into my left sneaker. *Shit!* It felt like applesauce with every step. I picked up the beer. There was still some left. *Bottoms up.* I discarded the bottle and pulled my pen and envelope out of my inner pocket. A short girl with blonde hair caught my eye. I pressed through the crowd again until I stood behind her. She was so invested in her dance that I didn't want to bother her right then. I decided to look for Althea. A girl tapped me on my shoulder. I didn't know her, but was nonetheless happy to see her. She might grant me an interview.

---

[7] For good?

I didn't hesitate. "Can I interview you for a book about roller derby?" She poured a shot of some kind of alcohol into a red plastic party cup and handed it to me. I drank it down.

"Thanks," I passed the cup back. "Can I intervi ..."

"You talk too much," she interrupted, pouring a large shot and throwing it down her throat. She then poured another and handed it to me.

I put my hand up to decline her offer. "Well I used to carry a good conversation. Then I dropped it and it shattered. Now I can only speak broken English." I awaited her laugh. She squint her eyes and shook her head; she caught the pun, but it had caused brain damage.

"What? Shut up!" She yanked my hair back and rained the alcohol down my mouth. I choked and coughed out a mix of sauce and saliva. When some of the spittle hit her shirt, I gasped. *She's gonna clobber me!* With a chorus of apologies, I reached into my pocket, pulled out napkins, and handed them to her. I expected her to punch me or, at the very least, get pissed and walk away. She didn't do either. She poured another shot.

"Whatsamatter? Can't keep up?" she pitched the shot down her mouth. Two wet lines guttered down the sides of her chin. "Pussy," she gargled.

I'm sorry—did you just challenge an ex-Long Island Roller Rebel to a drinking contest? I snatched the bottle from her hand and took a sizeable inhale. After several good glugs, I shot her a *top that* sneer and handed her the bottle. She threw the plastic cup on the floor—ready for battle—and took a deep breath of alcohol. She then wiped the drips from her lips with her wrist. Saying nothing, she raised her left eyebrow, mirrored my previous snicker, and handed me the hickory.

I swan dove into the intoxicating abysses of the bottle. When I finally came up for air, I could barely stand up straight anymore. My dive, I realized, had been more of a belly flop.

Only a few drops remained at the bottom. She grabbed it, drank what was left, and tossed the empty bottle into the garbage.

"Can't ... I ... inderbew you floora booghk?" My words dizzied and danced.

Another girl grabbed Shot Girl and started to grind up against her. Shot Girl danced off deeper into the sea of rollergirls. Somewhat choked up on the transitory madness, I felt as if I had unwittingly damned myself on some poisoned brew. They were all around me—rollergirls, I mean.

Terra NüOne from B.A.D. told me that she enjoyed my card trick.[8] Fighty Almighty, a girl who had bouted up and down the west coast (and coined The Vagine Regime phrase "If you ain't strickly dickly, you're one of us"[9]), was the first person to ask me for a card at the party. Suddenly, many were asking me for cards. I was enthralled; they wanted magic. Despite their requests compromising the walk-away-post-card-pick, I acquiesced. How couldn't I? I felt elated—swimming in an ocean of Derbylove. And to the detriment of my right leg, I started to dance in the very fires that would consume me.

Terra me Sue, Layla, and I left the party to head back to Layla's place. My leg hurt now more than ever. I had left without the stories—without interviewing Althea N. Hell or Cash Money. It was okay though. There was still one more day of Northwest Knockdown. I'd find 'em somehow.

The Wave:
Or How I Almost Killed Jerry Seltzer

Although there were only two bouts that next day, the arena swarmed with derbyfolk and fans alike. The first bout, the Grudge Match, pit Philly against Texas. "Grudge Match" was

---

[8] Terra, that made my weekend.
[9] See Switchblade Siouxsie (2008).

an understatement. Both teams had played that whole weekend with extraordinary amounts of heart. Now they only wished to rip out each others' hearts and skate all over them.

When the bout started, I watched as Ozzy Zion revved up his chainsaw and the crowd. The battle was on! He had whole sections in the arena chanting "Texas! Texas! Kill! Kill! Kill! Texas! Texas! Kill! Kill! Kill!" Not to be outdone, I started my own "Philly! Philly! Kill! Kill! Kill!" chant. The Texas fans didn't much care for my little modification of their mantra and booed as I passed. *Good. Blind Regional Hatred—just like Ozzy likes it.* Their jeers simply made me work harder. "Philly! Philly! Kill! Kill! Kill! Philly! Philly! Kill! Kill! Kill!" I pressed on around the track through the wall of screaming fans. Not to be outshined, Ozzy, too, continued down the trackline screaming for Texas. Chainsaw to bullhorn, Ozzy and I fought for applause; fought for our girls. By the time we made our respective ways around the track (crossing paths between the second and third turns), Philly and Texas fans were trying to out-scream each other. From different corners around the track, cries of either "Texas! Texas!" or "Philly! Philly!" with the tagline "Kill! Kill! Kill!" pounded us from all corners. I smiled across the way at Ozzy. *Well done, old bean.*

After two brutal periods, the score was close—actually, it was tied 95 to 95 with only two minutes (one jam!) left in the game. But the Philly girls were ready. They had heart. They had speed. They had style. They had Mo Pain on the jammer line. Beside her, Rice Rocket. I couldn't cheer. I couldn't even breathe. At the sound of the whistle, Mo skated around the track creating such a frenzied whirlpool that we, the audience, couldn't help but sink down in her undertow. Our screams, earsplitting currents that resounded throughout the arena, weren't desperate scrambles to grab onto some loose tree branch or rocks along the central nerve of the rapids; they were screams of ecstasy. We wanted this fate. We wanted to die in Mo's rip tide and tumble into the underworld, reliving the bliss of her jam for all eternity. Mo didn't disappoint. She took lead jammer and scored an unbelievable fourteen pointer, ending the bout 109 to 95!

Enraptured, I jumped up and came down on my leg—hard. I tottered back and fell over. A man standing behind me stopped me with his body, my weight almost knocking him to the floor.

"Oh! Shit! Sir! I'm so sorry!!" I apologized.

"Idiot!" yelled a lady over my right shoulder, daggers flying out of her throat. "Look what you're doing! Do you know who this is?!?!"

"No, I don't! I'm sorry!"

"That's Jerry Seltzer! His father [Leo Seltzer] invented roller derby, you fool!! Are you trying to kill him?"

"No! I'm really very sorry! It's my knee! I came down on it wrong yesterday! I'm really really very very sorry!"

They walked away to congratulate the Philly girls on their win, and I escaped to the back changing-tent area and waited for the main event: Gotham Girls vs. Windy City. When the whistle blew signaling the beginning of the end of the bouts that weekend, the crowd had blurred into one gigantic roller derby entity. At no point did we, the audience, do "the wave"—we had become the wave. The Texas Rollergirls must have looked on with pride as Chicago and New York duked it out on the ring of their creation.

Gotham had an assembly line of revolving skaters with which to destroy any takers. Bonnie Thunders skated with her back arched like the pointed entrance of a cathedral, creating a one-woman work of art through the pack that reminded me of the Duomo in Florence and its intricate sculpting of forgiveness and judgment; only, Bonnie had left forgiveness off the track and she didn't apologize for it. I couldn't tell if she understood something the rest of us just didn't get; or if we understood it, but only enough to admire her mastery over it. She possessed some ancient esoteric knowledge about roller derby combat that most others didn't get and guarded that knowledge, carrying an eight-wheeled torch that was passed down only to the few, only to the worthy.

Following her was Suzy Hotrod. She existed outside of the matrix and looked on the rest of us with pity. Was the pack really moving that slowly, or was she moving through it so quickly? I stood in awe as the Hotrod comet streamed through the galaxy of rollergirls around her and burst through them like a star exploding in the purple of a late afternoon sky. Blocker Ginger Snap tied up any loose ends in the pack. What could be said of her style? She skated like a piece of wedding cake—everyone wanted a slice, but nobody touched it.

The competition remained fierce throughout, but unfortunately too many penalties often left Windy City without a jammer. In the end, like the Empire State Building lit up on a warm summer night, Gotham rose above the rest. I wanted the bout to go on forever. A thought, I truly believe, that was shared throughout the Portland Expo Center.

Gotham danced their well-deserved victory dance to Queen's *Another One Bites the Dust*. Windy City had put up a hell of a fight, leaving us all talking over each other about our favorite moments in the bout and who we thought rocked the house that night. Truth was, they all had. The Eastern Division teams had swept the awards, with Gotham in first, Windy runner up, and Philly in third. When all the teams assembled before the announcers' booth to claim their medals, we all chanted one last "East Coast! East Coast! East Coast!" at the tops of our lungs. The chant quickly turned into "Where's our beer?! Where's our beer?! Where's our beer?!" Persephone passed a bottle of Champagne around to the rest of Philly.

Violet Temper took a sip, handed me the bottle, and said "Good job." Then, in a New Years Eve fashion, Malice with Chains sprayed us all with Windy City's Champagne. Who was going to tell her to stop? Who would have wanted her to?

Mad Rollin' Dolls founder and WFTDA president Crackerjack approached me after the awards ceremonies, handed me a small badge, and said, "You are our most dedicated mascot." It was an official WFTDA iron-on patch! I must have sounded like a slobbering fool as my "thank yous" salivated out of my mouth. I realized that moment that there are many different threads in the roller derby story. It is not the story that is universal, but rather the quilt that all the stories combine to tell. Somewhere in the fold individual threads will cross, sometimes pleating a patch of perfect peace.

Good 'ole Crackerjack.

Attack of the Fairy and Gangsterette

The after-party bar was large enough to house a small army. Three large floors filled up with rollerfolk. The live band karaoke caused near-whole leagues to get on the stage and belt out songs. We were rambunctious. Everywhere I looked, beers were getting knocked off tables, and derbyists were stacking themselves on top of each other, constructing human pyramids. And here, I couldn't join the dancing merriment. I looked on enviously at those on the dance floor and then decided that I should try to find Althea N. Hell. I held myself up on the banister and tried to glide down the stairs as best I could. I found some Outfitters and asked them if Althea was about. Turned out she hadn't even gone to Nationals, so all attempts to track her down that entire weekend had been fruitless *a priori*.

She eludes me again.

Scrappy Go Lucky, a Rose City Roller, ran up to me after I grabbed a beer.

"Fairy Brutal is looking for you."

"Why?"

"Beats me."

Then a Carolina Rollergirl—Fairy Brutal's league—approached me. "Fairy Brutal wants to lump your ass."

"Why? What did I do?"

"Nothing. She just wants to."

"But my knee still hurts from yesterday."

"Oh, don't be such a pussy!"

I didn't know who Fairy Brutal was, but apparently, she had an itchin' for beating up the banana. Supposedly, she had beaten up several mascots in her day and played roller derby in lieu of taking anger management courses. Usually, I take derby "bios" with a grain of salt; this time, I wasn't so sure. I needed to avoid this killer from Carolina at all costs; only, I had no idea who I was trying to avoid. If a fervent Fairy found me first, I was fucked. On the other hand, I couldn't avoid her because I didn't know what she looked like. Eventually, she tracked me down.

"I'm going to fight you," she declared, robbing me of any say in the matter. "You better just do as I say—let's not make a scene."

We are going to fight and not make a scene?

There was nothing I could do. She had me in check. *Rollergirls.* At least this time I got a warning. Usually, they just tackled me. We backed up like sumo wrestlers and crashed into each other. Both struggling to stay on top, we undercut our balances and fell to the floor. The nerves in my leg started to scream at me. Just when I couldn't take anymore, the notorious Windy Citier Val Capone jumped into the mix. Then Scrappy Go Lucky. *A setup*! It was a full-on banana pile up with me, beat red, somewhere on the bottom fighting my way through rollergirls, screaming and laughing, all while slowly getting crushed. Val Capone pulled me off the floor in a headlock and I started to feel faint. My grandfather's last words to me echoed through my mind: "Since we all gotta go one day, it wouldn't be so bad to go out suffocating in a woman's breasts." *Oh grandpa, so fatidic.* So there I was, walking towards the light, the portal, suffocating to death between the Spartan bosom of Val Capone. With one last effort, I pushed back and she fell over. I went down with her. The impact cracked her shoulder blade. I had forgotten that roller derby injuries can occur just as easily off the track as on it. After-parties are full contact. No sooner had I picked myself up clenching to a bar stool when a girl took me outside to smoke a bowl with her.

"Need some medicine?" she asked.

I shook my head "yes."

As we walked out of the bar, I turned my head as J. Crush, Belle Star, and Electra Blu took the stage and started the first lines of AC/DC's *Shook me All Night Long.*

After the smoke I went back inside the bar and caught up to Layla who asked where I'd been.

"Smoking with ▮."

"Oh my God!" exclaimed Layla. "Did she show you her tits?"

"No."

"Then you haven't *really* smoked with her yet!"

Eventually, the party started to wane, and Layla and I went back to her place. I left Oregon the next day; on the plane ride home, my seat, coincidentally, was next to Philly Roller Girl Euro Thrash's in the very last aisle. As the engines growled louder and louder, I felt that old unease about the takeoff creep into my nerves. I tried to make small talk with Euro as my heart pounded from deep within my chest. We started for the runway.

I began to sweat more and more. Finally, I couldn't take it any longer and simply grabbed Euro's hand, closed my eyes, fell back into the seat, and breathed as loudly as the plane's engines. I didn't say a word. I could only imagine what she thought of me at that moment. After we were in the air, I released her hand, apologized, and explained the whole thing.

From New York to Baltimore to Austin to Phoenix to Los Angeles to San Francisco to Chicago to Madison to Portland (and all the states connecting them), I witnessed the beating heart of roller derby—*Derbylove*—that which redefined the sport into the cultural phenomenon it is becoming. I sat in my plane seat holding my WFTDA patch. My journey was over. Not with a whimper but a bang!

XII

ALTHEA ON THE DARK SIDE OF THE MOON

The Quest is ended, but it never met its end.[1]
ANDY LETCHER

Two months after Nationals and a few dozen pages into my initial draft, I caught a whiff of something. *What the fuck is that smell?* My banana costume was rife with decay. I prepared it for the cleaners, and while digging through the inner pockets, I found The Vagine Regime itinerary flyer that Althea had given me back at RollerCon.
Shit.
Finding Althea had been a side mission ever since she and I met. I still had nothing about The VR, a rather important contingent of the modern roller derby culture. To write this book without it would be to miss the point. I needed the damn story, and she was the rollergirl said to know it.
Furthermore, I hadn't gotten the Windy City Rollers story either. Ranked second in the nation that year (and some would say, by default, the world) and no mention of their origins? *No, no, no, no, no*—that would not do. As it turned out, luck smiled

---

[1] Telling the Bees, "Untie the Wind," *Untie the Wind*, Black Thrustle (2008).

its fortunes upon me, and The Chicago Outfit was hosting a fundraiser the night before the opening bout of Windy City Rollers' home season that January of 2000Fine. I figured I could kill two jammers with one blocker. I was going back to Chicago.

Talk Derby to Me

By the time I secured Val Capone's phone number from Butterscotch Cripple, Val had already left for Mexico to celebrate her 30th burfday. I didn't know how she would react to my impromptu call—when I tried to dig up any information on her, all the reports came back the same: "Case File Sealed." When we finally spoke, Val opened her Door-bylove to me.

I was enthralled. *Staying with the Val Capone?*

Not wanting to impose, I left my banana outfit home. I felt like I was pushing myself a little too much on leagues. Nationals with Philly had been a blast, as had been Regionals with Charm City. But it was time to settle down with one league. Moreover, mascoting for the Windy City Rollers (WCR) was just plain intimidating; the league had a huge fan base. The story of WCR's success was easily demonstrable by the size of the venues it played. During its first season (2005), WCR outsold all other leagues in ticket sales. To accommodate the masses of fans, WCR moved to The Stadium in Cicero, which seated 1,500. Soon even that wasn't enough, and the collective relocated to the University of Illinois at Chicago Pavilion, which can house up to 10,000 fans.[2] That was a bit overwhelming for me. The Alliance Energy Center back in Madison held the same amount, but that was for an enormous

---

[2] Authored unnamed, "We Are WCR," *Windy City Rollers Season Program* (2009), p. 2-3.

event. WCR was one league! *Nope. Can't do it. Too big. Too much.*

I arrived on a chilly Chicago night; Val took the train to O' Hare to meet me so I wouldn't get lost. We went back to her apartment and rested for a while. She showed me one of the tattoos on her arm—small red slashes like the kind one sees in a prison cell. "I get one for each time the Manic Attackers win."[3]

Windy City Rollers is comprised of four teams: The Manic Attackers, The Fury, The Double Crossers, and Hell's Belles. That night, Val's team, The Manic Attackers, held a team meeting at Manic captain Malice with Chains' apartment. I only stayed for a short while because team meetings were for team members only. I snuck out unnoticed. Nothing would stop me from interviewing Althea this time. Val had arranged for Ref Raff, a Chicago Outfit ref, to give me a lift back to her place from the Althea mission. I need only get to the bar safely and get the damn interview. I pulled the crumpled up paper out of my pocket and unfolded the scribbles: "Mentrose stop. Mentrose and Cicero. Memories."

While waiting, I decided to step on and off a metal bench to practice so that I wouldn't accidentally fall onto the track when I boarded the train. A barbershop collective kept the time signature in my muscles and loosened my tendons; my feet dropped in lockstep to the deep soul vaulted in the quartet's harmonies. Up and down I went, dancing to their moving voices.

"What are you on?" a voice behind me inquired.

"The bench."

I turned to a pair of cops standing over my shoulder. *Fuck.*

"Acting pretty weird tonight, no?"

---

[3] Bane-ana, *Interview with Val Capone*, 30, January, 2000Fine.

Actually sir, this is all quite normal for me. "Weird? What do you mean? Who's acting weird? I'm not acting weird. I'm just practicing for Althea N. Hell."

"You'll see me where?!"

Shit! "No, no ... I won't 'see you' ... Al-the-a!"

The train rolled by and stopped. I looked over the officers' shoulders. "That's, um, my train."

"You're, um, not getting on it."

No! Althea! I don't have time to play with you guys! "Why? What did I do?"

The quartet stopped singing.

"You're behavior is suspicious."

"So gimme a breathalyzer test! A pee ..."—*wait, you fool! Don't take a pee test!*—"... I was just goofing around with the singers. That's all! I'm a writer ... sort of. I'm on my way to interview Althe ... someone."

I heard the "bloop" that signaled the train doors were closing. With (almost) all aboard, the train slowly pulled away.

"Identification."

I reached into my pocket and pulled out my driver's license. He took it and ambled away talking into his walkie-talkie while the other stood "guard." Over cop jargon and mumbles, I overheard "possibly high." *I'm not!* He came back, pulled a mini flashlight out of his belt and flashed it in my eyes.

"Necessary?"

"Very!"

It could have been worse, I guess. These officers could have been out stopping a murder or a rape somewhere in the city. Luckily, I was there to make sure they didn't have to, and that I would be late for Althea. *Mission accomplished, assholes.*

"You check out. Stay out of trouble." He handed me back my license.

Stay out of trouble? What the fuck did I do? "Whatever. And my train?"

"Wait for the next one."

Maybe twenty minutes later, the next train arrived. I looked over my shoulder for any fuzz, and not seeing any, boarded the train without further incident. I was already late. Ten minutes, and Mentrose, my stop, approached. I disembarked with all deliberate caution and slowly, steadily, safely, and surely walked to the fundraiser. The directions in my pocket lead me to the corner of Mentrose and Cicero. The sign above the door read "Memories." I pulled my pen, pad, and tape recorder out of my bag.

I walked in and didn't see Althea. *Maybe she got held up by a cop too?* I saw Outfitter Suzie Crotchrot and said hello. She was standing by the merch table with Dee O.A. and Leonora Da Bitchy. I introduced myself and told them that I had chased them through four states trying to get the story of The VR.

"Oh, did you talk to Althea?" asked Da Bitchy.

Easy, old man. "That's why I'm here. Four states. Four cities—Las Vegas, Wisconsin, Portland, and Chicago—twice! I've chased her across the United States in hopes of finding out about The Vagine Regime." I puffed up my chest and pointed my finger into the air. "And tonight is the night!" Da Bitchy shook her head.

"Well, I hate to tell you this, but Althea is not coming tonight. She can't make it. Sorry."

I stared blankly at her for a moment. Then, excusing myself, I walked out onto the arctic Chicago streets. "AAAAHhhhhhHHH!!!!!" I screamed into the cold, uncaring sky.

A few teenagers heard me and approached. "You 'aight, son?"

"Althea isn't coming tonight!" I blasted at him. "She's not coming tonight!! Don't you get it? I'm never getting this fucking interview! Four cities! Four fucking cities!" I raised my fist at the sky and shook it violently.

"Slow down, son," the kid said. "Dat chore girl? She wit anotha man? Das bitches fo ya. The second you turn yo back …"

"She's not my girl! She's a mirage! A figment! I made it all up! THERE! IS! NO! AL! THE! A! N! HELL!!!!!! She doesn't exist!"

"I don't know what cha'll smokin', but I gots betta shit. Peep it?" asked another kid.

"No! I … I …," I was so fired up I couldn't find a word to say anymore. The only thought I could piece together was that line from *A Christmas Story* after the father's fishnet-legged lamp crashed to the floor. "… NOTAFINGA!!"[4] I screamed at a wall.

"Whateves," said another kid. The group shuffled on to wherever and left me there. I sauntered back inside—beaten.

I sat at the bar and ordered a beer. When Daddy's Girl (a recent export to The Outfit from Sacred City) arrived, I spent most of the evening hauled up at the bar chatting with her about this and that. Shot after shot, I bitched on and on about my failed search for Althea N. Hell. After we left the fundraiser, Terra NüOne (another recent west coast—B.A.D.—export to The Outfit) granted me an interview at the Beat Kitchen, a bar underneath Val's apartment. It was here that I encountered arguably the funniest derbynumber story I ever heard.[5]

Ref Raff convinced Val to come down and join us for a drink. Shortly thereafter, we were back upstairs. I cuddled with

---

[4] Bob Clark, "A Christmas Story," *Metro-Goldwyn-Mayer*, (1983).
[5] See Appendix 12: On Numbers and How I Got Mine.

Val's puppy, Yippie KayYeah, and passed out rather quickly. I woke up suffering from a brutal mix of bad hangover and the realization that I had failed to get the Althea interview. I showered and readied myself to enjoy a Windy City Roller doubleheader later that night.

Manic Tards

A new season meant a new uniform for the Manic Attackers—baby blue and yellow unitards ("manic tards"). That left Val's 2000Great season uniform (a straightjacket one-piece dress) open to me. I told her that I would wear it as fan support for the Attackers during the bout.

I hadn't spoken to anyone about mascoting; I didn't want to show up and invite myself in to WCR's scene. Stupid move. After I arrived, Belle Diablo, Chrissy Fiction, Dayglo Dago, Stegascorus, and several others asked me when I planned on changing. I felt like a dick. My concerns over imposing myself had turned into what I think they took as an insult. It wasn't meant to be that. I still wasn't comfortable with inflicting myself onto leagues; in the process, I might have slighted them. *Can I do anything right?*

The arena looked a few seats shy of sold out. From a spectator's point of view, I could see why. Windy City brought all the best elements to the track: speed, hard hits, glorious skating, and of course, manic tards.

During the Hells Belles and The Fury bout, Eva Dead (The Fury) jammed as an exhibition unto herself. I'd never seen a jammer take off with such velocity at the sound of the whistle. Following her, Belle Diablo cut through the pack like a demon's scepter through sinners' flesh. I don't know how Belle and Eva are towards each other off the track, but they seemed to have a perpetual "unfinished business" with each other on the track.

Remember when Freddy finally fought Jason? That was *Child's Play* compared to the *Massacre* that was Belle and Eva that night.

Up until this point, there wasn't a fan in the stands that wasn't floored by the performance of all four teams. Yet, Manic Attacker Wreck N. Shrew still opted for pleasing the crowd further and started her last jam against Blossom Bruiso twenty feet behind the jammer line. After dancing to Michael Jackson's *Beat It*, she cartwheeled into the jam. The crowd went nuts! I know that as time passes on, the sport itself is nullifying the theatrics, but I must admit that I still enjoy catching these moments every now and then. Final score: Manic Attackers 120, Double Crossers 51.

Not to be outdone by Shrew's dance number, Athena DeCrime of the Hell's Belles boogied down to *December, 1963* as it played through the loudspeakers—Frankie Vali's sweet vocals guided DeCrime into the lead when The Fury and the Hells Belles retook the track to finish their bout. DeCrime racked up the points and then fled the scene.

Although both teams brought more than enough action for the fans to talk about for days to come, there could only be one winner. The Belles took The Fury straight to Hell with a 122 - 80 final score. Outside of major roller derby events, Windy City had the largest crowd I'd ever seen.

While at Bottom's, the bar where Windy City held their after-party, Helsa Wayton, Skaytr, a few others, and I tried (unsuccessfully) to start up a dance-off. But after such an intense doubleheader, it was obvious that everyone was tired. Even the fans—it was exhausting sitting on the edge of our seats for two hours.

Just as the evening started to wind down, I went to use the restroom still dragged as a 2000Great Manic Attacker. A guy at the adjacent urinal told me to use the girls' room. When I asked him why, he said rather bluntly, "Would you like me to beat the reason into you?"

"There's really no need for that. But if you must, there is a small army of girls outside who might not take too kindly to it."

He paused. "Oh, you're with the rollergirls?"

"Dude, look at me. I'm in a dress for Christ's sake."

"My mistake." He zipped his fly and scurried out the door.

Good 'ole Windy City Rollers.

Manic Tards: The Sequel!

I returned to New York early the next morning and stewed for days over my two failures. *Why didn't you bring the goddamn banana suit? Why didn't you just ask Val?!*

And Althea! You just gave up! You could have put in a little more effort! You didn't even try! Fuck ...

Lack of funds found me Amtraking my way back to Chicago that Thursday afternoon in March. It was gonna be cold—*Chicago in March kind of cold.* But I needed to make things right: First, mascot for the Manic Attackers. The last text message I received from Val read: "Call me when you're nearing Chicago. Please tell me you brought your banana outfit!" I smiled. *See, old man?* That still wouldn't be too easy—the size of the crowd from last time had been fishnet-burned onto my mind. Second, as easily guessed, was to finally speak with Althea N. Hell. It had been a bigger pain in the ass than finding a place to bury Jimmy Hoffa. *Althea, I'm getting this damn interview.*

With Chicago hundreds of miles away, I found my seat and tried to sleep. I couldn't get comfortable in the seat. I just kept thinking of the size of WCR's audience.

I stepped off the train in Chicago at 10 o'clock the next morning with both missions vying for space at the forefront of my mind. I had one other very important thing on my mind as well: a Kuma burger. When I arrived at Kuma Corner, Outfitter Suzie Crotchrot greeted me at the door. *Yes*! *The gods have chosen it fit that Ms. Crotchrot put me in touch with Althea.* This she did; I was to call Althea later that night.

After my amazing, delectable, scrumptious, superific, still-the-best-god-damn-hamburger-I've-ever-eaten Kuma burger, I took a quick hour nap at Val's apartment. When I woke up, we parted ways. She went to her usual pre-bout Manics' meeting. Due to my nap, she arrived late.[6] I left for WCR's practice space to help rip up the track, tie the individual pieces onto palates, and load the palates onto a truck. A rather tall fellow, Igor, was assigned to be my lift-and-carry buddy. Once the track was safely inside the large moving truck, I called Althea. She told me to meet her at, of all places, a barbershop. Igor kindly gave me a lift.

Arriving at the salon not twenty minutes later, I walked up a narrow staircase and through a door at the top. Focusing intently on every step, I made my way into the main room fearing that a hit could be called on this banana at any moment. A cloud of smoke hung over the air. In one of the stools was Althea, The Godmother. The head honcho of the family. The *capo di tutti capi*. She sat there all red-eyed looking at me like an empty suit. No one checked to see if I wore a wire, but I trembled as I pulled out my tape recorder and sat beside her. My knees clicked with every question. *Would I ask her too much? Would I wake up in a potato sack at the bottom of Lake Michigan?* So, after several hundred dollars in airfare and miles of highway over and within four different states, I finally present:

---

[6] Sorry, Val.

The Birth of The Vagine Regime

I wanted to get a feel for The Vagine Regime's roots, which sprung from The Chicago Outfit. The Outfit had grown out of the now defunct league The Chi*Town Sirens, which had, itself, loosely grown out of an earlier league, The Wreckin' Rollers. The Sirens had formed one cold winter night in Chairman Meow's apartment. When that league folded, some of the girls went on to join WCR. Those who stayed became The Chicago Outfit.

Whenever I'd asked Chairman about the Sirens his response was, "Yeah, I dunno ... yeah." In roller derby, these things happen. Was the Texas Rollergirls' Great Idea not the outgrowth of overhauling the league, and in its wake, the sport itself?[7] I asked Althea the same question.

"[The Sirens] just didn't work. There are too many reasons why it didn't work, none of which bears repeating. Next question."

I'd touched a nerve. *Fuck*! The Sirens had been off'd, and from the tone in Althea's voice, speaking of the league posthumously was rude. I had disrespected the family. My eyes darted around the room for a gun barrel sticking through a curtain. Not seeing any, I turned off the Sirens and concentrated on undressing The Outfit.

"The Outfit is Chicago's only all-travel roller derby league—we do not hold intra-league bouts, just inter-league ones."

"Why?" *Still scanning the room.*

"We all prefer it that way. Really, for us, Windy City is a huge factor in a good way—they push us to have to work hard. We respect them. We are trying to do something a little

---

[7] See Joulwan (2007).

different and we are as passionate as they are about it; Chicago already has a home team league that rocks the track."

Althea felt that as a hometown league, The Outfit would stay in the closet. "We're working really hard to brand us as a serious league in the roller derby community and in the city of Chicago. With regards to the history of Chicago, The Outfit was the little gang that came out of nowhere and took the city by storm; it seemed that's kinda like us in a way. We're The Outfit, and we're a family, and we're little, and we love it."

"And what's the deal with The Vagine Regime? Everyone told me to talk to you specifically about it. That it grew out of the league overhaul ..."

"When The Sirens dropped the name, every future Outfitter was supposed to come up with a possible name to be submitted and voted on. Someone came up with '312 Beat Down Crew.' Gaygan ... ya know—*Gaygan* ... came up with 'The Vagine Regime.' The 'VR' received several votes, but we ended up being 'The Chicago Outfit.' The Vagine Regime became a joke and was ultimately swept under the rug. Gaygan moved to Sacramento; the idea and the name went with her. She hooked up with Angel City Derby Girl Injure Rogers, who wanted to unite the queers of derby under one flag at RollerCon '07."

"One rainbow flag, I presume?"

"Yeah, Injure and Gaygan decided to make The Vagine Regime a real team."

And thus, the first all queer roller derby team was born.[8]

"One last question: What's that thing you all do with your fingers?"

Althea looked cross-eyed at me.

Poor choice of words. "I mean, what's that symbol thing?"

---

[8] Credit for starting the VR is attributed to many rollergirls the world over. See Switchblade Siouxsie (2008).

"Oh, the Vag symbol? It's a weird finger thing. I don't know ... it looks like this." Althea raised her hand to demonstrate. She just showed it to me without explanation. But it goes something like this: "First you make a peace sign closing all other fingers, then you bring the middle finger over the pointer so that the tip of the pointer is pressed into the tip of the middle, arching the middle so there is a hole between."[9] Instant finger-vagina![10]

Althea continued. "The Vag symbol is now being used across the nation, and that's so fucked up cause it started here but we never get any credit for it. We should cause Chicago is the shit, bitches!" Althea exhaled from the pipe. "So that's how The Vagine Regime started. And that's how the Vag symbol that all you gay and non-gay bitches are using started."[11]

Althea's interview, and The Vagine Regime, reminded me of how different a sport roller derby was from, say, baseball. I was reminded of the uproar by some game-goers at San Diego's Petco Park two years earlier. July 8th had been dubbed "Pride Night" at the stadium (where discounted ticket prices were offered to homosexuals), a night that coincided with a kids floppy cap giveaway. The "insult" was further agitated by having the Gay Men's Chorus harmonize the National Anthem to kick off the 'ole ball game—*heavens no*! And even though the Set Free Ministries development director J.D. Loveland said that he had "no hard feelings with the gays and lesbians, the Padres or anybody," many parents in the stands fumed over the

---

[9] Gaygan, "The Story of the VAG," *Hellarad: Cali's Most Ignaceous Skate Zine*, 2008 Rollercon Edition.
[10] Pun intended.
[11] Bane-ana, *Interview with Althea N. Hell*, March, 2000Fine.

open display of love by two, consenting same–sex adults.[12]

I got to thinking how making love illegal was a sign of the end of all once-great nations. But not Derbylove! And that seemed to be the umbrella that leagues like The VR could skate under. Though it was not the first queer-inclined sports organization to exist (as the "Gay Games" first kicked off in 1982 in San Francisco), roller derby was the first *new* sport to say loudly and clearly that all were welcome to participate. The outrage felt by some people at Petco Park in San Diego would never be tolerated at a bout. The roller derby culture wasn't straight or gay; it was *stray*. I wanted in; Althea told me to ask Injure Rogers—the Matron of Muff—about mascoting for The VR. I said I would and thanked her for the interview.

I could barely sleep when I got back to Val's apartment. But I finally realized the role The VR played in the new derby revolution. Derbylove was what redefined the roller derby *cultural* revolution. This orientation pluralism seemed to be the linchpin of roller derby's *athletic* revolution. These two idiosyncrasies bolstered the sport up from its grass roots below and appeared most manifest in The Vagine Regime. That's why The VR *must* be with us always. *Finally ... finally got that fucking interview ... but now I had to find Injure. The quest hadn't met its end.*

The Serendipitous Synergy of Kelsey and Kat Von D' Stroya

I didn't wake up until late Saturday afternoon. Brad Habit, the Manics' bench coach, picked Val and me up, and we drove to the arena. As the WCR teams took photos, I stretched and

---

[12] Author unnamed, "Parents Plan to Protest 'Gay Pride Night' at San Diego's Petco Park," *California Catholic Daily*, (3 July 2007). Accessed via: Calcatholic.com.

warmed up behind a large black curtain. When I felt nice and nimble, I went to find a bathroom to change in. Fernando, one of WCR's board directors, asked me if I'd like a dressing room to change in. *Really?* I lit up. He led me to a back room and asked if it was adequate. Hell yes it was! But changing in a changing room changed my elation to fear. It reminded me that I was playing in the big leagues. This, after all, was not only a "sports-crazy city" as Val told me but also the birthplace of roller derby. Would the fans welcome a banana? *Only one way to find out.* I emerged decked out in yellow then went back out to the track to find head ref Dr. Vroom and let her know that I knew what I was doing as a mascot. I didn't have to look far. Dr. Vroom skated over to me and said in not so many words, "I know I don't have to explain the rules to you and that you know what you're doing—have a good bout!"

Good 'ole Dr. Vroom.

Despite the warm welcome from the girls and Dr. Vroom's sweet compliment, I still felt intimidated by the multiple dimensions of my charge. During the first half of the Manics/Belles bout, I was much reserved; the crowd was as massive as I had expected, and individuals in the audience couldn't hear a word I said. I tried to elicit rounds of "Man-ics! Man-ics!" from the crowd. Someone in the front row asked me, "What do *sandwiches* have to do with anything?"

It didn't get any easier. When I returned to the Manic's bench area after a few runs, some girl sitting in the stands started to throw peanuts at me. I'd grown accustomed to the "fuck with the mascot" bit and it really didn't annoy me, but some of the peanuts were getting perilously close to the track. I picked them up and told the girl that she was endangering the skaters and asked nicely that she please stop. Ten seconds later, another peanut hit my back. I kept cool and told her that after the bout she could throw whatever she wanted at me, but to please not put the skaters in any unnecessary danger. The asshole persisted. One peanut hobbled just over the outside line and onto the track. To the right of me, Roe de Leon, one of the Windy medics, turned red. She approached the fan and bitched her out. Presumably, the girl lost her appetite; she sunk back into her seat and the peanut projectiles ceased.

Good 'ole Roe de Leon.

I shut down easily. Even with Roe's intervention, the asshole had caused me to fall into self-deprecation. Usually that's what's needed to mascot, but this time it was different. The audience was simply too overwhelming. I barely moved the rest of the period.

My poor mascoting didn't go unnoticed. At halftime, Val approached me and insisted that I amp up the crowd. I explained that everything I shot out bounced off the bulletproof audience. "Well, take it up a notch," she advised. *But how?* All my little gimmicks to get fans to cheer (i.e. "the girls will fire me if you don't cheer" and "Malice will beat me with her chains if you don't scream") didn't work at all. Nonetheless, I had to step up my game in the second half—lest the Manics turn their skates on me.

During the transition from the Manics/Belles first half into the Double Crossers/Fury second half, one guy called me over to his seating area. "It's my friend's birthday, and she wants to meet you."

"I'll do ya one better! Which one is she? What's her name?"

The guy pointed to a girl in the nosebleeds, "Kelsey."

I found Kelsey, knelt before her, and sung an operatic version of "Happy Birthday." She gave me a big hug and said thanks. *Windyfan Derbylove.* Even if Peanut Bitch hated my guts, at least I knew that Kelsey and her friends didn't; that alone would be enough to spark a psychic kick to my ass. I decided to watch the Fury/Crosser bout from the stands. I'd watched bouts from the stands before but never studied how it looked from various angles. *What do the fans see from this vantage point? What can I see from here? What would I want to see from here? Where could I place myself so that I would be visible to Manics fans but not directly in the audience line of sight?* I studied the bout from a fan's perspective—for Kelsey and her friends. *How can I make sure Kelsey, and everyone like her, enjoys this bout?* I also went looking for some mascot houses. As I moved from one seat to another, I saw Kat Von D'stroya from Detroit Derby Girls sitting in the stands by the third turn. Kat and I had a name thing. We had met several times in the past but could never remember each others' monikers. To her, I was "The banana-guy"; to me, she was "Kat V... Somethingorother."

"Kat!" I yelled. "What's my name?"

"Ummm ... Banan ... Banana Mannn ..... Bane-ana! What's mine?"

"Um ... Kat Von D'stroya!"

Finding Kat might prove a good start to finding my mascot houses, as I doubted she held any allegiance to either the Manics or the Belles. After all, her league, Detroit Derby Girls, would meet Windy City Rollers from both teams next week in her home city. For now, a little silliness might coerce her towards the Manics. Between Kat on one end and Kelsey on the other, I might be able to make some magic happen in the middle.

When the Fury/Crossers bout ended, the Manics took their place by the benches. They sat right across the track from where I had seen Kat. I stood beside the Manics and broke out my chatter ring and bullhorn. On the track, Wreck N. Shrew had a sweet jam and I ran over to my little (hopefully) Manic house screaming into my bullhorn, "Where the Manics at?!?!" The section between Kelsey and Kat went nuts and chanted "Man-ics! Man-ics! Man-ics!" in unison with me. I propped myself up onto the security gate and screamed over the fans as loudly as I could; I almost fell over. As I caught myself and reflexively looked to see if anyone noticed (*no, no one just saw me almost break my ass*!), Melissa, a friend of Skaytr's, caught my eye. She went ape-shit and really helped me out by screaming louder than everyone around her. Others in that section, in turn, tried to scream even louder, and before I knew it, the section cheered for the Manics. *Thanks Melissa.*

As for Kat Von D'stroya, either she really liked the Manic Attackers, or out of sheer kindness, screamed for the Manics as well, which caused several in her section to join her. For the rest of the bout, I didn't really bother with anyone else, comfortable as I was in my sweet mascot house. Between Kelsey and Kat Von D'stroya's cheering, I was finally in a good headspace. They had never met each other, Kat and Kelsey, but in a moment of unwitting mascot coalescence, Kat's "derby" and Kelsey's "love" kissed me on both cheeks. The smile on my face in between them made the connection.

An hour later, we were back at Bottoms again. This time around, the dance party rocked. Malice, Wreck N. Shrew, Shocka Conduit, Blossom Bruiso, and a host of others too many to list here made sure of that. Even Val abandoned her post up in the elevated D.J. booth to come down and tear up the floor with us. I had heard a rumor that night that a certain song caused WCR tractician Al Natural to get naked and dance. This is true. Val played Nelly's *It's Getting Hot in Here* for just the occasion, and Al Natural lived the subtitle to that song.

Unfortunately, we bananas are a festive bunch and I woke the next day with an excruciating hangover. The train ride home, too, was equally apocalyptic. But it was worth it. I got to mascot for a WCR home team and had the story about the birth of The VR. But something still felt missing. Where had The VR gone since its nascent days? I realized that getting Althea's take on the origins was nothing more than a good start to a larger story. Injure Rogers would have to supply me with the rest of it. I didn't know when or where I would be able to get in touch with her, but the desire for some of that VR magic was enough to push me forward.

On the train ride, I sat next to a music history professor who taught at the University of Chicago. His name is Jason, and as I transcribed bar napkin thoughts of the bout to my journal, he asked me what I was writing. After I told him of this book, he informed me that his friend had actually been at the WCR bout on Saturday! The encounter made me realize how far this sport had reached in such a short time. To be sure, a year earlier, whenever I mentioned roller derby, I was often met with a confused, "What's roller derby?" And now, there, on a train ride home from Chicago, a gentleman whom I'd never met had not only heard of roller derby but had a friend who was a fan. It would seem that after decades of vamping and revamping the sport into a cultural-athletic revolution, it was in Chicago that roller derby had finally come home.

XIII

C<small>OALITION OF THE</small> R<small>OLLING</small>

> *This is so exciting ...*
> *I can't think of a thing to say*
> *... and I'm an announcer!!*
> M<small>ISS</small> S<small>AVAGE</small> C<small>AT</small>

Just let it out, old man.

My sweaty hands clenched the bag before me. Pressure; so much pressure in my forehead. Edging towards complete muscular shut down. *Get it out before you can no longer hold the bag.* My throat was so dry. But it was the damn water that interrupted my otherwise quiet stomach. The dry heaves were tiny convulsions; preludes to the purging. I could actually feel my skin growing paler. Death itself was a welcome holiday. Sitting in coach for four hours is good preparation for eternity in a coffin.

I'm coming, Slice!

Rumors of a budding European roller derby community just past German-ation left me with little option other than traveling to Europe and seeing the first petals myself. I contacted Slice Andice and asked her if I could finally make good on my promise to mascot for London Roller Girls during Europe's first derby event in history: Roll Britannia. She green-lighted me!

I also had another mission: WFTDA's *Five on Five Magazine* didn't have anyone going to Roll Britannia to cover the event. I contacted Rocky Mountain Roller Girls skater Assaultin' Pepa (who handled submissions for *Five on Five*), and I was sent on my first journalistic assignment.

I walked into Heathrow International Airport in England and sat down in the empty waiting area just as the sun smiled at me. *Go'way, fucker*! I had taken the red-eye flight with the silly and whimsical notion that I'd just sleep on the plane ... or spend nearly eight hours trying to find Jesus before ending my own life.

For reasons that can only be described as ridiculous, airport seats have immovable arm rests—even though the designers and manufacturers know perfectly well that we tired travelers would rather lay down than rest our elbows! So from seat to floor, I sprawled out. When I awoke about two hours later, some people had collected around me, waiting for their next flight to wherever. I got up and bought a cup of coffee. I found the Tube to London and headed to Earl's Court, where Roll Britannia would commence. I was still out of it, and the movement of the Tube didn't help. I needed to make myself laugh before I delved into being just another cranky prick (not-so) fresh off an airplane.

'Bollocks'! I yelled.

A lady sitting across from me put her newspaper down and stared at me intently for a moment. 'Bloody Americans ...', she mumbled and returned to her newspaper.

'Just practicing', I smiled.

A man got up from his seat and approached me. 'You mad'?

'No, I'm a banana'.

He pulled a badge out from under his shirt. 'S'plain'.

Was he a bobby? An off-duty Tube conductor? I didn't want to find out. 'I'm here for Roll Britannia. Europe's first ever roller derby tournament. I'm just a little out of it from the flight. Sorry'!—I pointed to my chest—'Stupid American'!

He sighed. What could he say to that? He left me.

Ah, Europeans ... works every time.

Earl's Court was walking distance from my train stop. I asked a security guard where, in that vast building, Roll Britannia was held. He pointed to an escalator that wasn't running. I walked up the stairs, excited to join the Roll Britannia brigade. Instead, I entered a big empty room. *Uhhh, where the fuck is everyone? Is this the right venue? The right city? The right country?*

Even as I sipped my coffee, my eyes started to close again. Since no one was about anyway, I decided (and was somewhat urged on by natural forces) to sack out again. I stuffed my banana costume into my Chicago Outfit hoodie and stretched out on the concrete floor. I rubbed my hands over the hard ground. *Roll Britannia ...* Soon I was off to sleep.

Sometime later, I felt a punting against my rib. I sat up immediately. The janitor stopped kicking my side. 'Sorry mate, didin' know 'fewer deadur no'. Can I help you'?

'I'm here for Roll Britannia'.

The janitor didn't know to what I referred and walkie-talkied his boss, who in turn contacted Misha Naccomplished, one of the chief organizers of the tournament. She would be arriving at Earl's Court at 4 o' clock. I looked up at the giant clock above the entrance. 1 o' clock. The janitor left, and I fell asleep again.

I woke a few hours later and reached for my now cold coffee. I went to the bathroom, washed my face, and brushed the coffee-stank off my teeth and breath. When I walked back to where I had set up camp, a girl walked in. Misha was sweet and thanked me for coming. Soon, Ballistic Whistle, LRG Head Ref, arrived; the three of us began measuring out and laying the tracks for Europe's first roller derby tournament. The floor was choppy in some areas and looked like waves from a sea-storm frozen in place. To combat this, we cut up pieces of cardboard and duct-taped them over the more compromised areas. Furthermore, due to the size and shape of the bout space, one of our two tracks had a large support beam in its center.

Slowly but surely, LRG skaters, refs, and support-staffers joined our ranks. I was introduced to Danny and Erin No Bra, my weekend hosts. From there we all trekked to the recreation center where LRG practiced. To my pleasant surprise, Gothamites Ginger Snap and Hambone were there. We exchanged hellos, and Snap told me that Johnny Zebra (whose name would be pronounced 'Zebra' with the short 'e' all weekend long) and Philly/Charm City ref Miss Trial were also in tow. Further, Rat City bout photographer, Axle Adams, and *Blood and Thunder Magazine* founder, Black Dahlia, would be shooting the event. After watching the practice, Danny and I retired to his flat for some pizza, beers, and a good night's sleep.

I woke to a beautiful morning and took the Tube to Camden-Town, a hardcore/punk enclave that reminded me of the East Village back in the early 90s. I had been practicing juggling for some time (and scored several impromptu lessons from Rat City announcer Randy Pan in different US cities) but used fruits like lemons and oranges instead of balls. They had a good weight to them but would sooner or later spoil. Or I would drop them too many times, turning them into little balls of goo. I remember realizing, as I watched another tangerine splatter on the floor, a simple truth: *juggling takes balls.* Most American kids are programmed to believe that England is a romantic place of knights, and princesses, and dragons, and Merlin, and magic, and minstrels (and somewhere juggling fits into all that). I am no exception. I needed to buy my first real juggling balls in merry 'ole London. On the corner of a crowded street, not far from The Stables (an outlet center), was the appropriately named 'Odd Balls'. Set in rows of containers towards the back of the store were an array of juggling balls of various colors and sizes. I found three balls that were of comparable size to small oranges. From there, I met up with many of the refs for some pints and the ref meeting at the London Pub.

In the Mix

That Saturday morning, as I walked through the parking lot of Earl's Court, I saw lines of people dressed like super heroes, witches, and 'treckies'. I ran up to a witch.
'Wow! You guys really go nuts for roller derby out here'!
'What's roller derby'?
Earl's Court is comprised of two large buildings, one of which housed Roll Britannia that weekend; the other hosted a comic book convention. Some of the comic convention folks were interested in roller derby, and my first job that Saturday morning involved giving a group of Ghostbusters a tour of Roll Britannia. I walked into Earl's Court with Peter Venkman, Ray Stantz, Egon Spengler, and Winston Zeddemore, and saw a sight a million miles from what I first saw as I lay on the bare concrete floor two days earlier. Rollergirls from all across Europe had convened in London to test their abilities, hearts, and endurance on the track. I used tour-guiding the Ghostbusters as a way to acquaint myself with the teams. The first merch table we stopped by belonged to the Royal Rebel Rollers (RRR).
I opened my Roll Britannia program to the RRR page. 'The first stop on our tour is the "super-pimped version of Captain

Planet"[1], Royal Rebel Rollers. Like several other competitors this weekend, the RRR is a mix team of Windsor's Royal Windsor Rollergirls, Bedford's Rebellion Rollergirls, and Middlesbrough's Middlebrough Milk Rollers. Inky Minx is one of the Royal Rebel Rollers' star players. She and the rest of the rough and rambunctious Royal Rebel Rollers will skate against Edinburgh Scotland's Auld Reekie Roller Girls travel team the …' I glanced back at the program, frantically skipping to the correct page '… "Twisted Thistles"'.

By and by, the Ghostbusters went back to their convention, and I wandered back and forth between the two tracks, taking notes for *Five on Five*. Over by track one, I lost myself in a bunch of screaming fans dressed in green and black. Their chants of 'Auld Reekie, yer su foin'! Yer so foin' ya blow my mind! Auld Reekie! [clap clap] Auld Reekie! [clap clap]', echoed throughout the hall.

I only watched for a short time, as I had to be over by track two for my first bout: London Roller Girls vs. Stuttgart Valley Rollergirlz. I happily anticipated mascoting my first Euro-bout, but was all the while hoping that Stuttgart had brought a mascot (or maybe two?!). The bout started and I looked around the room but saw no one in any kind of costume. I was happily surprised by the amount of fan support Stuttgart brought. One of their fans even did his best to make up for the lack of mascots. During one particular jam, a Stuttgart fan with long dread locks chased after me. The crowd roared, egging us on—a derby mascot's dream!

London had a steadily mounting lead, and by the end, the differential was staggering. LRG jammer Ninjette skated like a freshly woken dragon after eons of slumber—once roused

---

[1] Author Unnamed, "Royal Rebel Rollers," *Roll Britannia: Official Programme* (2009), p. 27.

nothing—nothing—stopped her; her blockers made sure of it, and unleashed a mediaeval wrath upon the Stuttgarters. Yet during the entire bout, I never once saw a Stuttgarter lose her cool or snap at a teammate. After the bout, I caught up with Stuttgart captain Dolly BustHer, one of Stuttgart's more formidable skaters. I was curious as to what methods the girls employed to remain so calm in the face of such a considerable defeat. Meditation? Marijuana? The answer was surprising, to say the least.[2]

TEA Time

'Ow! What the fuck'?!
Fuzzilla didn't say anything, just hit me again.
'Wha?! What the fuck did I do'?
What I had done was ask if I could mascot for mixed Team East Angrier (TEA) in its bout against Stuttgart Valley Rollergirlz. Fuzzilla must be a Stuttgarter who thought that I had something against her league. I didn't. It was really just a coincidence that I happened to be mascoting against Stuttgart twice in one day! When Fuzzilla tired herself out, I discovered that she wasn't from Stuttgart and wasn't mad at me at all! She was, in fact, from TEA. She was giving me my initiation, in answer to my query. After her beat down, I became (for a short while) 'Bane-Angrier', changing my number '1 Bunch' to '1 Punch'.

After the LRG bout, I had been speaking with London Roller Girls blocker Bête Noir. It was she who first told me of the 'Golden Underdog Unicorn Team'.

'Golden Underdog Unicorn Team'? I was enthralled.
'Yeah! Best boutfits at Roll Britannia'!

---

[2] See Appendix 13: Trials and Times of Stuttgart Valley.

Team East Angrier was a fusion of two leagues: Romsey Town Rollerbillies and Brawlin' Angeles Roller Girls. Decked out in gold and neon-colors, large gold jewelry, and a Tank Girl attitude, TEA had quite the origins tale to tell. Apparently, the cartoon heroine She-Ra visited the Rollerbillies and hooked them up with the Brawlin' Angels. As many of the girls hadn't skated before, they were urged to don 'leopard print spandex [to] add some serious super powers'.[3] I don't normally believe roller derby team 'bios' but this team's story seemed plausible to me.

TEA was the artistic side of roller derby taken to eleven. It was like England's answer to Montréal's New Skidz on the Block, The VR, and Team Dance Party all rolled into one. I couldn't resist; I asked if I could mascot TEA's bout against Stuttgart Valley Rollergirlz.

Stuttgart wanted revenge for the loss against London. They also had that dred-locked Superfan dude for me to go to battle against. Some TEA girls told me that they were intimidated by the size of the crowds—many of them didn't have much skating experience, and some were skating for the first time. Stuttgart quickly took the lead and held it throughout the bout. But all good skating comes from the heart, and Team East Angrier had plenty of that! At one point, TEA blocker Hermaphrodite smashed a Stuttgarter right into their fan's stronghold, breaking down the wall! I went ballistic, grabbed Auld Reekie announcer Miss Savage Cat, and waltzed around the track with her. Back out on the frontlines, another TEA blocker, Munchin Mong, executed some of the most brutal backwards whips I'd ever seen. When she was called to the box, I complemented her on them.

'Damn. Those Stuttgarters are rough'!

---

[3] Op cit., p. 31.

'It's cool', replied Mong. 'I love the learning experience'.

After the bout, I went to get my Roll Britannia program. That was where I kept my field notes of the bouts for the *Five on Five Magazine* article. It was missing! I ran around Earl's Court trying to find it. No one had seen it anywhere. *What the fuck am I going to do? Assaultin' Pepa was counting on me*! I was saved by the conscientiousness of two heroes: Pat the Butcher and Char Char Gabore stopped a janitor just as he was going to throw my program in the trash, saving my article for *Five on Five*. Char Char handed me the program. 'My notes'! I grasped it in my arms with merriment! I held it close to my heart and spun around joyfully like a total nitwit. Earl's Court came alive with the sound of music!

Good 'ole Pat the Butcher and Char Char Gabore.

Later that night, I was back in Camden-Town meeting Misha Naccomplished, Bette Noir, Raw Heidi, Nuke Leah, Axle Adams, and several others for drinks. Over brews, Axle told us how hard it was sometimes for bout photographers to capture such high-speed moments on film. 'Refs and other officials yell at you to get out of the way', Axle said.

I was taken aback. 'Really? Cause it's always the photographers yelling at me to move'.

'Ha! That's cause we're being told to move'! It's a jungle for us out there, too'.

Maybe bout photographers and mascots had more in common than I thought. We were both vying for a better position to do our respective jobs along sideline trenches at noisy and confusing bouts; and we were both trying to make roller derby all it can be. I also admired Axle's zeal for the Pants Off Dance Off. 'I bought special underwear for the Pants Off Dance Off [at Northwest Knockdown]', he told us. 'I wanted to wear something ridiculously colored! So people would say, "Holy shit! That fat dude's got Pants Off Dance Off down"'!

From a derby cultural perspective, we were kindred spirits.

And what about Danny No Bra? A confirmed bout photographer, Mr. No Bra had hosted me that weekend. And what can I say? I liked the guy. And Bagel Hot from Toronto—he'd always been cool to me. And what about that dude from Charm City? Craig Lammes!—he was always chill towards me. It was in that moment that I realized I got so keyed up at bouts making sure that I never got in a rollergirl or ref's way that, here and there, I might have forgotten to consider the bout photographers. *Sweet shit! I was doing the same thing to them! Well, not anymore!* We all need to work together for our sport. A track divided is not skateable!

So, bout photographers ... truce?

Five on Fire

The next morning at Earl's Court, London Roller Girls gave me a small rectangular piece of brown cardboard that read 'Poop'.[4] 'Everyone will get the joke', Slice Andice assured me. But I felt that the sign was missing something. I flipped it over and wrote on the reverse side, 'Free Hugs from Bane-ana'. Black Dahlia suggested I tally up my 'hug score' with slashes on the bottom. I did and within twenty minutes, I had received nineteen. I stopped counting after that.

After a morning of running from track to track to cover Roll Britannia for *Five on Five*, I suited up to mascot for London Brawling against the IRN Bruisers, Scotland's other represented league that weekend. When I stepped onto the elevator to go from the lobby to the bout space, it was filled

---

[4] The league's website features a dancing banana holding up a 'poop' sign.

with IRN Bruisers. On the ride up, these Wilma Wallaces' screamed for blood. I heard that Team Awesome skaters Trish the Dish and Ivanna S. Pankin had flown out to Scotland to help the IRN Bruisers. The Bruisers were ravenous indeed but lacked the bout experience of London. The score was another blowout, with London leading eighty-four to the IRN's zero for most of the first half. But it didn't matter; the Bruisers played with such gusto that the two Team Awesomers' influence was clearly visible in them—not only with the skates on their feet but also the fire running through the veins of the five girls on the track each jam.

It was a tough bout to mascot. The fans had taken to the underdogs, and the IRN Bruisers received an overwhelming amount of fan support. For the first time in my mascoting career, it was the crowd *vs.* me. I didn't know what to do. The situation had never come up before. I was saved when I located a LRG mascot house just around the third turn. I grabbed the LRG flag, ran over to the London fans, and shook my ass for them a la Flo Shizzle from back home.

The Bruisers had almost won me over too; they returned to the track smiling every time a la Flo Shizzle ... *from* ... *back* ... *home*. They sent Jaci Dodger to the jammer line. At the whistle, she detonated. From yellow to orange to combustion-blue, Jaci moved like fire through a kerosene factory—not just setting off the fuses of those around her, but engulfing them too, making them a part of her, and growing with each pass of a screaming fan. When the wind of the pack moved, she danced right along with it, feeding without remorse, swallowing all she could. She wanted those points. The crowd was on its collective feet by then and cheered her along the track. But London knew all too well how to handle such uprisings on the outskirts of the empire. By halftime, the score was 130 to 6 in favor of London. The Bruisers fought like warriors for every one of those points.

But the London girls had one thing on their side that catapulted them into the lead every time—experience.

But it was an experience that they shared with others that weekend. The whole point of Roll Britannia was, as Misha told me after the bout, to 'foster league interaction and start a European derby community'. And that is exactly what they did that weekend. The European leagues proved that they had what was needed for long-term success—*heart*. And that is where it all begins, as it is the heart that pumps the wellsprings of zeal and fertilizes any culture—sports or otherwise. The European leagues had imported the Derbylove along with the sport, ensuring its success. Or, as Ginger Snap put it while announcing the Leeds Roller Dolls/Berlin Bombshell bout later that day: 'There is so much Derbylove in this room, I could vomit'!

Maybe half an hour later, a man approached me. It was the guy who told me not to yell on the Tube on my way out of Heathrow—he had come to Roll Britannia! He was pretty lit up, and I answered his zillion questions about our bizarre little roller derby. I would start to answer one question when something would happen on the track, and he'd ask me about that instead. I couldn't keep up with him. Between questions (or whenever a big hit would send a rollergirl flying through the air) he would ask me the same question I've answered a million times in the affirmative: Is it real?

'Sa foin' spoort ya got 'er', he said between sips of beer.

'Aye 'tis', I responded in my best English accent.

London After Midnight

The walk to the after-party was a party in itself. A long parade of derbyists laughed, danced, and shouted down the winding streets of London. I looked around for landmarks to find my way back to Earl's Court; that was the only way I knew how to get back to Danny and Erin's flat. I passed a place called The Scotch Shop and wrote down to make a left there as a signpost for getting back to the right bus to the No Bras'. As I charted streets and storefronts, I heard a commotion behind me. LRG announcer Big Cat Merv picked up a large traffic grater and carried it with him down the streets, knocking over garbage cans.

The troupe arrived at the after-party bar, and Merv put the grater down on the sidewalk. The bar was very fancy and reminded me of the kind of place yuppies frequent in Uptown Manhattan. We danced much, celebrating not just London's victories on the track but Roll Britannia's victory for roller derby as a whole. Misha Naccomplished was in exceptionally high spirits: 'I can't believe we pulled it off! All we wanted to do was spread the word that roller derby is here! Look at this! Look at everyone who showed up'! *Misha Naccomplished, mission accomplished*! There was still one last challenge of the weekend—the dance off. I had to represent the after-party character of the American roller derby leagues. Eventually, the dance-off narrowed down to just two challengers: a European rollergirl and me. After we both silently decided that neither was going to give an inch, we called it a draw.

But then something weird happened. As we danced, she kept asking me when the 'banana' would leave and the 'man' would arrive. I didn't know to what she referred, but she said it again: 'You're still being the banana; where's the man'? I didn't know what to say. I thought I was being the 'man'. It dawned on me that although some derbyfolk developed roller derby 'personas', I never had.[5] *This was me.*

When the after-party waned, I wandered the streets of London all night, taking bus after bus until I finally arrived in

---

[5] See Joulwan (2007), pgs. 125-50; Mabe (2007), pgs. 74-5.

West Dulwich—the No Bras' neighborhood. I slept for about three hours, said my good-byes, and left for the airport.

I arrived at Heathrow on time, and as I took a seat in the waiting area, I felt a tap on my shoulder. 'Twas Black Dahlia; she had a ticket for the same flight. As we walked on the plane, Dahlia asked if I had any water so she could take an airsickness pill. I didn't. But fear not! As we walked through first class, we passed an aisle seat that had a bottle sitting within arm's reach. I pretended to drop my Chicago Outfit hoodie on the first class seat, and picked it up with the water bottle firmly entrenched in my palm, concealing it under the hoodie. My last act in England was Robin Hooding a bottle of water from first class for Dahlia. When we found our seats, I gave her the bottle. Our seats were right across the aisle from each other. After asking the person sitting next to her to switch seats, we ended up sitting together on the plane. My stomach was a cauldron spoiled organ stew. I didn't want my flight home to be a repeat of my flight to England. I humbly asked Black Dahlia if she wouldn't mind holding my hand during take-off. She looked at me crossly for a moment, but when she saw the desperation in my face, obliged. Eyes closed, and with deep breaths, I took her hand. As the plane left the ground, she squeezed it tightly to let me know she was there.

Good 'ole Black Dahlia.

Once in the air, I'm usually okay. *It's those damn takeoffs and landings.* For the first three hours or so we talked about this and that. She told me jokingly that she didn't like bananas. I replied that I couldn't stand rollergirls. Before trudging our separate paths into Sleepland, I leaned over to her.

'Can I tell you a secret'? I asked.

'Sure'.

'I don't like bananas either'.

XIV

The Banana Monologues

> *That's a happy face that looks through that banana costume.*
> HEIM

    I hadn't intended on a *Lord of the Rings: Return of the King* ending, but I am being urged on by forces beyond myself to retell this last anecdote. My journey to interview Althea N. Hell only ricocheted off into a new mission—find Injure Rogers and see where The VR had gone. I realized that the only way I was going to get this story was to mascot for The VR itself. Over the course of my travels, I had befriended several Regimists. *Maybe I should find a way to ask?*
    But as I looked over my abysmal funds, it became apparent that I couldn't possibly make it to RollerCon, where The Vagine Regime would once again face off against the Caulk Suckers. Luck smiled upon me when my favorite aunt (c'mon, we all got one!) used her frequent flyer miles to pay for my plane ticket. I decided to make my case for mascoting as directly as I could—I made up a mascot résumé. Also, in the event that The VR gave me the go-ahead, I spent the Sunday night before my flight with my friend Michelle making posters in case God's Warrior (or someone like him) wanted a show down. The first poster depicts a banana flipping a person off with the words: "Another Fruit

for Gay Rights." We colored *"For," "gay,"* and *"rights"* red, white, and blue. The second, and perhaps more controversial poster, portrayed The VR's logo—two hand-holding female silhouettes, like the kind one sees on "Women's Bathroom" signs—with a slight addition: Jesus, positioned between the two girls, holds their hands. Above the three heads are the words: "Jesus Loves Queers." If any psalm-slamming, Bible-banging misogynist-fascists God's Warriors wanted another Holy War on Fremont Street, I would be ready with more than jokes this time.

Three weeks after landing back in New York from London, I was once again enjoying a vomit-riddled ride to Vegas. Several hours later, I was at the Maui Bar enjoying Wednesday night drinks with those friends who I only see a handful of times a year, one of whom was Terra NüOne. I handed her my mascot résumé.

"It really comes down to what Injure says. You know I want you to mascot for us, but she has the final word."

Twenty-four hours of merry RollerCon hell later and I still hadn't heard anything. Sure, it had only been a day, but I felt like a kid on Christmas Eve drooling over gifts that cannot be opened. That night, as had become custom in so many cities in America, I was parked on a barstool for 3 am drinks with Daddy's Girl talking about life, love, and roller derby (the essentials). I didn't say anything for awhile, as I didn't want to come off as a pain in the ass. Eventually, one too many shots of top shelf got on top of me, and (to top off the night) I toppled into a topsy-turvy pile of drunken mess.

Deej could see it in my eyes. "What's wrong?"

With words worthy of Wordsworth, I unloaded my long journey to get to the heart of what revolutionized roller derby—the redefinition of the female athlete and how The Vagine Regime played a crucial role in that new paradigm.

"Fuck it!" she said. "I'm making an executive decision! You're mascoting for us tomorrow and that's final. If anyone has a problem, they can take it up with me!"

Good 'ole Daddy's Girl.

Elated, I bought us another round and maybe an hour later, went back to my room. I climbed into bed but couldn't sleep. I reached for my bag, pulled out my juggling balls, and warmed up. I then tried to think of more Bible-related jokes. I did push-ups and sit-ups. The next day, I would be ready.

How the Vagine Regime Saved the 'Nanner

The shuttle to Fremont Street couldn't come quickly enough the following afternoon. However, despite Deej's "executive decision," I still wanted Injure's approval out of respect. When I arrived at Fremont Street, I set about finding her. I saw a Vagine Regime stronghold around the fourth and first turns. Injure was amongst them. I got down on one knee, buried my face in my forearm, and declared my vow to go to battle for The Vagine Regime.

"Of course you can!" she smiled. She handed me a bunch of small handheld rainbow flags and asked that I hand them out to VR fans in the crowd during the bout.

Hand to forehead, I saluted her. "Oh, hell yeah! I'm at your disposal. Now stick those Caulk Suckers where the sun don't shine!"

I slipped into my peel and did some warm up cartwheels and juggles. I then took two of the small flags and taped them to the ends of my pompoms; I could now go back and forth between black and yellow plastic strings and rainbow flags with a flip of my fingers. I unfurled my "Another Fruit for Gay Rights" and "Jesus Loves Queers" signs. Out on the track, a Regimist was already waving The VR ensign—a rainbow flag with VR silhouette-girls holding hands. I went up to join her and she started to "boo" me.

"Why are you booing me?"

"Get with the Caulk Suckers, Banana Man! Boooooooo!!!"

"Um ... I'm on your side," I said and held up my Jesus Loves Queers sign. "I made these in case protesters show up."

The girl looked at the sign. "Oh ... Well let's go get 'em Banana Man!"

When the bout began, I mascoted it from on high. I ran around the track screaming "Where's the queers at?! Where's the queers at?!" with the VR flag-holder following close behind me. Together we handed out the flags to VR-crazed fans. When anyone booed, I laughed it off. One prick, an "I'm straight and I want everyone to know it" tough-guy, threw small crumbled pieces of paper at me. "Fag!" he yelled.

"Fag?" I asked. "You're the guy cheering for sucking cock!"

I pointed at him and yelled, "This guy likes to suck cock!!" I grabbed my Jesus sign and flashed it in front of his face. "Don't worry," I yelled, "Jesus loves you!" The guy actually surrendered; and I moved on.

During one jam in particular, as Swede Hurt rounded the track as lead jammer, I jumped up waving my pompoms and must have gotten stuck in the ether. Floating vast distances above the lovely desert, I was caught up in a whirlwind that slowly shaped itself into droves of skaters flowing towards a sunset. Swede seemed to move with these apparitions, formed as they were by the loud cheering and clapping coming from The VR fan stronghold. A feeling that was at once brilliant and moving amassed a peace that I never knew before—*so what if I didn't have a derby persona? So what if I couldn't separate the "banana" from the "man?"* It's not like The Vagine Regime skaters out on the track had developed a "queer" persona to skate under that they abandoned once the bout ended; they just were who they were, and the sport was open to it. I was just who I was; finally sufficient unto myself. And so, the story has now been told of how The Vagine Regime saved the 'Nanner.

Good 'ole Vagine Regime.

Unfortunately, I didn't get to cheer The VR to victory on the track. But I can't help but feel that the presence of The VR on the athletic cultural stage meant a different victory—for equality. As VR skaters slaughter-graphed my Jesus Loves Queers poster, I was handed a copy of *Hellarad: Cali's Most Ignacious Zine.* The cover featured a baby picture of B.A D. skater Mötley Crüz; under her portrait, the zine's tagline read: "Sometimes Derby Isn't About Skating."

Indeed.

The next day I saw Injure Rogers at the Vagine merch booth at the Las Vegas Sports Center, where other bouts were held. I wanted to buy one of the silhouette girl shirts to commemorate one of my happiest mascoting moments since I started derby roughly four years earlier.

"We don't have any here to sell. Those shirts are actually for VR team members only," said Injure.

"Oh. No doubt. Well, thanks again for everything."

"...But I guess that means we'll have to get you one."

"Wow! Really?" I wanted to tell her that she made my day, my week, my month, and my year. She gave me an address to email for the shirt. "Just tell them I said it's cool. Hope you'll come out again for us in the future."

I assured her I would and walked to the bouting area to watch Team Artistic shake its brushes and strokes at Team Speed. There was still some great roller derby action to be had; and hopefully many more adventures waiting patiently for me on the other side of the purple ...

XV

ON THE CUSP OF REVOLUTION

*I've got stories that you'll never believe.
And I know it. I wear it, I wear it on my sleeve.*[1]
TIM ARMSTRONG

*There is that common connection of roller derby ...
we all touched the ground-wire and connected
through roller derby and it's a beautiful
connection. We're all here enjoying
each others' company, making
lifelong friends, having a
good fucking time.*
JIM "KOOL AID" JONES

Roller derby continues to grow. Indeed, little pockets of roller derby leagues are sprouting in every city and town of our country. I have since visited many of these leagues, spoken with, passed bowls to, cracked beers with, danced alongside, cried with, bandaged, held hair back as puke met toilet, and hugged many of the people involved.

I cannot say what derbyfolk *are*, but I can certainly say what derbyfolk *aren't*. They are not a generic image or facsimile of what a rollergirl ought to look and act like. Roller

---

[1] Rancid, "Old Friend," ... *And Out Come the Wolves*, (Epitaph, 1995).

derby as a culture has no material identifications (like clothing styles, movie and music tastes, past experiences) but rather exists as an idea hanging in the atmosphere.

Derbygirls come from a variety of athletic backgrounds. After falling in love with roller derby, Jayne Manslaughter of Denver's Rocky Mountain Roller Girls had to come to terms with this new development in her life: "*Me, an athlete? Me, playing a team sport?* [italics in original]"[2] Others, like Gotham Girls skating extraordinaire Suzy Hotrod, played sports growing up but "didn't like the jock crowd."[3] Texas Rollergirls blocker, Desi Cration, played "the non-traditional girl sports" like ice hockey and rugby.[4] Moko Loko from Texas's Lonestar Rollergirls played softball, swam, and played track and field. Her take on them: "They were all so super serious, so alike. Roller derby ... is a weird-ass sport. I mean, a really weird ass sport—it's very 'out there,' and a lot of fun. It's not normal at all."[5] For the seasoned sports players of roller derby, there is something that separates roller derby from sports they have played in the past. Puffy Bangs from New York's Hudson Valley Horrors told me the major difference between roller derby and other sports she's played:

> For people who love sports, what's really amazing about roller derby is that an individual player is playing both offense and defense simultaneously. And her team is doing the same thing, so you have this dynamic interaction; an individual player playing offense and defense under the larger umbrella of her own team playing that same

---
[2] Mabe, 16.
[3] Wachter, p. 20.
[4] Bane-ana, *Interview with Desi Cration*, 3, August, 2000Great.
[5] Bane-ana, *Interview with Moko Loko*, 30, July 2000Great.

dynamic. You have these two integrated circles—for lack of a better term—on an individual level and on a team level as well. ... If your offense is lacking your teammates are picking up for it, if your defense is lacking, your teammates are picking up for it and it's happening in this really fluid way. ... I know of no sport where an individual player and a team have that sort of energy.

And Puffy Bangs would know. She told me she's "a diehard football fan, basketball fan—[she has] played softball, played everything, individual sports to team oriented sports and nothing," she assured me, "has the same edge as derby."[6]

After all is said and done, after the last jam of the bout has ended, the last piece of track tape has been ripped up, the last slaughter-graph has been signed, the last picture taken, the last dance has been danced, the last shot from last call for those who have lasted the night has been drunk, the question still remains: athleticism aside, what is it about the roller derby culture that makes it such an interesting sport? Why is it, as Injure Rogers commented, the "sport that non-sport people are drawn to play?"[7] To me, it is the inability to prune derbyfolk into a single Scissorhandsian shrub that defines the revolution as so unique and special. And it is this uniqueness that bled into the sport and redefined the female athlete. There is no dress code, there is no piss test, resumes are unnecessary, hair length and color don't matter, past doesn't really matter, and criminal records are sometimes proudly displayed like rink rash scars. There is no derby girl image; not anymore. Derbygirls represent something deeper than that—a culture that transcends looks and lifestyles,

---

[6] Bane-ana, *Interview with Puffy Bangs*, 1 August, 2000Great.
[7] Switchblade Siouxsie (2008).

and taps every Western lifestyle that I am aware of. Germany's Stuttgart Valley Rollergirl Dolly BustHer commented, "The girls that are in our league listen to all sorts of music, and [have] all sorts of jobs, and all different backgrounds, and consists of girls from all walks of life, and when we combine these things it creates this wonderful community that it is amazing to be a part of."[8]

Georgia W. Tush from Montréal Roller Derby believes the answer to what makes roller derby different is actually simpler than that: "It's our cocky strides and musky odors! ... Basically, we stink and there are weirdoes everywhere."[9]

Touché Ms. Tush.

I had gone across America and then halfway across the world in search of a climactic ending only to realize that there will not be one. Roller derby is on the rise. Each year, more teams form and senior teams move to bigger and bigger venues. Not everyone gets along all the time, or sometimes at all. However, there is an undeniable mist that hangs over the sport that I feel most derbyfolk recognize. That "mist" has a name, too. I have heard many different derbyists call it many different things, but the most oft-heard expression has been dubbed "Derbylove." Derbylove, although not always as potent as it could be, can be seen in a multitude of ways: In what other sport do players wake up the next day hung over because they got married to another player from another team from another city during a crazy weekend at RollerCon? How often do players from all over the world get together and crash on each others' couches only to knock each others' teeth out the next day? What other sport has as much pizzazz as beautiful and strong athletic women on roller skates? In what other sport is

---

[8] Bane-ana, *Interview with Dolly BustHer*, 19, July, 2000Fine.
[9] Bane-ana, *Interview with Georgia W. Tush*, 30, July, 2000Great.

the idea of a "don't ask, don't tell policy" laughable? In what other sport is everybody invited to participate regardless of size (small or large) and age? Texas' Great Idea consisted of a single founding rule: that the leagues should be skater owned and operated. This meant that every girl in every team had a voice. The mellifluous tone echoed from that collective voice shaped a clever, dynamic, and colorful sport.

Roller derby is still in its infancy phase. Whether it survives remains to be seen. How it evolves is equally questionable. Even if it turns out that we are all just part of something that passes right on by—a footnote in sports history—I will nonetheless look back on my days as a roller derby mascot as one of the most fulfilling and rewarding times of my life. I will know that for a brief moment in an infinite time, we all stood for something that was special beyond our explanations—beyond us as individuals. We stood for unity, for art, for athleticism. For love.

Many years from now, I will tell stories to young women and men over a chessboard in Tompkins Square Park of all night drives across the country, broken bones, wardrobe malfunctions, sisterhoods, and how I witnessed a cultural evolutionary jump in how future generations will define female athleticism—and how my heart still thumps to the sound of skates spilling love all over the track. How the inspiration and kindness of strangers didn't just help me become a better mascot, but a better person as well. How there was always a home for me when home was thousands of miles away. How I was able to, if even for a brief moment, walk in a waking dream. I will tell them that I was fortunate enough to watch the growth of the first female dominated sport. They might still speak of other sports like "women's basketball" or "softball," and I will remind them that no one said "women's derby." Quite the contrary; we say "basketball" and "men's derby." I do not know where roller derby is heading. No one does. But if future generations can feel how I've felt and see what I've seen, then Texas' modern roller derby revolution will be with us for years to come.

Beneath the sport, under the shitty calls, the prolonged timeouts, below the travels and frustration, and frustrations of travel, there is a camaraderie that cannot be denied. Through trial and error, tribulation and good fortune, rejoice and rejection, I hope that this book has portrayed the sport's cultural underpinnings in an uncontaminated way.

So, I raise my glass in a toast. To The Long Island Roller Rebels, for everything. To the Philly Roller Girls, for Northwest Knockdown, and your tireless efforts to bring us ECDX. To Charm City Roller Girls, for adopting a lost banana. To London Roller Girls and Team East Angrier, 'twas a wonderful Coalition, indeed. To The Vagine Regime, I am proud to be your mascot. To Texas Rollergirls, for the beautiful sport they ignited. And, of course, to all the skaters, refs, NSOs, announcers, mascots, and volunteers the world over who make roller derby the exciting and spectacular sport that it is; I can only say "thank you" for bringing this into all of our lives.

My deepest gratitude for the open doors, free beers, burritos, conversations over long drives, couches, hotel room floors, late night after-parties, early morning practices, unbelievable bout moments, broken bones, dried tears, rink rash, fishnet burn, abundant laughter, spilled blood, and (most importantly) that indomitable torch carried by you all every time you roll onto that track. See ya on the sidelines; I'll be that guy dressed like a banana screaming his heart out for you all.

To the derby. To the love.

Good 'ole Derbylove.

APPENDICES

APPENDIX 1: *USEFUL TERMINOLOGY*

For those unfamiliar with roller derby, I offer this quick paragraph that gives a *very* basic concept of the sport for clarity, as these terms will be used throughout the narrative. The sport is infinitely more multifaceted than the simple definition I present. For the most updated (and thorough) rule set visit: www.wftda.com/rules. Also useful are the roller derby books found in the selected bibliography.

In roller derby, five girls from both teams assemble on an oval-esque track. Each team is comprised of four *blockers* and one *jammer*. Of the four blockers on each team, one is a *pivot*. The pivot does her best to control the speed of the pack and is known as the "general" on the track. The two jammers start their position thirty feet behind the blockers. At the first whistle, the pack of blockers—herein called *the pack*—takes off. When the last blocker has crossed the pivot line, the second whistle sounds for the jammers. The jammer that first makes it through the pack (without fouling) is awarded *"lead jammer"* status. This initial pass also changes the status of the blockers—they are now points to the opposing jammer. Each time she passes a blocker she receives a point. The blockers, somewhat schizophrenically, play offense and defense simultaneously—at once assisting their jammer, while trying to stop the opposing jammer.

The jams are timed at two minutes each. However, this can be shortened if a girl takes lead jammer first and (for strategic reasons) calls the jam immediately. If both girls pass through the pack but incur penalties along the way, neither jammer is eligible for lead jammer, and the jam will go for the full two minutes.

APPENDIX 2: *DON'T SHOW ME THE MONEY*

What must be stressed throughout all this is that these girls do not get paid. When they are carted off on gurneys, they may not have insurance to land on.

I remember my first trips to different states. Upon my return, friends, coworkers, and strangers alike would ask me how much money I made mascoting.

"Nothing," I'd reply.

"*Nothing?*" they'd repeat. Then they'd ask about the skaters. Mascots aren't that important, but surely the girls bring home a sizable wad of cash?

"Nothing," I'd say again.

"*Nothing?*"

Nothing. In fact, we often returned home in debt. Trish the Dish, one of the founders of Las Vegas' Sin City Rollergirls (currently skating with San Diego Derby Dolls), said that one surefire way to tell if someone is involved in derby is simple: "She's broke. Physically *and* financially." They take a beating on the track, pay out of pocket (sometimes) for their injuries, recover, and are back on the track as soon as possible. "I played a lot of sports in my day, and this one takes the hardest toll on your body," said Trish.

> We keep breaking ourselves and coming back, and breaking ourselves and coming back, and we don't have insurance, we don't make any money so you have to love it to spend this much time, [and] this much energy. Even if you don't travel around the country, to

still spend three or four nights a week for two or three hours away from your family, practicing; or if you're doing bout production, or setting up sponsors, or doing the leg work that it takes to run a league, you're a volunteer. Volunteers don't do things because they hate it; they do things because they want to make a difference.[1]

And yet, derbygirls can't stay away from the sport. Captain Morgan's doctor, for example, told her to take three months off from derby because of a sprained wrist—that lasted about a week. Crash Hartless from Omaha Roller Girls told me that derby "saved and ruined my life. It gave me access to a lot of people I wouldn't have met otherwise, so I have a bond with a bunch of bad ass chicks. At the same time it ruined my knees for the rest of my life. But I don't regret it."[2]

Val Capone sustained more injuries than anyone I'd ever met (roller derby or otherwise) both on and off the track. One of her earliest injuries occurred in a—and I never thought I'd see these words printed together—"Spice Girls related incident," in which she broke a rib. She tore the cartilage in her left knee twice, separated one shoulder, dislocated the other, snapped her clavicle, popped both her thumbs and her jaw (causing hearing loss in her right ear), nearly suffered a broken shoulder blade courtesy of yours truly, and was even hit by a hardware truck. She told me proudly that she is "uninsurable for life."[3] To me, she was more. She represented that unconquerable spirit that makes up roller derby. Indeed, roller derby would not have gotten as far as it has come without her efforts, and the efforts

---

[1] Bane-ana, *Interview with Trish the Dish*, 16, November, 2000Great.
[2] Bane-ana, *Interview with Crash Hartless*, 1, August, 2000Great.
[3] Bane-ana, *Interview with Val Capone*, 30, January, 2000Fine.

of countless others like her. All working *pro bono*. All working for the love of derby.

APPENDIX 3: *AFTER-PARTIES*

> *If rockstars were athletes,*
> *they'd be rollergirls.*
> SWAN

Most victories (and loses) in any sporting event have after-parties. How many of those after-parties are *competitive* though? In roller derby, the after-party is a cutthroat extension of rivalries not left on the track. The objective is simple: party harder than the other team (or league if after travel bouts). Drink more, dance longer, do whatever it takes! Still be buying rounds, singing off-key karaoke, and dancing after the other team has passed out.

Admittedly, it's harder to win the after-party if you are the league that did the traveling. After all, you might have driven all day (or night, or both!), helped set up, played a bout, and still came out to crack a few brews. You do, however, get a second chance at the after-after-party to prove your celebratory-worth.[4] The Roller Rebels, no matter where in the country, always won. "That's okay, we'll just kill them at the after-party," remarked a confident Captain Morgan religiously whenever we lost a bout. Ref Joey Jager, much like Jenna Fiesta, lived up to his name and bought rounds regardless of who won. In one instance I remember particularly well, Montréal's New Skids on the Block handed the Roller Rebels our collective asses in August of 08. Jager dumped $400 on the bar so that both leagues, as a whole,

---

[4] In my travels, I have yet to see a league throw a better after-after-party than Texas Rollergirls.

could do a roller derby "solidarity shot." We lined up around the island-shaped outdoor bar and on the count of "bottoms up," maybe fifty of us bottoms upped. "Who wants another one?" yelled Jager. This time only a handful received shots; Joey dried the bar out of the very drink from which he derives his name.

Moreover, the victorious team usually bought rounds for the losing team several times during the night. "Shouldn't the loser have to buy the rounds?" I asked trying to understand this custom.

Butterscotch explained:

> At the after-party, it's important to show the league that there are no hard feelings; that you left it on the track—that you are happy with where you are. Party with them; let them buy you a drink, cause they feel bad for you—hell that's great! As the loser, you get more beer than the winner does. The winner buys you a beer. They know they kicked your fuckin ass, ya know ... you earned it.[5]

Sometimes the after-party lasts all weekend—before, during, and after the bout(s). Enter Team Dance Party. Spawned at Roller Con 2000Great, Team Dance Party was the brainchild of Sacred City Derby Girl Cash Money, who birthed the team the first night of RollerCon 2000Great. Team Dance Party is just something that spontaneously happens. Whether at RollerCon, or really anywhere that Cash Money is, you just drop what you are doing and start dancing. At RollerCon, Team Dance Party danced in between the endless aisles of slot machines, on top of the bars, in the elevators, everywhere! After the hotel security told Team Dance Party a hundred or so times

---

[5] Bane-ana, *Interview with Butterscotch Cripple*, 1, January, 2007.

to "take it somewhere else," they finally relinquished their demands and just let Team Dance Party do what it does best.

As early as 2006, some new kids on the block have stormed the after-party scene—Montréal Roller Derby's New Skids on the Block. Decked out in early 90s neon boutfits, the New Skids not only brought an eye-catching team but also impromptu synchronized dancing numbers to the after-parties. You've seen those movies: Kids at a prom suddenly take command of the dance floor and move like they are all members of a dance troupe. Avid after-party dominators, The New Skids have a routine that puts any would-be opponents to shame.

APPENDIX 4: *COMMUNITY BASED, COMMUNITY BASTE*

Charity used to begin at home. These days, it begins on the track. For example, Virginia's Dominion Derby Girls have used proceeds from bouts to donate to charities as diverse as Help and Emergency Response (HER), which aids victims of domestic violence, and the Special Olympics in 2007; Dominion raised $8,100 for the latter cause.[6]

Roller derby leagues have donated to various youth services, rape victim centers, animal shelters, adopt-a-highway programs, child abuse/neglect centers, art fairs, the American Red Cross, Planned Parenthood, political awareness organizations, breast cancer research foundations, Leukemia research groups, mental health associations, kids' scholarship programs, AIDS walks, environmental groups, and various local families that need financial help in one form or another. *Impressive.* What's even more impressive: all the above

---

[6] Kip Wadlow, "Pulling Double Duty: Coast Guard and Skater, Tsunami Tsue," *Blood and Thunder: All-Girl Roller Derby*, Vol. 1, 5 (Fall 2007), p.19-20.

mentioned groups have received support and donations from just *one* league. Madison Wisconsin's Mad Rollin' Dolls has contributed time, effort, and money to roughly seventy community organizations since its inception in 2004![7]

There is also the charity that occurs under the radar. Countless examples abound, but my favorite occurred at RollerCon 2000Fine. The story comes to me from Kalamazoo Derby Darlin captain, Terrorhawk. While on the shuttle heading back from a bout at the Las Vegas Sports Center to the hotel at RollerCon, derbyists saw a lady struggling with her children and crying as she pushed a stroller down the street. Derbyfolk ordered the bus driver to stop and pick up the lady; they paid her fare. The lady didn't speak English, but one of the girls (whose name I do not know) luckily spoke Spanish and acted as translator. Apparently, this unfortunate lady's husband had just dumped her off with the children and disappeared from their lives. *Prick.* She had no source of income and no way of getting to family and friends that lived outside of the Vegas city limits. The derbyfolk on the bus took up a collection—not chump change mind you—"I gave fifty dollars alone," Terrorhawk told me. By the time the bus dropped her and her children off at a bus stop, she had over $300 dollars in her pocket and a smile on her face.

But derbyists don't just limit their labors to charities and the less-fortunate. They also donate their time to smaller up-and-coming leagues. Though this is not always the case, it more often than not is. Although I realize the inherent limitations on speaking only from my own experiences, I have seen more established leagues help than hinder the up-and-comers. For example, the Gotham Girls supported the Long Island Roller Rebels from the beginning. Gotham wrote one of the WFTDA

---

[7] Accessed via: http://madrollindolls.com/charity. (3/13/2009).

letters of reference, Gotham blocker Ginger Snap would sometimes come and announce the bouts, Gotham refs Hambone and Flying Squirrel would officiate, and so on. There was also the Hudson Valley Horrors, who would loan the Roller Rebels skaters when necessary, the Jersey Leagues (Garden State and Jersey Shore), and now the Yonkers based league, Suburbia. With all these leagues, there was always a bout to go to, a couch to sleep on, and a person to crack a beer with. It was wonderful. I asked Trish the Dish of San Diego Derby Dolls why that was:

> It's a community type thing, a sisterhood. All the beginning leagues started because a girl knew someone in another city and got her to start a league, and then that girl knew someone else and got her to start a league. It's very community-based. It's like another family. I think it all comes back to the beginning, when we played interleague [bouts]. It was because I knew someone in another city and I said, 'Start a league and let's play!' Then you want to introduce your friends to their friends, and I think that's where it started and stuck. A lot of the traditions that we carry on are from the beginning.[8]

This was evident from early on. In 2006, after Arizona Roller Derby hosted the world's first flat track roller derby tournament, Dust Devil, they sent a portion of the net profits to the participating leagues for travel expenses.[9]

On an individual level, derbyists try to also take care of their own. At RollerCon 2000Great, I came across a donation

---

[8] Op. Cit.
[9] Joulwan (2007), pg. 266.

basket for one Tequila Mockingbird, a Windy City Roller who suffered a terrible back injury. We had never met, this Tequila and I; in fact, I'd never even heard of her. Yet, I felt compelled to sink a twenty into the bin in hopes that even my modest donation might get her back on her feet sooner.[10]

With all of these fund raisers, charitable donations, and acts of kindness towards each other (and strangers), rollergirls provide the "baste" not only to the sport but also to their towns, cities, and other communities as well.

APPENDIX 5: *CHALLENGE TEAMS*

Challenge teams only exist while the girls are out on the track giving each other hell. Girls from a multitude of leagues play side by side even if they have never so much as met in passing before. These makeshift teams, I feel, display the diversity of derbyists. Challenge bouts are usually played at derby conventions like the East Coast Derby Extravaganza (hosted in Philadelphia), RollerCon (hosted in Las Vegas), and other events. Challenge bouts pit two teams of opposites against each other: *Vegetarians* vs. *Meat Eaters*; *Caulk Suckers* vs. *The Vagine Regime*; *Team Party* vs. *Team Straight Edge*; *Tattoos* vs. *No Tattoos*; *Team Awesome* vs. *Team Douche Bag*; *I'd Rather be Swimming* vs. *I'd Rather be Golfing*; *Team Loudmouth vs. Team Quiet; Gingers vs. The World,* and so on.

If one wants to make the argument that the girls can then be reduced into these narrow feeds, think again! A Meat Eater might just as easily skate alongside a Vegetarian on the Tattoos Team in another bout against a fellow Meat Eater without tattoos.

---

[10] For the full story, see: Barbee and Cohen (2010), pgs. 122-25.

Appendix 6: *On Guys in Roller Derby*

Although roller derby (post revolution) is still in its infancy phase, some ideas have seemingly already gone to pass. One such idea is that which suggests, "Women only! No guys." What I've learned, and experienced firsthand, is that most rollergirls (at least the ones I've met) have no problem with guys being involved in the sport. Some, in fact, like and encourage it; as one reporter wrote in her *Top Ten Things Learned at RollerCon 2009*, "Guys + roller skates = wow."[11]

I don't speak for all guys in derby, but I can honestly say that the ones I've known in this sport are sincere in their dedication to their leagues and roller derby in general. Like the girls, the guys volunteer their time, help out at bouts, donate money, and perform a host of other tasks in hopes of making this sport all it can be. Their leagues, so far as I can see, appreciate and enjoy their support.

I've heard once or twice that guys are only involved with roller derby to get laid. Well, no. When and if it does happen, I can assure you that the encounter was probably more an unforeseen byproduct of derby life. Sure, it happens, but to say that that's the *only* reason guys like roller derby is, for lack of a more suitable word, stupid. Moko Loko told me at RollerCon '0Great, "Whether or not they are trying to get laid isn't really important to us as long as they put in their hours. And you can't blame them; we got some amazing females!"[12]

Another girl at RollerCon ▮▮▮ said that guys only want the sex and not the sport. Mind you, she said this as her girlfriend

---

[11] Tiki Timebomb, "RollerCon 2008, Las Vegas," *Blood and Thunder: Women's Roller Derby Magazine*, (Fall 2008) Issue 9, p. 27.
[12] Op. Cit.

nibbled on her ear. I asked her if her girlfriend played roller derby.

"Whatdayathink?" she cracked. "I *only* date derbygirls."

"Why?" I asked.

"Because their fucking hot and bad ass."

'Nuff said.

"Guys in derby don't bother me," Dolly Rocket told me over beers in Baltimore. "I mean, the guys who aren't serious about the sport won't be able to keep up with the hectic pace of it all. Plus, we know—the girls I mean—we're not fucking stupid; we can tell if someone isn't serious about the sport and is just a douchebag trying to get laid. Those guys don't last very long. They'll be out the door rather quickly."[13] Rocket's sentiments were later echoed (in a somewhat less Dolly Rocket way) by Kasey Bomber and Axels of Evil and should serve as a caveat to any guys thinking about joining a derby league: "Don't think for a minute that you can pop into a few practices, snag some tail, and get out with your reputation, your pride, and your safety intact."[14]

But there is also the inverse. ▮▮▮ told me that she knew several girls who played roller derby in hopes of attracting a guy. When I asked her if she thought that that was an insincere motive to play a sport, she said, "It's just like back in high school—the girls wanted that cute, rough, built guy that played football. Now, with derby, she wants that rough, cute football guy to drool over her. I mean, it isn't insincere, people are going to want to hook up and fuck no matter what sport they play—roller derby or any other one. I don't mean to sound mean, but that's a stupid question. Next."[15]

---

[13] Bane-ana, *Interview with Dolly Rocket*, 27, July, 2000Great.
[14] Barbee and Cohen (2010), p. 172.
[15] Bane-ana, *Interview with* ▮▮▮, 1, August, 2000Great.

Are *some* guys only involved with roller derby in hopes of nocturnal action? Probably. Are *all* guys involved for that reason? Yeah, right. Trust me; there are easier ways to feed one's delights than laying sport court, lifting amplifiers, sweeping tracks, and getting yelled at by refs and fans. I only mention all this in hopes that the whole notion of "no guys allowed" and "guys are only involved with roller derby to get laid" can finally be put to rest.

APPENDIX 7: *WITH THIS RING, I BLED THEE*

With Texas' Great Idea came the advent of the derbywife—a roller derby relationship between two or more derbyfolk. The derbywife tradition started on a long desert highway between Los Angeles and Phoenix back in November 2003. The Los Angeles Derby Dolls embarked on a road trip to Arizona to check out Arizona Roller Derby's (AZRD) first bout. Kasey Bomber and Evil E, both of the L.A Derby Dolls, instigated "the world's most ill-advised drinking contest," smothering each other with "I love you mans" and coining the term "derby wife" during that drive. Two years later at RollerCon aught 5, AZRD skater Deez Nutz procured her ten-year-old's Elvis costume and presided over the marriages on the steps of the Double Down Saloon in Vegas. Literally hundreds showed up for the event, waiting to marry the derby love(s) of their lives.[16]

The role of the derbywife can be summed up in the vows that are exchanged at the Double Down Saloon in Vegas during RollerCon. Said vows, written by L.A. Derby Doll Kasey Bomber, are as follows:

---

[16] Kasey Bomber, "The Origins of the Derby Wife." Accessed via: http://rollercon.net/register/derby-wedding-registration/

Dearly Beloved, Ladies, and Broads ...

We're gathered here tonight to honor the union of these skaters in the grand tradition of derby marriage.

As you look to your future wife or wives next to you, know that you are entering a very unique and special union.

It is one based not only on friendship, honor and loyalty, but also on tricking each other into ill-advised late night situations, reminding each other to always recall with relish your best takedown if ever you doubt your skill before a bout, and advising you to always select the "daily digest" option on all twenty nine of your yahoo groups.

The skater or skaters beside you may not be your best friends, but they have that special quality that no other in roller derby possesses for you. They are the ones who "complete you." They are also the ones who will not hesitate to punch you in the mouth if you ever said that out loud. So, without any further ado, please join hands and repeat after me:

> I, state your name, take you, state your partner's name, to be my derby wife.
>
> I promise to ride with you in the ambulance if you ever break your arm in a bout even if the EMTs are all ugly.

I will always tell you when your pads start to smell like a goat's ass in summer.

I vow to always take pictures up your skirt at after-parties, and to hold your hair back while you puke on the sidewalk.

I will always be your first phone call from jail, even if I was the one who got you there in the first place.

I will always remind you about the amazing last bout if non-skating matters start to annoy you.

I promise to be your biggest fan. Unless we face off in a bout, then I promise to hit you harder than anyone else on the team, because I'd never insult you by going easy.

So, with the power vested in me by Ivanna S. Pankin, the Double Down Saloon, and Col. Tom Parker, I now pronounce you derby wives.
You may kiss the brides.[17]

What this all means can be summed up by Moko Loko's experience at RollerCon in 2000Great. She had told her (soon-to-be) derbywife that she couldn't attend RollerCon that year. "[Her derbywife] was like, 'Just get in the van! Get in the van and go!' We're getting married!" The band that played at RollerCon that year was part of their league. "So we're in [the band's] van, cause our girls are always looking out for us. They

---

[17] Reprinted with permission. Thanks, Kasey!

got us a room, and you know, I'm really not too worried about it. We look out for each other. I don't know how other leagues are, but we look out for each other. And now, on Saturday, I'm getting married."[18]

Sometimes whole leagues got married. At RollerCon '07, Sacred City Derby Girls proposed to B.ay A.rea D.erby becoming the first inter-married leagues in roller derby history. Sacred City supplied the wedding cake. Wrestlers and waltzers tore up the suite's makeshift dance floor. Sometimes (okay, more often than not) colliding into each other, knocking over furniture, breaking lamps, and spilling drinks all over the carpet.[19]

APPENDIX 8: *THE SAGA OF TEAM DOUCHEBAG*

There was still one more challenge bout that weekend between Team Awesome and Team DoucheBag. Lexie Deluxe, Philly Roller Girl and Team Awesome founder, first put the team together to play Team N.E.R.D (New England Roller Derby). According to my sources, Team DoucheBag originated with the No-Cal ladies. They wanted to challenge the "Mighty, [A]ll-American" team, Team Awesome. Since every team has a skater who "does whatever it takes to win, whether that means breaking the rules, making fun of their competitors' mamas, or giving the opposing teams' fans or refs a big 'Fuck You!',"someone thought it a good idea to band all these douchebags together to take on the Awesomes.[20] Comprised mostly of

---

[18] Op. Cit.
[19] For the full report, see: Mathemortician, "RollerCon 2007: A Whole Lotta Hella," in *Hellarad* (2008), p. 22-4. Additional information was supplied to me by Brawllen Angel from B.ay A.rea D.erby (9, August, 2000Great).
[20] Taxi Scab, "Team Profile: Team DoucheBag," in *Hellarad: Cali's Most Ignaceous Skate 'Zine*, V. 1,1, RollerCon 2008, p. 16.

Sacred City Derby Girls, B.A.D girls, Angel City, San Diego, Rat City, Arizona Renegades, and some other randoms tossed in, this team was set to scrimmage Team Awesome during the halftime of the Salt City/Duke City bout.

This did not necessarily work out as planned. Most of the members of Team DoucheBag did not purchase RollerCon passes as a protest to the high price of the pass ... or because they were broke ... or all of the above ... or whatever. As such, the pass-less members of Team DoucheBag were not permitted to scrimmage against Team Awesome. This left a problem for the Salt City/Duke City halftime entertainment, as Team Awesome now had no one to play against. Luckily, some very brave ladies stepped up at the last minute and formed a new team, which was to be called "Team Awesomer." Now Team Awesome was not very pleased with this particular name, and in turn, forbade their new opponents to use it. After much debate and many suggestions, a new team name was created: Team Awe ... Fuck it.

The name would have to suffice. After a brief clobbering by Duke City and Salt City, Team Awesome and Team Awe-Fuck it faced off. Since this bout was open to all spectators, RollerCon pass or not, Team DoucheBag, "in the spirit of true douchebaggery," made an appearance.[21] They came to cheer for the team that stepped up and against the team they rightfully should have been playing. Armed with cocktails and dressed in black and gold, with derby aliases printed on their shirts and foam fingers that flipped off, well, themselves since they accidentally printed the finger backwards, Team DoucheBag was quite a sight to behold. They screamed, and they yelled, and they cheered for Team Awe-Fuck it at the top of their lungs. Unfortunately, in the end, their team lost to the original Justice

---

[21] Ibid, p. 16.

League on wheels, Team Awesome. We cannot say at this time whether Team Awesome would have tasted their first defeat at the hands of Team DoucheBag ... we'll never know. But I doubt that's not the last the derby world has seen of Team DoucheBag.[22]

APPENDIX 9: *THE HEAVY KIDS*

Besides the aggression of the girls, the rowdiness of the after-parties, the camaraderie, and the overall demeanor of what some might call a "stereotypical" rollergirl, there is a problem in this country that roller derby might be able to help fix. Texas Rollergirl announcer, Jim "Kool Aid" Jones and I have had several talks in several states about this next point. Namely, the positive self-image that roller derby bestows on the more or less marginalized of our populace: the heavy kids.

During one of our talks, Kool Aid turned serious—almost solemn. "This country puts a lot of negative spin on big kids," he said. His daughter had recently joined the Derby Brats, a league for adolescent girls to vent their pubescent aggressions. At one of the Derby Brat practices, Kool Aid watched these rollergirls-to-be skate with the intensity we have all seen in other derby leagues. One of the girls, he added, was noticeably heavier than the others. "The kid was about 13 or 14 and was basically 'the heavy kid.'" I listened intently as the paternal essence that is Jimmy Kool Aid Jones flowed out of him. "It hit me as I watched the Derby Brats how positive an influence this sport will have on her. Without derby, she might feel negative about her size ... she might not feel accepted. With derby in her life, she'll be strong and agile ... like once she sees the big girls

---

[22] Special thanks to Cherrylicious for recounting this bizarre tale to an inebriated banana.

that kick a lot of ass, she will know she has a place to be amazing! Even years from now, when she quits derby, she will have had this positive influence for the rest of her life."[23]

Fellow Texan 8 Track agrees. As she tells it, "[My daughters] get living, breathing proof that you do not have to fit any image you see in a magazine to be smart, sexy, or athletic."[24]

Derbygirls are roll models. No matter what her age, size, or past is, a girl need only "strive to her highest potential and try not to be an asshole" according to Rose City High Roller, Layla Smackdown.[25]

APPENDIX 10: *PEANUT BUTTER SILLY TIME*!

This wasn't the first time such a request had been made to me by a roller derby ref, skater, fan, or otherwise. I have been asked to do the Peanut Butter Jelly Dance so many times, and in so many different states; the first request occurred in 2006 when a derbyfan asked me to do it. I didn't know to what he referred.

"C'mon man! You're the banana! Peanut butter jelly time, peanut butter jelly time!" He sang the song, emphasizing the lyrics by dancing.

"Don't follow." I said. Again, he sang the song and asked if I ever watched the cartoon.

"I've heard of the show, but don't really watch it."

"It's hilarious!" he said. "YouTube it."

I went home, and the idea fell into the recesses of my subconscious mind. I forgot to YouTube the video; the opportunity was almost completely lost until The Roller Rebels

---

[23] Bane-ana, *Interview with Jim "Kool Aid" Jones*, 3, August, 2000Great.
[24] Quoted in Mabe (2007), p. 64-5.
[25] Bane-ana, *Interview with Layla Smackdown*, 15, November, 2000Great.

next bout. Somewhere between telling jokes, waving pompoms, and running around with Furious George, another fan asked me to do the Peanut Butter and Jelly Dance.

"Oh, shit man. I'm sorry. Someone told me to watch it and I plumb forgot," I responded.

In a brazen display of innovation, the guy did the dance and sang the song for me. I even joked to him saying, "You know, some other guy asked me to do that too."

"Oh, dude! You *gotta* do the Peanut Butter and Jelly Dance! You're the Banana Man! Know what? You can probably YouTube it!"

I told him that I would watch the video and learn the necessary words and gyrations.

I never did.

And so it went. Every bout, after-party, or fundraiser that I attended someone (or someones) asked me to perform the P B and J Dance. The encounter always ended with the petitioner showing me the dance, and me saying that I'd learn it. I never learned it. Since the requests never ceased, I thought it might be funny to turn the tables on all the P B and J lobbyists. I decided to see how many people *I* could trick into doing it.

Nearly six years after receiving my first request to get funky with the P B and J Dance, I still haven't seen it—not once. I have furthermore withheld ever watching the show—lest I unwittingly catch the episode that the dance appears in. However, I can lay claim to one thing that in its own little way might be a world record: I'm fairly sure that I have tricked more people into performing the Peanut Butter and Jelly Dance and in turn, have actually seen it more times than anyone else in America—quite probably the world. To quote the starring bunny from a cartoon I do watch: "Ain't I a stinker?"[26]

---

[26] Bugs Bunny, "Duck Amuck," *Warner Bros. Cartoons*, (1953).

APPENDIX 11: OF SPORTS AND SPECTACLES

> *I knew that the sport would be rich subject matter for my next paintings.*[27]
> CORY OBERDORFER

I know I might catch some crap for this from some derbyfolk, but here goes. Yes, in my humble view, roller derby is a spectacle. It's a sport, no doubt, but a spectacle as well. It is, by definition and sight, "unusual, notable, [and] entertaining."[28] Some derbyists think recognizing that the game of roller derby is a spectacle cheapens the sport itself. I offer a different interpretation. From the derbynames, the fabulous "boutfits," the sticker covered helmets, the halftime shows, Tank from Ohio Roller Girls wearing a wrestler's mask when he announces, and Justice Feelgood Marshall reffing in a dress ... hell, just go to RollerCon for an hour and you will see that roller derby is both a sport and a spectacle. My question is: *Why is that a bad thing*? Is it not all these accoutrements that makes the sport not only different from every other sport that ever existed, but also different from every version of roller derby that came before Texas' Great Idea? Find any roller derby flyer from any league from anywhere in the world. What does it look like? Is it unusual? Notable? Entertaining? Have you ever seen a flyer for a sporting event that looks anything like a flyer for a roller derby bout? For myself, I can say with certainty that I have never come across a poster or a flyer for a baseball or football game that portrayed zombified versions of the athletes eating

---

[27] Author Unnamed, "Cory Oberdorfer: Derby Artist," *Five on Five: The Official Magazine of the Women's Flat Track Derby Association (WFTDA)*, (Spring, 2009), Vol. 2, 1, p. 51.
[28] See Webster. Any edition.

the brains of their rivals. I feel that roller derby is simply too visual and artistically inclined to not, by default, be a sport *and* a spectacle. Other derbyfolk recognize this as well. Violet Temper from Philly Roller Girls states that "[t]he inherent nature of the sport is very showy."[29] Puffy Bangs says, "[Derbygirls] bring an individualistic flair to a sport that allows for that sort of freedom of expression that is under an umbrella of athleticism. ... You see a lot in professional sports ... You get certain personalities, certain players get a name and personas that are associated with them, but in roller derby, I think we take that to a whole other level. [Roller derby] allows you to tap into a part of yourself that you may not be allowed to tap into under normal social or professional situations."[30]

And does this all not work in favor of roller derby? An onslaught of dazzling maneuvers executed by extraordinary athletes on wheels coupled with flashy boutfits, and catchy names? I think it does, but this view is certainly not shared by all.

For instance, some leagues have recently debated giving up the derbyname aspect, and some skaters already have. Windy City Roller (WCR, Chicago) Julia Rosenwinkel used to be known on the track as Lucy Furr. Julie changed her name back to the one on her birth certificate because she felt that "playing for real with a fake persona was sending a mixed message." She does admit, though, that derbynames are part and parcel of derby tradition.[31] On the other hand, others like WCR league mate Val Capone feel that "names are part of the fun of derby

---

[29] Quoted in Mabe, p. 73.
[30] Op. Cit.
[31] Julia Rosenwinkel, "What's in a Name?" *Five on Five: The Official Magazine of Women's Flat track Derby Association (WFTDA)*, (Spring 2009), Vol 2, 1, p. 41.

... the bad puns are classic."[32] And Val would know. She hasn't just named several rollergirls such as league mate "Amy Nonamey" but also coined the phrases "grand slam" (she is an avid baseball nut) to indicate when a skater passes all five blockers in the pack and "false start" when a skater takes off before the ref blows the whistle. Colt 45 of Jet City Roller Girls has written that the names are more rooted in history than anything else: "[D]erby names became especially popular in the eighties ... the era where the term 'sports entertainment' was coined. ... Having a derby name is not only fun and exciting for the crowd but also gives the normal, everyday women who play roller derby an opportunity to have an alter ego and a bit of notoriety on the track."[33] Mercy Less from Derby News Network feels that brandishing an athletic "name" goes back further than the 80s and "is a time honored sports tradition," citing Babe Ruth and Ocho Cinco as examples.[34] Still others, like B.ay A.rea D.erby jammer Brawllen Angel, fall somewhere among all schools of thought: "The names don't make you, you make the name. ... If you're a good skater and you make a name for yourself around the nation, people are gonna remember that name, and that's just the way it goes."[35]

Are the names necessary? Of course not; they are simply fun. For example, I've never once met Rat City Rollergirl "Jalapeño Business" but smile at the witty wordplay pressed on the back of her jersey at every derby event I've seen her. The spectacle should never replace the sport, mind you, and I applaud many of the leagues that keep the theatrics down to a minimum and the athletic requirements high.

---

[32] Op. Cit.
[33] Josie "Colt 45" Moody, "Something Old, Something New," *Blood and Thunder: All Girls Roller Derby*, (Fall 08), Issue 9, p. 62-3.
[34] Quoted in Barbee and Cohen (2010), p. 158.
[35] Bane-ana, *Interview with Brawllen Angel*, 9 August, 2000Great.

Until everything that makes roller derby unique is eliminated, than it's kind of hard to say it isn't *partially* a spectacle. To me, these aspects don't delegitimize the sport; they simply decorate it.

So take away the aesthetic of the fliers, the names, the boutfits, the fracas of the after-parties, the wit of the announcers, the halftime shows, take the cat ears off Gotham blocker Hyper Lynx's helmet, remove Ohio Rollergirls announcer Tank's wrestlers mask, wipe off the skull that swallows half the face of Oly Rollers blocker, Rettig to Rumble, stultify the fantastically blinding boutfits of The New Skids on the Block, turn a deaf ear to the pre-bout live music as girls spin right round, baby, right round the track like records spun by DJs pumping the crowd with Iron Maiden, and then yes, I will concede that roller derby is not a spectacle. I will, however, miss seeing Justice Feelgood Marshall ref in a dress.

APPENDIX 12: *ON NUMBERS AND HOW I GOT MINE*

Derbygirls have numbers on the backs of their jerseys and on both biceps during game time (often sharpied on). Like all sports, this is done for the refs' and other officials' sake. But unlike other sports, some numbers are plays off the girl's names. Long Island Roller Rebel Régine Bull's number is "8 seconds." "1492" has colonized itself on the jersey of Carolina jammer extraordinaire, Princess America. Charm City Roller Girl Rosie the Rioter is numbered "100%." There is also Gotham Girls' Cheap Skate: "2 cents."

Some "numbers" are plays off the name without even using numbers. Take Mortician Murphy from River City Rollergirls. Her jersey sports not numbers but letters: "R.I.P." Long Island Roller Rebels blocker Missy Nigma has "OG," which actually stands for a variety of things like "Original Gangster," "Oh God," and "olive garden."

Other numbers have deep meanings to the girls. Butterscotch Cripple's number is 42 because, as she told me, "that's the answer to everything"[36] according to Douglas Adams' *Hitchhiker's Guide to the Galaxy*. Some are downright hilarious! My favorite tale comes from Chicago Outfit/Vagine Regime skater Terra NüOne. She chose "1111" because the number had been mysteriously following her around during her usual day to day activities. Don't believe me? I'll let her explain this one:

> I was seeing 11:11 all the time! I'd look at a clock and it would say '11:11.' And then one day I looked at a clock that had the seconds, and right as I glanced at it, the time read '11:11 with 11 seconds!' There was an OCD thing about it; like if I looked at a clock and it said '11:12,' I'd get really pissed. I would feel like I missed something, but if I saw '11:11' I'd feel like everything's okay … [laughs] … I'm such a psycho! I'm okay now, but there was a time in my life that it was almost a problem. I'd be at work and checking my phone because I was looking for that time. I don't do that anymore, but every now and then I'll see 11:11 and be like, 'Oh! There it is!' But I no longer feel like my life is falling apart if I miss it. Actually, I kinda like 11:12 now![37]

I finally adopted a number I liked three years after I joined the Roller Rebels at the 2000Great Eastern Regionals "Derby in

---

[36] Op. Cit.
[37] Bane-ana, *Interview with Terra NüOne*, 31, January, 2000Fine.

Dairyland" tournament hosted by the Mad Rollin' Dolls. Up until then, I had an arbitrary number assigned to me. So arbitrary in fact that I don't even know what that number was. I wanted my number to be "13" based off one of comedian Mitch Hedberg's jokes. The late-great comic once remarked that the letter "B" looks like a "scrunched together '13'."[38] I planned to ask the shirt printer if he could put the two individual numbers close together as a makeshift "B." Unfortunately, Heart Breakher from The Roller Rebels already had a "13" making the number off-limits for me. But then I had what I thought was a better idea anyway. And, unlike the "13" Mitch Hedberg line, the number would be wholly my own joke. I figured that since the numbers are on the jerseys so that referees could more easily identify penalties (and I don't receive penalties), I settled on "No Use for a Number" after the early 90s punk band "No Use for a Name."

When I told the number to Mr. Pistol, Charm City's bench coach, he said, "I figured your number would be 'a bunch' or something."

I loved it! But wanting a number in the equation, I said back, "What about '1 bunch'?"

"Perfect!" he replied.

APPENDIX 13: *TRIALS AND TIMES OF STUTTGART VALLEY*

Stuttgart technically formed a month or so before London Rollergirls, but the latter is referred to as the 'big sister league' of European roller derby. Via an interview with Stuttgart Valley's star skater Dolly BustHer, I found out some of the obstacles that her league had to endure before they could start skating. By Roll Britannia, Stuttgart had only bouted eight

---

[38] Mitch Hedberg, *Mitch All Together* (Nov. 2003).

times. 'Eight times'? I asked. 'But you've been a league for four years'.

The reason for Stuttgart's lag in bouts was purely bureaucratic. Outside of the normal stresses that come with forming a league (like locating a place to skate and finding girls to fill that place), Stuttgart Valley Rollergirlz had to do something that no American team ever had to do—register with the government. Germany has a strict bureaucracy that doesn't allow organizations like a roller derby league to exist without first registering as a *Verein*. To put it <u>very</u> simply, this means that the government recognizes that organization as a non-profit one. The process usually takes a few weeks to finish. The Stuttgart Valley Rollergirlz trudged through a yearlong linguistic battle making sure that all the 't's' were crossed and 'i's' were dotted on the paperwork. 'The wording [of the request] has to be perfect', Dolly BustHer told me. 'We had to 'rephrase this' and 'rephrase that' and our request kept coming back, and every time [we] had to pay, too'!

If I may be allowed one stereotype: rollergirls are persistent. Stuttgart Valley Rollergirlz attests to this. 'In Germany it is different than in America. No one ever heard of roller derby', said BustHer. 'There was no Roller Derby before we created it. Actually, Stuttgart Valley Rollergirlz was the first league in Europe. That's what made it so hard, because we were trying to pull something up and no one knew what the hell we were talking about. So you always had to do a lot of explaining when you were fliering for parties and events. [People asked,] "Roller ball? Where's your ball? What do you do"'?

I guess roller derby is so ingrained in American culture that when I heard about it years earlier, I hadn't *really* first heard about it. I mean, I knew the sport existed; I just hadn't known that it was coming back into public consciousness. In places like

Germany, explaining roller derby to the public was like explaining baseball to Eskimos.

'It's cool now because, like I said, no one had ever heard of roller derby in Germany and we spent so much time explaining it to people, but by now, people actually recognize us on the streets and say, "Oh! Rollergirls! Rollergirls"'! BustHer laughed. 'And we've become well known in the area, and you don't have to do so much explaining any more. They say, "Oh! Roller derby! I heard about it! Cool"! It's become pretty well known in Stuttgart'.[39]

It all made sense. Many of the Stuttgarters were just happy to be playing that weekend; they didn't care if they won or not. After hearing Dolly BustHer speak of the trials Stuttgart Valley Rollergirlz endured just to be able to bout, the girls' calmness in the face of the heavy lose became clear to me. Indeed, that seemed to be the case with many of the girls out there on the tracks. Some of these girls had to trek a few extra miles that no teams on our side of the pond had to. Stuttgart taught me a lesson. Sometimes I got so emotionally invested in watching my team win a bout that I forget that roller derby mascoting has been the best period of my life since potty-training—win or lose.

---

[39] Op. Cit.

Selected Bibliography

Books

Barbee, Jennifer "Kasey Bomber," and Alex "Axles of Evil" Cohen. *Down and Derby: The Insider's Guide to Roller Derby*. (New York: Soft Skull Press, 2010).

Gladwell, Malcolm. *The Tipping Point: How Little Things Can Make a Big Difference*. (NewYork: Little, Brown and Company, 2002).

Joulwan, Melissa "Melicious." *Roller Girl: Totally True Tales From the Track*. New York: Simon and Schuster, 2007.

Mabe, Catherine "Jayne Manslaughter." *Roller Derby: The History and All-Girl Revival of the Greatest Sport on Wheels*. Denver: Speck Press, 2007.

Martin, Steve. *Born Standing Up: A Comic's Life*. New York: Scribner, 2007.

MAGA(ZINES) AND PROGRAMS

Author unnamed, "B.ay A.rea D.erby Girls: Short Skirts, Shorter Fuses." *WFTDA Dust Devil '07: Western Regional Tournament Event Program*, (February, 2007).

Author unnamed, "Cory Oberdorfer: Derby Artist," *Five on Five: The Official Magazine of the Women's Flat Track

Derby Association (WFTDA). Volume 2, Issue 1, (Spring, 2009).

Author unnamed, "Parents Plan to Protest 'Gay Pride Night' at San Diego's Petco Park." *California Catholic Daily*, (3 July 2007).

Author unnamed, "Royal Rebel Rollers." *Roll Britannia: Official Programme* (July, 2009).

Author unnamed, "San Francisco ShEvil Dead: From the Cradle to the Grave and Back Again: A History of the ShEvil Dead." *B.ay A.rea D.erby Girls: War on Wheels* (August 2008).

Authored unnamed, "We Are WCR." *Windy City Rollers Season Program* (2009).

Barbee, Jennifer "Kasey Bomber," "The Vagine Regime: Queer Pride and a Raucous Good Time," *Blood and Thunder Magazine*, 12, (Summer, 2009).

———— "L.A. Derby Dolls in Three Acts," *Blood and Thunder: Women's Roller Derby Magazine*, 9, (Fall 2008).

Black, Bobby. "High Rollers." *High Times* (October, 2006).

Crüz, Mötley. "RollerCon 2006: Kind Of Not That Awesome." *Hellarad: Cali's Most Ignaceous Skate 'Zine*. Volume 1.1, (July, 2008).

Drop, Lemon. "San Diego's View on the Bank," *Blood and Thunder Magazine: Women's Roller Derby Magazine*, Issue 9 (2008).

Gaygan, "The Story of the VAG." *Hellarad: Cali's Most Ignaceous Skate Zine.* Volume 1.1 (July, 2008).

Hix, Lisa. "Club Land," *SFGate* (October, 2005).

Kuma's Corner. "Burgers," *Menu* (2008).

La'Vicious, Tricia. "Roller Derby Announcing: How Hard Can It Be?" *Five on Five: The Official Magazine of the Women's Flat Track Derby Association (WFTDA)*, Volume 1, Issue 2, (2008).

Long, Taylor. "Roller Derby League Blows Off Steam." *The Chronicle* (Dec. 15, 2005).

Marshall, Justice F. "2008 Nationals." *Five on Five: The Official Magazine of the Women's Flat Track Derby Association (WFTDA).* Volume 1, Issue 2 (Winter 2008).

Mathemortician. "RollerCon 2007: A Whole Lotta Hella." *Hellarad Cali's Most Ignaceous Skate Zine.* Volume 1.1 (July, 2008).

Moody, Josie "Colt 45." "Something Old, Something New." *Blood and Thunder: All Girls Roller Derby.* Issue 9 (Fall 08).

Pankin, Ivanna S. "History of RollerCon." *RollerCon: Official Information Packet and Desert Survival Guide* (August, 2007).

Philly Roller Girls. "Welcome to the East Coast Derby Extravaganza," *East Coast Derby Extravaganza* (Event Program, March, 2007).

Rosenwinkel, Julia "What's in a Name?" *Five on Five: The Official Magazine of Women's Flat track Derby Association (WFTDA).* Volume 2, 1. (Spring 2009).

Scab, Taxi. "Team Profile: Team DoucheBag." *Hellarad: Cali's Most Ignaceous Skate Zine.* Volume 1.1 (July, 2008).

Timebomb, Tiki. "RollerCon 2008, Las Vegas." *Blood and Thunder: Women's Roller Derby Magazine.* Issue 9 (Fall 2008).

Thomas, Katie. "A Bruising Beginning." *Newsday.* (Jan. 2, 2006).

Wachter, Paul. "You Just Can't Keep The Girls From Jamming." *The New York Times Magazine.* (Feb. 1, 2009).

Wadlow, Kip. "Pulling Double Duty: Coast Guard and Skater, Tsunami Tsue." *Blood and Thunder: All-Girl Roller Derby.* Volume 1, 5 (Fall 2007).

Internet Sources

www.Calcatholic.com

www.derbybrothers.com

www.madrollindolls.com

www.sfgate.com.

www.prostamerika.com/Rollerderby

www.wftda.com

ACKNOWLEDGEMENTS

Many people contributed directly and indirectly to the making of this book. Thank you to Melissa "Melicious" Joulwan, Catherine "Jayne Manslaughter" Mabe, Jennifer "Kasey Bomber" Barbee, and Alex "Axles of Evil" Cohen for their inspiring books and unwitting literary kick to my ass to finish this project. Thank you to Kerry McClain and Nicolas Charest for allowing me to reproduce their photographs as drawings. All the rollergirls and guys the world over that let me interview them, bought me a beer, and offered a couch or a hug. WFTDA for letting me do my thing. Daddy's Girl for 3 am shots in exotic cities and for her "Executive Decision." Roller derby announcers and mascots for warm words and interstate hospitality: Jake Steele, Dirty Marty, Jimmy Valentine, Randy Pan, Jim "Kool Aid" Jones, Miss Treat, Tank, Ozzy Zion, Dirty "Rat Man" Houllahan, Megatron, Pelvis Cosetllo, Dump Truck, Lumber Jill, and Hester - keep it kooky, kids! Leagues I've cheered for: Charm City Roller Girls, The Long Island Roller Rebels, Philly Roller Girls, New Skids on the Block, The Dairyland Dolls, London Roller Girls, Team East Angrier, Bay Area Derby, Texas Rollergirls, Windy City Rollers, and The Vagine Regime. Countless refs the world over for showing me the same consideration I show them. The New York Shock Exchange, for the second wind and new adventures—it is an honor and a privilege to skate beside you all.

Kerr, you're a part of everything that I do; I will carry your influence and love with me to the end - see you on that day. My lifelong buddies: David Barhome, Fernando Martinez, Derrick Burnett, Robert Murray, Jonathan Ross, Michelle Effron, Stephen Fudrowski, Robert Tuosto, Heim, Paul Timpone, Randy Ambroise, Donald and Tommy Russo, Wayne and Donna

Maggio, Josetta Foto, Lynn Counio, Lisa Bellino-Nixon, and Melissa Greensher - you all saw me through the worst of it, thanks for your friendships, and for still being there after all these years. Michelle Augello-Page for her insights into literature, love, life, and reminding me how to feel the inspiration all around me (sempre). The countless entertainers I've met at Penny's Open Mic for helping me get my performance chops up, letting me test my mascot bits on them, and giving me ongoing advice. And to those girls sitting around a living room dreaming of creating the next amazing roller derby league - you can do anything you set your hearts to.

There are also those people that need to be mentioned here with extra special thanks. First, Mom. A woman of your strength, character, and heart will make an excellent rollergirl in the next life; thanks for never letting me give up. Dad, for instilling in me a lust for adventure and for bestowing me with the cock n' balls to live by my convictions. My Aunt Diana, for her continued love and support of my efforts. My band, The Odortones, for dealing with my psychosis, while simultaneously keeping me sane and understanding that I love both music and derby. Karen "Sleeping Booty" Steinecke, for doing the job that had been promised would be done by countless others who never delivered—drawing the pictures for this book. Andreanna "Point N. Shoot" Seymour, for the last minute photo shoot. Michelle Effron, for turning the picture into a cover. And finally, my editor and book cooker, Robert Tuosto, for taking the time to help turn the rantings of a derby-crazed lunatic into a coherent work and for helping me see this project to fruition. I am in your debt. AD ASTRA PER ASPERA.

www.ingramcontent.com/pod-product-compliance
Lightning Source LLC
LaVergne TN
LVHW011415080426
835512LV00005B/63